CELEBRATE YOUR GOLD WITHIN

Kathy Burgum

(Kripadhara)

CELEBRATE YOUR GOLD WITHIN

By Kathy Burgum

(Kripadhara, a Sanskrit name translates; "flow of grace" was given to Kathy by her Guru)

Integrated Guide on:

FULLY *Living Your Life with Success, Happiness and Without Limitations*

Published by

Heart Space Publications
PO Box 1085
Daylesford
Victoria
3460
Australia
Tel +61 450260348
www.heartspacebooks.com
pat@heartspacebooks.com

ISBN 978-0-9924939-6-7

About the Author – Who is Kathy?

Kathy (Kripadhara) was born in the north of England, where she grew up, later travelling the world whilst successfully practising her profession – international tax accounting. After working in Europe, Singapore and other Asian countries, she made Australia her home. Her dad passed away when she was sixteen, leaving her to experience life's challenges without his mentoring presence. Kathy spent more than half of her working life outside England. What a contrast – an ongoing education that she continues to embrace with open arms and heart.

Kathy has faced and overcome many challenges during her adventure in life, choosing to accept each one as a learning experience. Throughout this book, as well as sharing her passion in life, Kathy shares some of those obstacles and lessons with you so you can become empowered by her tips and traps – to save you time in discovering Your Harmony and Your Gold. She understands that the only real obstacles to you achieving your gold are mainly those created within your own mind.

Kathy's real awakening and transformation came when she discovered, studied, practised, and experienced yoga, which deepened her awareness of life – an ongoing process.

> " Allow me to focus divine rays,
> Light the paths of fellow travellers;
> Inspire them with Hope,
> Birth their Joy;
> My small contribution,
> A legacy. "

Acknowledgements

This book is dedicated to my parents and the children in the world.

I am grateful for each of those people who have touched my life, and who are too many to name. You each know who you are – I love you all.

In particular, I thank all those who have supported and guided me in finalising this book – including: members of the National Speakers Association of Australia (now Professional Speakers Australia), in Adelaide, who kindly took time to read through the very first draft of the book some years ago; Es McNulty who gave me a copy of the book "Getting Your Book Published"; Pat Grayson of Heart Space Publications who inspired me to finish writing the book, edited and published the book; Jyotir Saraswati for reading through a few of the chapters and providing her constructive feedback on inclusiveness; Kate Bindu for reading the pre-edit draft; Robert and Becca McIntosh for their invaluable help and patience with computer and mobile phone issues; and other friends who have provided much encouragement during the journey. Sometimes, especially at the beginning, and towards the end, of the project, I felt it may never happen. Each time this feeling passed I gained a renewed passion, greater clarity and a deeper dimension, and the inspiration to continue, so that I can share it with you.

Ten percent of the proceeds of the book will be donated to The Salvation Army.

Shortly before Mum died her main legacy to me was – You do not need to look outside yourself as everything you need is inside of you. Unfortunately, as Mum was a lady of few words, who rarely explained what she said, it took me quite some time to discover exactly what that legacy really meant. Another of her legacies was When one door closes another opens.

All the people who feature in the list of *Resources* (at the end of the book) have enriched my life through me attending their courses and or reading their books. Without their knowledge and inspiration, I would not be who I am today. Allow yourself to be inspired by the people who have achieved what they wanted to achieve, and who are living their life with joy, and who are willing to share their love and passion, to bring them into your life. They can make your journey easier. In most instances, actual names of individuals, whose circumstances have been referred to throughout the examples in the text, have been changed to respect their privacy.

Most importantly, I thank you, my new friends, for inviting me into your life and allowing me to share my knowledge and experiences with you, empowering you to find *Your Gold* Within. May you enjoy reading the book and I hope you gain benefit from it.

Introduction

This book is intended for readers of all ages, irrespective of gender, religion, background, location, and present circumstances, who are willing to accept change into their life with an open heart and mind.

Reasons for writing the book:

Ten years ago, during the course of my work, in a routine job performance review with one of my team, I explained that frequent talking about non-work-related issues was disruptive to the team's work efficiency. I asked the employee whether they enjoyed their work. During our discussion, it became apparent that the employee was in the wrong job and, after reviewing their talents and interests, they chose to pursue a career in engineering.

Although, seemingly a prosaic interview, it had a profound effect on me, where I realised that change is inevitable in life. From this I had a vision to share my message – to empower each person to live life fully, with harmony and without limitations – and designed the skeleton of this book. During an extended sabbatical, after studying the science of Yoga and working with a not-for-profit organisation, it is time to finish writing the book, to share that vision, my legacy.

Uniqueness of the Workbook:

The book is an Integrated Guide on Fully Living Life with Success, Happiness, and Without Limitations, and empowers the reader to attain happiness and harmony in life by building a foundation in each area of life. The book is designed to provide a framework and practical system with easy-to-follow steps, to enable the reader to analyse and understand them-self, question and recognise their real needs in life, and challenge them to attain their ideal dream.

It encompasses principles relevant to achieving success and awareness in a concise, and easy-to-understand way. Quotations of successful people are included at the beginning of each chapter, to highlight the focus of the chapter and share their inspirational messages. Examples, in the form of stories, elaborate and enliven many of the concepts in greater depth. Space is provided at the end of each chapter, so you can write down your thoughts, for future reference. Exercises are included at the end of certain chapters, for completion, to record your input.

Experiences, ups and downs encountered along my journey in life and lessons learnt, are summarised at the end of each chapter. Writing the book challenged me to recall the events of my life, bare my soul, and show how the experiences impacted on my life path. I share my legacy from the depth of my heart.

Benefits to be gained from reading the book:

The book explores and summarises the two world concepts, the outer – material world, and the inner – spiritual world, and how they both can impact and balance our lifestyle when integrated. It will challenge you to mindfully analyse your inherent talents, focus on building a foundation in each area of life, set meaningful goals – as stepping stones – and take action, to establish harmony in each area of life; and share your success with disadvantaged individuals.

The book will empower you to challenge your status quo and real needs, recognise the gap between your ideal lifestyle and status quo, and allow change into your life as a link to bridge that gap. The focus is on mindfully adopting a wellness regime, attaining peace of mind, and embracing abundance, so you can experience prosperity, happiness, and harmony in each area of life.

After reading the book, and completing the exercises, you will have created your own unique Life Plan – your Blueprint for living life fully with Success, Happiness, and Without Limitations.

I hope to share with others how to create harmony in each area of life by building foundations as anchors, to help manage change in pursuing your ideal lifestyle during turbulent times encountered in daily life. The underlying concept throughout the book is conservation and efficient use of energy.

Testimonials

I first met Kathy at a meeting of the Investors Club (now the Property Club) in Brisbane early in the 2000s. My aim was to share my knowledge and success by showing that the average person can buy a new property and be cash-flow positive.

Early in life Kathy became aware of the need to be able to "retire" without having to rely on others, including the government. Creating financial freedom is important, more so now than ever before, due to the increase in age expectancy and uncertain global economic stability. When the time comes to stop working, either by choice or due to other reasons, including health issues and redundancies, you can then spend more time with your family, travel, and also leave a legacy for future generations and less fortunate people.

In this book, Kathy shares her knowledge to show you that financial freedom can be achieved by following sound advice with proven results and with help that is freely available; that you can meet like-minded people, working within their own limits in a supportive environment, who are focused and persistent in pursuing their ideal dreams without losing hope and without suffering the highs and lows experienced by less well-informed investors.

This book contains a system that can empower you to enjoy well-being, abundance, peace within and happiness each day, whilst focusing on attaining your ideal lifestyle, irrespective of your age or current circumstances. It provides tools, and focuses on the need to build a foundation in each area of life so that when you are faced with hardship in one area you can cope, with a quiet mind, and work through the difficulties encountered without losing harmony and balance.

Kevin Young, Property Club Founder & Director
Brisbane, June 2018

Kathy and I have known each other since infancy. We played and read together, attended the same Sunday school, and dreamed our dreams. The framed copy of Kipling's If that hung by the front door of her family home was also influential in my early development and, like Kathy, I have often referred to it in adult life.

From our late teens, we went our different ways. Although we have kept intermittently in touch – and I have lovely memories of visiting her in Singapore

– it has been something of an eye-opener, reading through chapters of this book, to discover just how many of our life experiences have parallels and how they have brought us to a similar place in our personal growth.

Harmony: that is the key concept I relate to here, a way of living in which all aspects are mutually supportive and complementary, able to flourish because they are grounded, truthfully and with integrity, in the meaning you find in or give to your life, as Kathy shows. This goes far deeper than the fashionable "work-life balance" advice so often heard. And it demands continual nurturing.

When external forces are pulling us away from our foundational core – and, though history is replete with such times, they seem especially threatening right now – we need tools such as those Kathy offers to help us focus, and stay mindful. She has successfully used her experience and skills to mentor younger colleagues as they searched for their own life's purpose. Her book offers that opportunity to a wider audience.

Angela Williams, CMG

4 June 2018

I first met Kathy in Adelaide when she attended my workshop "Beyond Words", and progressed from being a frozen puppet to communicating with the audience as an animated presenter with a smile. The "to be" exercises required Kathy to come out from behind a curtain into very bright lights and stand before the audience and simply "be" not "do" anything – a very challenging process that had a profound effect. This quality of stillness can be very powerful. It is about accepting yourself for who you are and not trying to be something you are not. Kathy began to "let go" and "to be" in her communication with the audience.

Kathy recognised the need to celebrate her inherent talents, her legacy, and this book empowers you to Live Your Life Fully with Success, Happiness and Without Limitations; to be totally in the moment, not worrying about what other people think about what you should be doing. It challenges you to attain your ideal dream by building a foundation in each area of life that can provide an anchor in turbulent times encountered in daily life so you can have social harmony.

Kathy challenges you to find your peace within and *Celebrate Your Gold*.

David Griggs – The Speakers Studio, Adelaide

June 2018

I first met Kathy at the Yoga Ashram in 2011. She was living as a full time resident and student of yoga for five years, initially taking 'time out' from the stresses of the outside world. During this residency, Kathy made a commitment as a 'spiritual seeker' to the yoga path and was given the yoga name "Kripadhara". Today she has successfully completed her teacher training and is a fully qualified yoga teacher.

This book is an honest and open account of turning points in Kathy's life. It summarises some benefits to be gained from integrating the regular practice of Yoga into daily life to enhance well-being. It also provides other tools that challenge the understanding of the 'Self', how to live life more fully, and how to strategically attain an aim or goal without 'perceived' limitations. Used in combination, these methods help empower one to face the challenges in daily life, with a more balanced and unaffected mind. Life and its obstacles may not change but one's perception and consequent choices, can and do make a difference!

Kathy's book shows how the material "outer" world integrated with the spiritual "inner" world can help balance one's lifestyle. Yoga (unity) and its principles applied to daily life begin to connect one to the true 'Self', making it possible to create harmony.

This book is unique in its East meets West approach to attaining harmony, coping with changes in life, and maintaining wellness. The law 'of nature is a living example of harmony. This key concept as used by Kathy refers to a way of living in which all aspects of life are mutually supportive and complementary. This goes far deeper than the commonly termed "work-life balance", demanding constant effort and nurturing.

In a society of 'business' where external forces pull one away from the true 'Self' and Dharma (life purpose), these practical tools, help guide one to become more present and aligned to the law of nature.

Mangala Saraswati
Accredited Senior Yoga Teacher
Yoga Australia (L3); SYTA
Dip. Yoga; M.Ed; B. Ed;
Melbourne, Victoria

CONTENTS

Chapter One
The Beginning –
Preparing for Success

All human beings are born free and equal in dignity and rights.
— Universal Declaration of Human Rights

People were created to be loved. Things were created to be used.
The reason why the world is in chaos is because things are being loved
and people are being used.
— Dalai Lama

How you spend your time determines who you are.
— Oprah Winfrey

The future depends on what we do in the present.
— Mahatma Gandhi

Act enthusiastic and you become enthusiastic.
— Dale Carnegie

He who knows others is wise; he who knows himself is enlightened.
— Lao Tzu

Your only obligation in any lifetime is to be true to yourself.
— Richard Bach

All that we are is a result of what we have thought.
— Buddha

Whatever you can do, or dream you can … begin it. Boldness has
genius, power and magic in it.
— Johann Wolfgang von Goethe

It takes courage to be grow up and turn out to be who you really are.
— Edward Estlin Cummings

Nothing external to me has any power over me.
— Walt Whitman

Go confidently in the direction of your dreams! Live the life you've
imagined. As you simplify your life, the laws of the universe will be
simpler.
— David Henry Thoreau

Learn to get in touch with the silence within yourself and know that
everything in this life has a purpose.
— Elisabeth Kubler-Ross

- My message to you
- What is your passion?
- Who are you?
- Where are you now?
- What is your dream?
- What is preventing you from living your dream now?
- How big is the gap?
- The Attractor Factor.

My message to you

My message is to wish each one of you happiness, optimum health, peace, and prosperity in your life, to enable you to live life fully, and to inspire you to change your world and make it a better place. It is the only home you have. Think about what this means to you.

Think about what success means to you. The areas focussed on in this book are: physical, mental, familial / social, vocational, financial, and spiritual. Each of these six areas needs to be in harmony within itself, and with each other to enable you to effectively gain the most from your life. You need to build a foundation for each area of life, which are inter-related. At one time, I recall thinking that the game of life was to keep all the balls in the air at any one time. Now, I realise that sometimes you may also need to focus more time to completely rebuild a foundation or develop a particular area, as circumstances change or as you evolve.

Your reason for living is the most important factor in your life. Discovering your purpose, and gaining an understanding of your uniqueness is the source of harmony and well-being.

This book is for you – whoever you are, wherever you are; whatever your age – you are likely to be young at heart – whether you are male or female; regardless of your religious beliefs, colour, upbringing, background, or current circumstances. It is never too late to make some changes or start anew. Excuses are unacceptable! You *will* need courage.

There is no new knowledge – all knowledge has been with us since the universe was created, and is available within each of us – it just needs to be rediscovered by each one of us. The uniqueness of this book is that it summarises and condenses all the relevant principles to achieving success and awareness in a way that is easy to understand.

When you have finished the book you can treat it as a guidebook to be referred to often, and updated as your journey in life evolves.

As my background is tax accounting, the two specific areas I have chosen to focus on in-depth in My Life (located at the end of each Chapter) to illustrate how I can have everything in my life – happiness as well as financial abundance – include principles of the science of Yoga, which encompasses the whole of the personality.

Now is the right time to share my vision – when the student was ready the teachers presented themselves in my life to help me release the message from within. My vision is based on truth and integrity, in all areas of life.

Read through the book and complete the exercises. Each exercise is designed to commit you to the process of change and transition. You need to sign and date each one so you will be able to look back at a later date and realise how much you have grown, thereby making you appreciate the inevitable change. The signing also shows your intent, and intent is imperative.

First, you need to give adequate time to reading the first three chapters and completing the relevant exercises – these form the heart of the book's message. Chapters Four to Nine can be read selectively, but it is important that you read them all as they do not stand alone – they are inter-related and inter-dependent, as all of life is. Chapters Ten to Thirteen are designed to help you effectively implement your goals into your lifestyle, celebrate what you have achieved to date, and consider how you can fully enjoy the rest of your adventure in life with happiness, and harmony.

It is important to write down your thoughts as you go so you can review them and update them later. You may have found that most books do not provide space for this purpose (provided at the end of each chapter) and thus you have ended up with numerous pieces of loose paper – most of which get lost.

My heart goes out to those people, who appear to be so blessed with success in their lives, yet are apparently unhappy. Why are they unhappy – it's likely because they lack harmony in certain areas of their lives? You need only read the latest celebrity magazines and newspapers to become aware of such outcomes. Publicity is focused on those people who are sup-posedly rich and famous, yet appear to experience a lack of harmony in their relationships, or other areas of their lives, and as a result, their self-es-teem is low, and their health suffers. They seem to think that by taking a magic pill all their problems are resolved. Things do not work that way – it is the cause of the disharmony that needs to be diagnosed and treated ac-cordingly. Happiness comes from within.

Examples:

- *Marlene, who had attained her PhD, had lots of knowledge and education, and yet committed suicide. Sadly, other areas of her life lacked harmony. She had no confidence in applying and sharing her knowledge and never worked outside her home. She felt depressed and isolated from the community. Her family was devastated. Marlene had no self-confidence, had never learnt to love herself and seek professional help to resolve her personal issues and gain inner peace. What a tragic ending!*
- *Andrea, no matter how much money she has, how much she travels, or how good her health is, always has to be busy doing things. Her mind never seems to be at peace, and she is unable to relax. In a nutshell – her life seems to lack spiritual and mental harmony.*

From my heart to your heart, I hope you can enjoy success and harmony in your life. Discover your Gold – your inherent talents and spirituality within. Enjoy each day on your special journey. You live only once. There is no dress rehearsal for life. Activate your Gold – play full out and have fun. Get into the game, stay in the game, and learn as you go. Have courage to jump off the roller-coaster ride you may currently be experiencing; take time to appreciate the real you, as you recognize and realise your true passion. Celebrate your life, and expect something good to happen every day. It is your journey that is important, not the end result. Remember to keep your sense of humour as you go, and have patience.

What, then, is harmony? This concept is analysed and discussed in Chapter Three.

What is your passion?

People and their motivation always fascinated me. I have noticed that when people are passionate about their work they excel and are happy; when they are bored their performance deteriorates and often they become sick. I have worked with people like this and mentored them to help them find their passion in life. You spend so much time at work or in conducting your business – make sure it is your passion. What you do, how you act, and how you spend your time, will determine your future and who you are.

Examples:

- *Paul, a young graduate accountant had a delightful personality but spent too much time during office hours socializing with his colleagues and impeding their work progress. Clearly, he was bright and talented but in the wrong profession. During a career counselling session, it was revealed that he would be more suited to training as an engineer. He appreciated the opportunity to change his career direction and was much happier in his new role.*
- *John was persuaded by his father to work in the family business. In his heart, John knew that he wanted to become a medical practitioner. He persevered working in the family business but, at the same time, analysed his strengths and weaknesses and managed to convince his father that he would be happier pursuing his chosen profession as a doctor.*

Are you passionate about what you are doing? If not, then why not search for something you are passionate about? This could be a huge step as it may mean moving out of your comfort zone. Embrace change – you can become a happier person. Various career books are available to help you in this process. Take time, to analyse your inherent skills, and the career where they can be best utilised.

Who are you?

The first rung / step on your discovery ladder is for you to take time out to become aware *who* you are (*not* what you do).

Example:

If you are asked — who are you — what will you reply? I am a teacher; I am a long-distance runner; I am a cyclist; I am a businessman?

If so, you need to look inside yourself and consider what makes you a happy person. For example, I am healthy, have positive-minded friends, love to spend time at the beach in tune with nature.

Where are you now?

Choose a quiet place where you feel at ease and can dream big, think independently, be alone and uninterrupted, in your own private space and time – maybe near the ocean, the hills, a forest, in a library, or wherever you feel the most inspired. This is *your* book, *your life*. It is for you to write in – yes – feel free to make it your own. When you take ownership of your life you will become more passionate! Enjoy being alone to appreciate who you are, without interruptions from the outside world.

You were born free. You were born with a beautiful mind. What has happened between then and now? Who has influenced your self-belief system? Likely – your family, teachers, and other people during your formative years. You still have that freedom and the beautiful mind but they may be currently hidden beneath a veil of ignorance and confusion.

Examples:

Do you recall when you were born whether both your parents were present for your first moment in this new world? Think about this adventure – for nine months, you had led a protected life in your mother's womb and then out you came into a new environment with a sharp and startling gasp – imagine how you felt. You may have had to fight to survive and that could have been the start to feeling a lack of security and self-esteem. For example, in a premature birthing the lungs may be challenged; and often newly born babies are turned upside down and patted on the back – in some cases they are taken into another room, and separated from their parents.

The initial bonding process can have a major impact on your feeling of safety, and bonding.

Understand that we came into this world with no material belongings, only our soul, and latent talents, which are to be discovered and used during our life, in a body – our vehicle for living our life. Upon death, our physical body will depart from this world with no material belongings – only our soul will usually continue its journey. Everything else – any material wealth – will have passed on to someone else. It is humbling to know and realise this, and understand there is no barrier, or limitation, to us experiencing success during our lifetime other than the obstacles imposed by our mind.

List all your successes to date, no matter how small, in Exercise One (at the end of this chapter) – this will help you to build your self-esteem.

List your strengths in Exercise Two and your weaknesses in Exercise Three (at the end of this chapter) – this will help you to better understand yourself – this is your starting point. Ask someone who knows you well to help you to complete this exercise. Be honest with yourself.

You need to know yourself well before you can get to know others.

What is your dream?

Believe in yourself as you deserve the best. You can do anything you want, within reason. Your mind is a powerful tool – whatever you believe you can achieve, and the converse is also true.

Examples:

1. Jane wanted to climb Mount Everest and started planning for the trip, whilst training her body before she attempted this adventure. Her family and friends thought she was out of her mind and that the adventure would be unsafe. Despite the lack of support, Jane believed in herself and persevered with her plan and succeeded. Imagine how she felt.

2. Donald wanted to take part in a local marathon. His family and friends had heard that this could be dangerous and he could injure his knees. So, Donald took heed of their doubts and did not compete in the marathon. He chose not to believe in himself. Imagine how Donald felt.

Dream BIG as you will always get what you ask for – do not limit yourself to less than what you really want. This is *your* life and *your* responsibility – do not give away your power to anyone. You may have several dreams and will need to work through the same process to manifest each one – over time. You need to be true to yourself, whatever else you do.

Example:

Your dreams could include outer space travel, learning to fly an air-plane, white-water rafting, hot air ballooning, sailing around the world in a yacht, becoming a public speaker, having a large family, inventing something that would benefit the community, building your own house, caring for less privileged children, visiting sick people who have no relatives, being happy, making the world a better place – in line with your vision.

Imagine you are sitting in a movie theatre watching your life story on the screen. What do you want to see? What are you doing, where are you, and with whom? How does it feel? Take this book and a pen with you and turn to Exercise Four (at the end of this chapter) to write down your dreams.

What is preventing you from living your dream now?

What obstacles are currently preventing you from achieving your dream? Complete Exercise Five (at the end of this chapter). These might include some of the following (*poverty* factors):

Lack of:

+ vision
+ mental focus
+ confidence
+ a plan
+ perseverance
+ clutter – either physical, mental, or emotional
+ action

List them all – remember that obstacles are created mainly within your own mind and can be overcome. First you need to recognise and list them so you have a starting point and understand the size of the gap between where you are now and where you want to be. Then, you can appreciate how the obstacles can affect your ability to manifest your dreams, and determine how to overcome them.

Ultimately, you need to reassess your current situation, move on from your fears and regrets, adjust your plans, and take action – that will determine what will happen in the future, together with hope and the perseverance to succeed. Although we are unable to change the past, we can change the way we relate to past events, and plan to allow change to manifest in the future. While change is happening around you, remain calm and honour your existing commitments with integrity. Do not make too many changes at any one time – you may become overwhelmed. Be enthusiastic each day and stay on track – you are bound to meet with some opposition along the way. Always be true to yourself. It takes time for new habits to form and replace old habits. The first step is the most important and need be only a small one. Once the ball starts to roll it will gain momentum.

Example:

John was forced to sell two properties, following a loss of income when his job was made redundant. He became angry and fearful. Fear, caused by attachment to transient material possessions and losing such possessions, can result in disease that weakens the constitution, and immune system, and intensifies the disease. It is a negative emotion that needs to be replaced by hope.

Losing transient possessions can cause anxiety, anger, and regret, and a feeling of inability to move on – and followed by depression. Regret can be overcome by John accepting the underlying event as part of his life experience, being kind to himself, and recognising that other people's adverse underlying circumstances and stress of time pressures could have been part of the cause – not just him. He needs to look for positives inherent in the result, talk with a trusted person about the experience, and acknowledge he may have made a poor decision by not taking into account an imminent global financial downturn before he decided to invest in the second property.

How big is the gap?

How can you get from where you are now to where you want to be? If you start introducing *abundance* factors and eliminating the poverty factors (refer above) this will help you to close the perceived gap. Abundance factors might include some of the following:

+ Give thanks each day for all you have
    + *example* – for the food you are eating, your family and friends, your health
+ Maintain a positive mental attitude
    + *example* – do not allow a setback from the past to limit your hope for future success
+ Keep an open mind and an open heart
    + *example* – ask for help if you need it
+ Live a healthy lifestyle
    + *example* – eat healthy food, exercise your body, and make sure you get enough sleep at night; Develop faith, trust, and integrity, that all will work out for the best
+ Develop compassion for others, who could be worse off than you
+ Maintain a sense of humour – do not take yourself too seriously
+ Be passionate about each day – live it as though it were your last
+ Meditate to focus, and reprogram the mind
+ Clear all the clutter from all areas of your life
    + *example* – belongings, thoughts, emotions, relationships, ingrained harmful habits
+ Build a supportive team
+ Set some specific time-lines for the goals and action plans. Act – without action nothing can change
+ Be patient, and allow time to take its course. Monitor the progress

There are no boundaries when you have an open mind and heart and a vision of what you want or need. It takes courage to become who you really are. Take time to recognise and celebrate the successful results you have achieved in your life. Do not dwell on isolated negative experiences – know they cannot adversely affect you achieving future success.

Example:

Julie lives with her two teenage children and has a full-time job. She was divorced ten years ago, yet still stores some of her ex-husband's belongings in her garage. She refuses to accept that she needs to cut the ties. Until she can do this she will be unable to manifest her dreams to start her own business and accept and experience love in her life to become reality. Those belongings from the past are a barrier to Julie's current needs becoming reality, and future progress. It saps some of her energy that could be conserved and used to manifest her dreams.

Julie needs to change her mind-set, recognise the positive aspects of her previous marriage, celebrate her decision to create a happy personal life and successful business venture, and remove the obstacles from the past. She needs to live every day in the present, as if it were her last.

The Attractor Factor

Energy waves vibrate throughout the whole world. Everybody and everything consists of vibrations that resonate on energy wavelengths that attract like-minded people and objects.

Example:

Materially-minded people generally resonate more with materially-minded people, and spiritually-minded people generally resonate more with spiritually-minded people — they are vibrating on the same wavelength.

Similarly, what you ask for is what you get. The thoughts in your mind manifest what you ask for. Thus, if you focus your mind on something you really need you will attract it; whereas if you focus your mind on something that you may only like but do not need you will attract that. You are created to be loved, to be free, and need to bear that in mind when you ask for what you need. Be bold, and believe in yourself. It is better to focus your mind on abundance and wellness, rather than on poverty and disease.

Your mind acts as a magnet within a magnetic field. That is why it is important to focus on what you need — otherwise you may end up with what you do not need. If you expect the best, you will attract the best; if you expect less than the best, you will attract less than the best. Why would you want to settle for anything less than the best?

Example:

Yvonne needed a new car to replace the one she had owned for over ten years, which required major mechanical work. She also had a passion for jewellery and mentioned to a friend that she liked the necklace her friend was wearing. Her friend gave her the necklace – hence Sue gained what she wanted, and was thinking of most, rather than focusing on her real need.

You need to focus your energy on what it is *you* need – you are the only person who knows yourself and what you need. Unless *you* are happy you are unable to make anyone else happy. You need to conserve all your energy to remain focused on achieving your dreams.

Example:

Sue's teacher managed to convince Sue she should become a teacher when she left school. In fact, Sue's real passion was to study law. Because of this disparity, Sue worried about her future and became depressed. She visited her doctor who determined the reason for her depression. Sue was advised to inform her teacher of her decision to study law, which she did, and subsequently the depression disappeared and never returned. Sue was not attracted to teaching as her latent talents resonated more with those required by a lawyer. She faced her concerns and cleared the disharmony.

Only when you have your big dream firmly fixed in your mind: proceed to the next chapter for additional clarification.

My message to you:

It is important you know a little about my background, based on my environment during the formative years. Had my environment been different, my life's adventure could have been different, and my current circumstances could have been different. Enough of that. I have no regrets − cannot change the past or the present but can always create a different future. Each of us is where we are meant to be now.

I was born in a large town in the North of England, near Manchester. Mum and Dad were in their late forties, and it was around the end of World War Two. My brother, John, was nineteen years of age when I was born. We lived in a semi-detached house, with a small yard back and front, in a cul-de-sac − a quiet environment. Mum dedicated her time to maintaining the house and caring for me − she had a deep heart, although she rarely openly showed much affection, expressed emotions, or communicated much. She was kind-hearted, yet a strict disciplinarian. She was also discerning and protective. Dad worked all his life in the nearby city with British Rail − he left home early in the morning and returned late in the evening during weekdays. He was quietly philanthropic − a Freemason − and spent time at the Masonic Lodge − becoming the Grand Master of Iron Road Lodge. Although I saw little of Dad, he understood me well and was kind but firm, and treated everyone fairly. I never knew my grandparents, who passed away before my birth.

My first recollection in life outside the home was whilst sitting in my baby pram, staring at the kind faces of the local vicar and his wife who were making strange noises in an attempt to communicate − sometime after the christening ceremony. I recall thinking that although I could not yet talk or walk, I might have felt more included hearing adult language. I also vaguely remember being cradled in Mum's arms and being taken to the local photographer's for a portrait photograph.

Although much was scarce at that time, our family lacked none of the basic needs in life − food, shelter, water, and love. I never felt poor, although I suppose we were.

My brother, John never recognized me as his sister. According to Mum, he was jealous of losing his status as an only child. He spent some time away from home in the Royal Navy, after which he got married and left home. The only contact I recall with John at our home was when he put his foot out and I tripped over it, when I was a very young girl.

John left behind three books – "Swiss Family Robinson" (Johann D Wyss), "Treasure Island" (Robert Louis Stevenson), and "Robinson Crusoe" (Daniel Defoe) – and I became an avid reader at an early age. I was grateful for that opportunity. I have always been fascinated by foreign countries, the indigenous people, and their different lifestyles and cultures. Learning from books was a good start to learning, although experience provides life enrichment and has enabled me to appreciate that "normal" can mean different things to different people. What is normal to me may not be normal to you, or others. Hence, I aim to have empathy and compassion, resulting in tolerance, and do not compare myself with others whose circumstances are different than mine.

~ ~ ~

I have fond memories of playing cricket and football with the neighbourhood children. We had fun. On one occasion, when I was practising my skill at throwing an overarm ball, I managed to throw a stone through the kitchen window of a neighbour's house and was not very popular. I kept a low profile for a while after that experience. We also went for long walks along a nearby creek and caught tadpoles. I put mine into a jar of water and hoped they would become frogs. In fact they were imprisoned in the jars and rarely survived for long.

Angela, and I, enjoyed horse-riding at a nearby farm, which we each fondly remember and treasure. Those were halcyon days. Angela later visited me in Singapore during one of her business trips.

On one occasion, I was looking out of a front bedroom window on the upstairs floor of our home, and observed the flowers planted in our front garden, and those of our neighbours'. Our garden contained mainly purple auricular, and the neighbours' gardens contained plants of other varieties and colours. I thought it would be more interesting if our garden could include a few plants of other colours. Hence, I dug up a few of our purple-flowering plants, visited the neighbours' front gardens – and dutifully exchanged one of the purple plants for one of their plants. Of course, when I planted the "new" plants in our garden, everyone realised what had happened, and, again I was unpopular for a while.

~ ~ ~

From an early age, I spent time at Sunday school at the local church, which became part of my growing-up ritual – I felt safe in that environment. It enabled me to witness the moods and nature of other children, and their suffering when maltreated by their parents. I felt compassion at an early age. Later on, I became a teacher.

During my teenage years, Sunday afternoons were spent discussing the morning sermon at the vicar's home, and he also taught me to play chess. He had two dogs – a golden labrador and a beagle. The beagle regularly escaped and I recall the vicar chasing after it, which must have been painful as he suffered wounds from a motor-bike accident. I joined the amateur dramatic society but was never given large parts as I had a lot of homework to complete. I served on the church management committee, as treasurer, my first accounting job!

~ ~ ~

School life was not something I really enjoyed – I found it tedious, slow and shallow – the learning process, boring rather than a joyous exploration, and the syllabus contained very few practical lessons. I accepted that it was a necessary part of growing up, and had to be tolerated in order to reach the next phase of life. There was an over intellectualism, rather than experimentalism, which prevented the body, mind, emotions, and heart from becoming fully integrated.

One of the primary school teachers was an extreme bully who threatened us with a cane if we were unable to provide an instant answer to his mathematical questions. As my surname was near the beginning of the alphabet I had little time to think out the answer so was a recipient of his caning – my hand hurt for several days, and I never respected that teacher.

The geography teacher commented that my map of the British Isles, which we had been asked to draw, resembled a frog – that put an end to that conversation. Needless to say, I failed the geography exam.

Other than that, most of the teachers were lovely, especially the physical education teacher at high-school, who also helped me to master mathematics; the Latin teacher who persevered teaching a very dry subject; and the history teacher who also played the flute. I attended the grammar school, part of a three-base campus that also included technical and secondary modern streaming. We were the first student intake – the guinea pigs.

The grammar school was co-ed and the boys seemed regularly to create chaos, which resulted in their detention. On one occasion, they hollowed out a piece of chalk with the pointed end of a compass, inserted a matchstick into the hollow chalk, and filled in the end of the chalk with the chalk dust — that was meant for the inexperienced young French teacher to use. Unfortunately, the science teacher was the first one to use that piece of chalk, and was he mad!

I always wondered why the subjects taught in our school did not integrate some of those skills required for survival in life, for example: exercise science, nutrition and mindful eating, basic finance, and communication skills.

What is my passion?

Our high school motto was "Ad Astra per Caelum", originating from Virgil, which means – he / she aims too low who aims beneath the stars. I was told by the Headmaster that my role in life was to become a teacher – that was his intention for all the pupils, and that was the extent of the careers advice available to me at that time. I had very little patience then – nothing much has changed – so knew I would not enjoy teaching full-time. I never liked being told what to do without a reason why, so I bought a book on careers and determined, by a process of elimination, that I wanted to become an accountant, which would enable me to travel, study international law, and work in the world of business – this has always been my passion.

When I had passed enough exams at school, I walked to the Headmaster's office with trepidation, knocked on the door, and entered his room. I sat down and waited for him to ask why I was there, looked him in the eyes, and boldly informed him of my decision to leave school. He listened and responded – "Will you become a Chartered Accountant?" I confirmed that I would, and then he said – "OK, that's alright", and off I went into the world! I did not give my power away to the headmaster.

Sometime later, during a discussion with a careers consultant, I was made aware that maybe my inherent talents could have been best applied to a career in architecture. With that in mind I have always endeavoured to use those talents creatively in whatever situation I find myself. They provide me with an ability to focus, see the big picture, and visualize the end result. Those abilities help me to remain objective and calm under most circumstances.

I love beautiful things, design, energy flow, and colour coordination, as well as being able to analyse and document facts, and plan strategies. I also enjoy leading by example and sharing my knowledge and experiences, for the benefit of others.

My passion from an early age was also to experience living life in a different country. I visualized living on an island in the sun – it was snowing on the day I was born – the sun rarely shone in the North of England.

Dad arranged a meeting with a local accountant and I became an articled clerk for five years, meaning I worked during the day for minimal pay, and studied at night – completing a correspondence course. I did not attend university.

~ ~ ~

Dad rarely said that he was ill so, one day when he advised he had an acute pain somewhere in his stomach Mum and I became concerned. He had been for an x-ray and nothing was shown to be irregular. The family doctor arrived at our home, together with another medical consultant. It was agreed that Dad be taken to the local hospital for observation as neither of them could determine the cause of his abdominal pain. An ambulance arrived later in the day, and I watched as Dad was taken away, his face ashen. He passed away in his sleep the same night. The cause of death was peritonitis, a duodenal ulcer that had burst. I had always feared that I may lose my parents earlier in life than most of my friends, due to them being almost fifty years of age at the time of my birth. But I was not prepared for this to happen. Dad was sixty four years of age when he passed away, and was due to retire the following year when the family planned to relocate to North Wales. I was inconsolable and felt numb.

I was sixteen when Dad died and was left to pursue my career path in life without his guidance – you never know what life has in store for you tomorrow. Mum and I were devastated by our loss. We supported each other, and worked hard in overcoming our grief. I decided to stay at home for a few years until she felt more able to cope with her loss and regain confidence. I thought the world had ended – life was never the same again. Nothing could fill the emptiness. Mum outlived Dad by twenty years and never remarried. Dad had provided a stability in my family life that is very difficult to explain – he never argued and always promoted a positive outcome in dealing with all issues.

Brother John's view was that I should find a higher paying job, but Mum insisted that I complete my accountancy training and studies, for which I am truly grateful. Due to the emotional distress following Dad's death, and the time it took to grieve our loss, it took me two years longer than envisaged to complete my studies, and then it was time to leave home to pursue my career.

Rudyard Kipling's poem "If" was displayed on the wall near the front door, inside our home, and provided inspiration to live each day calmly. I often referred to this poem for inspiration – it is reproduced below:

"If you can keep your head when all about you
Are losing theirs and blaming it on you,
If you can trust yourself when all men doubt you,
But make allowance for their doubting too;
If you can wait but not be tired of waiting,
Or being lied about, don't deal in lies,
Or being hated, don't give way to hating,
And yet don't look too good, nor talk too wise;
If you can dream – and not make dreams your master;
If you can think and not make thoughts your aim:
If you can meet with Triumph and Disaster
And treat those two impostors just the same;
If you can bear to hear the trust you've spoken
Twisted by knaves to make a trap for fools,
Or watch the things you gave your life to, broken,
And stoop and pick 'em up with worn-out tools:
If you can make one heap of all your winnings
And risk it on one turn of pitch-and-toss,
And lose, and start again at your beginnings
And never breathe a word about your loss;
If you can force your heart and nerve and sinew
To serve your turn long after they are gone,
And so hold on when there is nothing in you
Except the Will which says to them: "Hold on!"
If you can talk with crowds and keep your virtue,
Or walk with Kings – nor lose the common touch,
If neither foes nor loving friends can hurt you,
If all men count with you, but none too much;
If you can fill the unforgiving minute
With sixty seconds' worth of distance run,
Yours is the Earth and everything that's in it,
And – which is more – you'll be a Man my son!"

It is now displayed on the wall at my home.

~ ~ ~

Most weekends were spent walking on the moors and Yorkshire dales, or in the Lake District, staying mainly at youth hostels. I travelled there by local transport – train or bus. Although I was often alone I never felt lonely exploring the countryside – the miracles of nature filled my heart with joy. Frequently it rained, which was good for the complexion. I was happy.

Soon after I first started work, I planned a trip to Iceland with Mini-trek – an expedition organization. I read a lot about the country and decided the best way to experience it was by camping, it took me two years to plan the trip. None of my friends wanted to accompany me so I booked to go alone with an expedition. Upon arriving in Reykjavik, I met up with a group of like-minded people, each of whom had travelled alone to Iceland. The first thing I remember about the adventure was the aeroplane ride – it was my first. The beauty of the white clouds, floating alongside the aircraft, was a spiritual experience – they resembled cotton wool suspended below the blue sky – and the sound of silence was sublime – no beginning and no end. I felt at one with the Universe and have never been afraid of flying.

Iceland is where astronauts were trained as the terrain resembles the surface of the moon – the sands consist of black lava dust and the landscape is formed mainly by volcanic craters – it is surreal. The weather was freezing cold in July. The food was excellent, as we travelled with the chief chef of the expedition company. Each evening, after the evening meal, our group bathed in the hot springs, before jumping into our sleeping bags. I felt cosy and warm. I shared a tent with a Scottish artist, which was fun. We travelled round the island in a four-wheel drive, which enabled us to explore the beauty of the isolated iconic terrain, including the smouldering embers from the volcanic craters. I collected a few pieces of the cooled embers for my study at home. I also recall seeing a fluffy yellow chick, struggling to find its feet on the snow.

One evening, a few of us sat huddled upon the side of one of the volcanoes, watching the sun set at around 10.00pm, and patiently waiting for it to rise at about 2.00am. Although it was cold, and we were shivering, it was worth the wait – hardly a word was spoken. We were mesmerised by the silent beauty. The sun set and came up horizontally in the sky, rather than vertically, due to the latitudinal location. It was like watching a movie.

Flying home I witnessed an active volcano on Surtsey, one of the nearby islands. It resembled a huge smouldering cauldron in the sea. It is even more memorable as I was privileged to sit next to Magnus Magnusson – a well-known Icelandic journalist who spent most of his life in Scotland.

I have camped only twice, once in Iceland, followed soon after by an expedition to Mt. Snowdon in North Wales, with Jon – a fellow traveller from the Minitrek expedition in Iceland. We drove to the foot of the mountain, walked to the summit, and camped on the way down. It rained each day and rivers flowed prolifically through the tent at night. Nonetheless, it was an exhilarating experience.

My love of horse-riding took me pony-trekking to Perthshire, and the Isle of Arran in Scotland where we stayed next to a golf course; and the Brecon Beacons in Wales, where I rode one of the ponies bare-back – that was a bumpy experience on a small pony! The scenery was spectacular and each experience was exhilarating. I also rode along the beaches in Malaysia, and in the Australian bush country.

~ ~ ~

A few weeks before my final accountancy exams my friend Sue and I set off for ten days to explore the places we had witnessed in the movie, "The Sound of Music", which I saw three times. We flew on an old army air-craft to Munich, then travelled by coach, via Innsbruck, to Hallstadt in Salzburgerland, in Austria. Hallstadt was a chocolate-box village, nestled at the foot of the European Alps on the edge of Lake Wolfgang, with pastel-coloured chalets festooned with window-boxes full of colourful flowers. We climbed the mountains, like Maria in "Sound of Music", where the pretty white edelweiss flower grew, and descended into a valley where villagers from the surrounding neighbour-hood gathered for a celebration. They wore local costumes and played various musical instruments – what a colourful experience. We also visited Vienna – unfortunately the Spanish Riding School was closed during our visit. A visit to the school is still on my bucket list.

~ ~ ~

During this time David, my childhood boyfriend was studying psychology and languages at various universities. He had never discussed marriage plans. I chose to spend time working in Brussels, Belgium. David decided to visit and asked me at the airport on his arrival "when will we be married?" After the end of one week, and ten years in our relationship, he suddenly declared that "it would not work". I was devastated, heart-broken, at the time, as David was unable to verbalise why "it would not work". This emotional upheaval a short time after the death of Dad was traumatic and unsettling. I felt very alone in the world, and chose to focus on my future career development. I could not foresee a future in the role in Belgium so decided to return to the United Kingdom ("UK")...

~ ~ ~

My first car in the UK was a new teal blue Triumph Herald, my treat for passing my accountancy exams, and although it was a great car I never again bought a new car as they lose their value too quickly. Following that, when I worked in Belgium, I owned a red Triumph Spitfire — not the most comfortable vehicle for driving along cobble-stoned streets in Belgium, but it was fun. I sold that car before returning to the UK. In London — it was easier to use public transport, except on the odd occasion when no taxis were available late at night. I relied on public transport until I arrived in Australia, much later. Since then, I have owned a red, manual, Hyundai Excel, which is reliable and economical to maintain.

Who am I?

London was an expensive city to live in but offered the greatest opportunity to gain international tax experience. I enjoyed the challenging nature of the work. At weekends I visited the many galleries – I especially enjoyed the diverse nature of exhibits at the Tate Gallery; and attended some of the classical music concerts at the Royal Festival Hall, and the Proms at the Royal Albert Hall. Another activity I enjoyed was riding the police horses in the Hyde Park barracks – elegant and highly intelligent animals. Horse-riding provides excellent management training skills, due to the co-ordination required between the rider and the horse to become part of a team and achieve harmony in action.

For two out of my five years of life in London I shared a house, with four other people, south of the River Thames in Barnes. It provided a good home base at a time when we never knew when we left home in the morning whether we would all return in the evening. One day, I was waiting for a bus at Piccadilly Circus underground station – normally I would have waited at the Green Park underground station – when a bomb exploded at the Green Park underground station. It felt like being in a war zone – phew – what a near miss! Fortunately, none of my house mates were injured.

During the time I lived in London, I attended the Lucie Clayton College to learn deportment and etiquette. I had fun and met some interesting people – an opportunity not to be missed!

I joined the Lansdowne Club, which provided a safe base in the city where I could relax and read the newspapers. This was the first social club of its kind in London to admit women members. It has affiliation with clubs of similar standing worldwide.

I joined the London Jaycees and enjoyed working on the many community projects they implemented. One of my favourite projects was heading a committee to issue a book on "Women In City Life" for which ex-prime minister Margaret Thatcher wrote the foreword. A copy of this book was distributed to each secondary school in the UK. I attended a World Congress in Nice, France, which was great fun. We attended a ball at the casino in Nice, and a party in the castle in Monte Carlo.

While living in London I met Ken, an American friend, who was also an accountant, working in Europe. After attending a tax seminar in Switzerland, I caught a train to Milan, where Ken was working and together we explored that city – I enjoyed window-shopping and seeing the latest fashions there. I bought a dress that I always enjoyed wearing. Following that I visited Florence and explored some of the famed architectural buildings and art galleries and witnessed some of the exquisite paintings, before returning to London.

Samuel Johnson said, 'If you get tired of living in London you get tired of life'. I never tired of living there – there was so much to experience – but it was time to move on.

~ ~ ~

My overseas work experiences are highlighted in Chapter Seven, but for completeness the locations are referred to below to provide a complete outline of the tapestry of my travel experiences throughout the world.

After I left the UK and during my time working in Hong Kong, I travelled to Manila for a short break – to catch up with Johnny, a friend I had met in Europe at the Jaycees world congress in Nice – he was also an accountant. Johnny and his family welcomed me at the Manila airport and I stayed with them during my visit. Each member of the family spoke a different dialect of Chinese. Through sign language and Johnny's interpretations we communicated well amidst a few laughs. We attended the opening ceremony of the University of Los Banyos by Imelda Marcos, visited the American War Memorial, and the Chinese Cemetery. One of the Manila Jaycees was a member of the police force so we managed to escape the curfew when we attended a dinner party on board a boat in the harbour.

~ ~ ~

Following on from Hong Kong, and during my early years working in Singapore, Mum passed away in England. During our years apart we had become the best of friends. Brother, John did not inform me of her death in time for me to attend her funeral, which he had arranged. I was very angry at the time. Under the circumstances, I chose to visit England a few months later and, meanwhile, focus on the busy tax filing season at work. I stayed with Katy, a close friend – I had a bad cold during that time and did not contact John until after I had sold the contents of the family home, and listed the house for sale, through another friend who was an estate agent – John had done nothing about this procedure. I also arranged for Mum to have a headstone next to Dad's, in the nearby crematorium. Then, I suggested to John that we meet for dinner the following week at a nearby restaurant. At first, he seemed hesitant to accept the offer, as he was "too busy". I told him where I was staying and that he could contact me if he wanted to. He eventually accepted the offer to meet for dinner, throughout which he complained about how badly he had been treated by our parents. I had no comments. I felt compassion for his apparent unhappiness. I enjoyed the meal with my two nephews the following night, and catching up with all their news. I saw very little of John after that time, although we did stay in touch until he passed away.

~ ~ ~

Initially I found life difficult to survive in Singapore as I had no job upon arrival. I worked as a freelance tax consultant, and spent some time house-sitting, with very little income for the first eleven months. After that I was offered a full-time position with one of the international accounting firms, where I worked for the next twelve years, and six years working with another of the international accounting firms. I became a permanent resident of Singapore.

After the first year of my life in Singapore, for the next fourteen years I lived with my Singaporean partner, Philip, and his son Franco whose biological mum lived in Hong Kong. We lived in several different locations – firstly, in a second-floor apartment near to my office, where we stayed for eight years, until the landlord stopped paying his mortgage and the bank foreclosed on the property. It was located near a Hindu temple and I learnt much about the Hindu culture, including the various festivals and ceremonies. Our next apartment was located on the eleventh floor in a high-rise building in Chinatown, overlooking the Singapore River, where we stayed for one year, after which the Japanese landlord doubled the rent. The views from there were spectacular, but during the time we stayed there much construction work took place that continued throughout the night – it was cooler then – which meant the noise made by the builders and their equipment never stopped. The next apartment – also for one year – was in Holland Village, a bus-ride away from the Central Business District. Although the location was convenient and the community life enjoyable, I found a larger and more comfortable place nearer to the Central Business District for less rent and, hence, moved to an old town house off Balestier Road, where I stayed for eight years. It was situated near to a Sikh temple, and within walking distance of shops and other facilities. I was happy living there.

My main exercise was swimming at the Tanglin Club, where I managed to complete thirty laps in the Olympic-size pool in the morning before going to work, and again after work before walking home. That provided a calm beginning and ending to each day, and a feeling of well-being. I also practised tennis. On most Sunday mornings, I met two colleagues, Pat and Lydia, to practice golf at Lydia's golf club, followed by breakfast and a walk along the nearby beach. We remained good friends throughout my time in Singapore.

Whilst living in Singapore, I travelled several times to Malaysia, which is only half-an-hour across the causeway between the two countries – with Pat, and friends; Indonesia both for work and pleasure; Thailand to attend work conferences and for pleasure; PRC during a business trip to Hong Kong; and Perth, Australia to attend various work conferences.

I also spent a few months in Seattle, USA, where I sat the examination to become a Certified Public Accountant (CPA) in New York. I stayed at the home of Peter, one of my clients, and his family and was fortunate to explore that area, including Vancouver, and the Canadian fjords to the north of Vancouver, with the family. I learnt how to cook Asian food from experts.

Apart from the usual 'flu that everyone had several times a year, due to the air pollution within the high-rise buildings in Singapore = I had never been seriously ill (just the usual chicken-pox, measles, and mumps during childhood). Then, I had a shock – I was diagnosed with breast cancer. I felt numb, lucky to be alive after the lumpectomy operation, and determined to change my lifestyle. Following my breast cancer operation and during the chemotherapy and radiation treatment – I recognized that the humid weather and current working conditions had become too oppressive, which was the main reason I decided to move on. I chose Australia rather than the United States as I felt that, in the long-term, the living environment would be more suitable for my lifestyle, although I had more friends in the United States at that time. Hence, I requested a transfer with my first Singapore employer, to work in Australia, and they arranged to sponsor a visa for me to work in their Melbourne office.

Soon after my transfer to Australia, Pat and I met in Singapore and travelled via Bangkok, where we ate the delicious local food, to Osaka – from where we spent a memorable ten days exploring Japan. We adopted Osaka as our base and travelled by train to Kyoto – the cultural centre – with its many parks, gardens, and temples. I especially enjoyed sitting in the peaceful Zen gardens. The Japanese people were very friendly, and we learnt much about the ancient culture. The Japanese food was delicious, and inexpensive. The cherry blossom was beautiful – it lasted for a very short period of time on the tree before it was blown off. The trains always ran on time and were efficient.

One day Pat and I caught the train to Himeji to visit the castle, and mistakenly caught the bullet train on our way back to Osaka. It went so quickly it felt as though we were hardly moving. Fortunately, it stopped at Osaka, otherwise we would have ended up in Tokyo in no time at all! After my move to Australia, I visited Pat and her husband, Graham, at their home in New Zealand.

~ ~ ~

After living on a small island, with an average daily temperature of thirty degrees centigrade and ninety per cent humidity, with no real seasons, I did not know whether I would prefer living in the city, the bush, or somewhere in between. Also, I had no idea how my body would acclimatize to the various climatic conditions in Australia. I started my new adventure in a granny flat located in Eltham, Victoria, next to the home of James, one of my previous colleagues in Singapore who had relocated there with his family. We lived near to Montsalvat – the largest artist community of its kind in Australia – where I attended weekly painting class in the evening, once a week.

As I had not driven a car since leaving Europe I was required to take a driving test, which I passed on the second attempt after the help of a few driving lessons.

I had no first degree although, in a different way, my global travels could qualify as a degree – in the University of Life. Upon arrival in Australia, I decided to apply for admission to the Master of International Tax program, which was offered to me by The University of Melbourne, based on my working experience, and professional qualifications.

~ ~ ~

Some years ago, due to a job redundancy, I was forced to take a year's break from my full-time work in Australia, and used some of that time to recreate my Life Plan – like the one you are creating now. This time out enabled me to dream big, write a Blueprint for my life, attend courses and seminars, read books, set goals, and take actions to start a process of change. During that time, I drafted the skeleton of this book. Every day was a day of introspection and learning, a time to be grateful – for all the abundance in my life, and to thank the people who had helped me along the way. I felt privileged to have so many blessings to count. But life was not always like that, as you will see.

Where am I now?

Most recently, due to another job redundancy and global financial crisis, followed by a personal financial downturn, I was provided with another opportunity to reconsider my current lifestyle needs. I began to think, although perhaps it should have become obvious earlier, that maybe a hectic city lifestyle was not the best option for me in the long-term. It consisted of long work days, followed by frequent business social events, time commuting to and from work, and often irregular eating patterns, which left little time for any type of regular fitness activity or meditation routine. My colleagues appeared to be on a treadmill and although they earned high salaries it came at a high price – little time for family and friends, little time for appreciating the real joys of life, and little time to recuperate from the effects of this stressful lifestyle.

I needed time out to again review my Life Plan, reflect on my current needs, where I want to be in, say, ten years time, and how my inherent talents can best contribute to society. I chose to volunteer full-time at a not-for-profit organization, to rejuvenate, reconnect spiritually and undergo a transformation. I had no idea for how long I would stay there, which turned out to be almost five years. Then, I felt the need to catch up on projects that had been put on hold during that time, including finalising the draft of this book. It has taken some time to get it to this stage and now I am happy and ready to share it with you. The input for the book is an integration of head (intellect), heart (deep emotions and feelings), and the need to share my learning and experience, hands (action), and intuition. If it benefits only one person's life the effort will have been worthwhile.

~ ~ ~

In a nutshell, when my life commenced it had a basic spiritual foundation and when I moved away from home to pursue my career overseas, this crucial foundation became somewhat shaken. I was aware of the need to exercise to maintain physical fitness and the main two ways I met that need were by walking and cycling – I found they provided inner peace of mind and respite from the stress of the work experience in the outside world. After I started to travel away from home to work this routine was never regularly re-established, except for my daily swimming routine when I lived in Singapore, and for that reason, my lifestyle lost some of its overall harmony. I started to question the religious teachings gained early in life, as one does, and learnt more about comparative religions, and spirituality – I had a desire to question and understand the real reason for living. Eventually, I studied Zen Buddhism and connected with meditation practices, experiencing a greater peace of mind.

My real reason for living was to succeed at my career, do my job well, and spend time with like-minded friends, and family, which, in fact, did not happen very often due to my travel schedule and demanding workloads. My passion has always been to make the world a better place, and enjoy my work, at the same time as maintaining a balanced lifestyle. However, once I got onto the prover-bial roller-coaster I stayed on that ride for quite some time. My life often lacked harmony throughout the pursuit of my career. I had pursued my passion, and was successful in my career – but without ever feeling totally fulfilled. When I was diagnosed with breast cancer I realized my life lacked total harmony. Eventually, I was forced to change my lifestyle. That illness was a blessing in disguise.

When I arrived in Australia, my main focus was still to pursue my career, as well as integrating into the local community, but eventually it became evident again that this pattern would never make me feel totally fulfilled as it lacked a strong foundation in each area of life – hence, a lack of overall harmony. It was time to spend more time on me before I could meaningfully contribute to life outside. Upon taking a longer career sabbatical break I began to reconnect more with the spiritual side of life and review and reflect on the real meaning of my life with a view to adopting an integrated approach – synchronising the inner and outer worlds.

What is my dream?

My dream is to revisit my passion and assimilate what I have learnt in life; to connect with like-minded people, add value in the world community, and create a safe and beautiful place in which to live. There are no obstacles – I need to work my way through the potential options in a systematic way, with patience, and be guided along the way by my intuition into the next exciting phase of my adventure in life. With less, I have more.

Currently, I live in country Victoria – enjoying a tranquil community lifestyle, sorting through belongings and ruthlessly donating or selling all those items that are surplus to my needs. It is surprising how many books and paperwork have accumulated and it will take a while to sort through them all and keep only those that are of current use. I appreciate all I have learnt and experienced in life, whilst awaiting my new calling. I am excited. Being impatient by nature, all this can be challenging. I accept that I am in a state of transition, and for now completing the book is my main project.

What is preventing me from living my dream now?

I need time out to create space, appreciate what I have learnt, reconnect, and mindfully select where to focus my energy and time. There are no blockages, other than those created by my mind.

Pulling out the weeds, sowing new seeds, allowing time for them to germinate and grow, and living with hope in my heart – is an ongoing process.

How big is the gap?

There is no real gap, other than the time it will take for the ongoing learning and appreciation process, to enable me to ascertain how I can most effectively contribute my time and energy within the community, and live life fully.

The Attractor Factor:

I need patience to allow my mind to attract like-minded people who can help me manifest my dream.

Visualizing my ideal lifestyle at the end of the next five, ten, fifteen years – will be a very powerful tool, like living in the future and then bridging the gap between then and now.

Space for you to write in:

Be sure you know exactly what you need – what you ask for is what you will get – then go for it. Be true to yourself. Once you are satisfied that you have prepared yourself for success, proceed to Chapter Two.

Celebrate Your Gold Within

Exercise One – Your Successes

List all the experiences in life, which have made you feel good.

What exactly was it that made you feel good?

What blessings do you have? What are you grateful for?

Experiences that made you feel good:	How did you feel?
1.	
2.	
3.	
4.	
5.	
6.	
7.	
8.	
9.	

What are you grateful for?

....

....

....

(Remember to sign and date below when you have completed this exercise – for future reference)

Signature......................................

Name: ....

Date: ....

Exercise Two – Your Strengths

Listing your strengths will help you to determine which of your dreams you want to pursue. Be honest and truthful. Ask trusted friends to help you determine your strengths. Focusing on your strengths will help you to maintain a high self-esteem.

My strengths are:

1.

2.

3.

4.

5.

6.

7.

8.

9.

10.

11.

12.

Signature.......................................

Name: ....

Date: ....

Exercise Three – Your Weaknesses

Listing your weaknesses will help you to determine what development programs you may need to attend or work on to help you achieve your dreams. Ask trusted friends to help you determine your weaknesses. Do not be afraid. By recognising your weaknesses, you can turn them into strengths and overcome them.

My weaknesses are:

1.
_____

2.
_____

3.
_____

4.
_____

5.
_____

6.
_____

7.
_____

8.
_____

9.
_____

10.
_____

11.
_____

12.
_____

Signature....................................

Name: ....

Date: ....

Exercise Four – Your Dreams

My BIG dreams are:

Write down everything that enters your mind, no matter how far away it is from your current situation. Be courageous. What would you want to do if there were no limitations or restrictions? It does not matter if you do not have twelve dreams, or if you have more than twelve. The main thing is to list them all. Later (after you have completed the rest of the exercises in this chapter) you can choose which one you are most passionate about pursuing first.

1.

2.

3.

4.

5.

6.

7.

8.

9.

10.

11.

12.

Signature....................................

Name: ....

Date: ....

Exercise Five – Your Obstacles

Listing the obstacles that are in the way of you achieving your dreams can help you to determine how best these obstacles can be overcome.

My obstacles are:	*How to overcome my obstacles:*
1.	
2.	
3.	
4.	
5.	
6.	
7.	
8.	
9.	
10.	
11.	
12.	

Signature.....................................

Name: ....

Date: ....

Chapter Two
Dreaming BIG

He who looks outside his own heart dreams, he who looks inside his own heart awakens.

— Carl Gustav Jung

The future belongs to those who believe in the beauty of their dreams.

— Anna Eleanor Roosevelt

Those who live passionately teach us how to love. Those who love passionately teach us how to live.

— Paramahamsa Yogananda

It's kind of fun to do the impossible.

— Walt Disney

Happiness depends on ourselves.

— Aristotle

Don't judge each day by the harvest you reap, but by the seeds you plant.

— Robert Louis Stevenson

Open your arms to change, but don't let go of your values.

— Dalai Lama

Only the possibility that a dream could come true makes life worth living.

— Paul Coelho

Imagination is the beginning of creation. You imagine what you desire; and at last you create what you will.

— George Bernard Shaw

Go confidently in the direction of your dreams! Live the life you've imagined. As you simplify your life, the laws of the universe will be simpler.

— Henry David Thoreau

We should not let our fears hold us back from pursuing our hopes.

— John F Kennedy Jr

- Your purpose in life?

- What will make you feel fulfilled?

- How can you achieve your dreams?

- What are you willing / not willing to sacrifice?

- Attitude of gratitude

- Believe in yourself

- Visualisation

- Believe you have what you need now

Your purpose in life?

You may have expected this chapter to be all about setting and achieving goals. Goals are a tool to help you stay focused on discovering your Gold and are very important – but only after you have determined what you need from life.

Many books have been written about setting and achieving goals. But sometimes setting goals can put limitations on your creativity and hinder attainment of your ideal lifestyle. This is because goals are often not based on your inherent talents and real life needs but on what you may want, or what you have been persuaded to do by others, without being fully aware of your overall needs and focusing on those. That can be like putting a ladder up against the wrong tree. Then valuable time and energy is wasted and time needs to be spent to re-plan and start the process all over again. Together with Visualisation, and the Power of Attraction, your dreams will help you manifest your passion.

Hence, Dreams are initially more important than goals – as setting goals and achieving them before you are certain of what you really want to achieve may limit your true potential by aiming for lower expectations than you could otherwise achieve, which that would result in disappointment.

Before you can live your ideal life, you need to recognize your inherent talents and how they can be fully activated. Imagine: what if you were living your ideal life now – had optimum health, happiness and peace of mind using your inherent talents with passion, with abundance in each area of life – how would you feel? When you use your inherent talents fully, you can experience happiness and abundance in all areas of life. You need to open your heart to recognise your inherent talents, and realise the beauty of life.

Examples:

- *When Alan left school, his goal was to become a wealthy business executive. He achieved that goal and subsequently realized the money did not bring him happiness. His personal relationships had suffered, his wife had divorced him and he was unable to understand and accept that. He reconsidered his purpose in life and decided he needed to fulfil his passion to help others discover their purpose in life and become successful. He chose to achieve this by becoming a business mentor and*

> *sponsoring less-privileged children to achieve success in their sporting careers.*
>
> - *Although Alan has successfully accomplished his passion in life to help others, he has not yet factored into his life his own personal happiness. He continues to reflect on why his wife divorced him, without accepting that happened in the past and he deserves to be happy in the present. He needs to love and trust himself to be able to love and trust others.*

It is important in focusing on your ideal dream to encompass a harmonious lifestyle, rather than one that is lacking in optimum health, peace of mind, and happiness. This means that your dream is created from within your heart with a complete lifestyle in view, rather than based on changing wants that have no overall focus or anchor.

Examples:

- *Chris made a lot of money yet lacked harmony in other areas of life — she is unhappy. She had set a goal to make $1 million within five years, which she achieved but had not included in her plan the need to build a foundation and create harmony in all the other areas of life. Chris needs to reassess her ideal dream.*
- *Tom has optimum health yet no money to do what he wants, when he wants — he is unhappy. He had focused only on getting physically fit but had not included in his plan the need to create harmony in all the other areas of life. Tom needs to reassess his ideal dream and build a foundation in each area of his life.*

Your passion and determination, together with appropriate actions, to live your ideal dream, is what will make it all happen. The only limitation is what you program into your mind. First, you need to dream big, and be sure to include all the areas of life before pursuing the dream.

Goals are still very important — refer to Chapter Ten.

What will make you feel fulfilled?

Why is it important for you to be successful and discover / activate your Gold? What will it mean to you? How will it make you feel? What will it enable you to do that you are unable to do now? What will it take to make you feel fulfilled? What difference will it make to you and to those whom you love and care about? Write down your answers to these questions in Exercise Six (at the end of this chapter). By writing down your heartfelt beliefs and requirements in life you can commit to changing the status quo and move forward.

Happiness is found inside and not always outside – it is based on peace of mind. Money alone does not provide happiness, although it can help you to enjoy life more fully provided you use it wisely, are not greedy and do not worship money.

You need happiness and peace of mind to experience harmony in all areas of life. In this state, you can experience passion in everyday living. Spiritual harmony (refer to Chapter Nine) is especially important in enabling you to experience connectedness and total harmony in life.

Your current situation is based on your perceptions of past thoughts and actions. You can build a new foundation, by sowing seeds of hope, and allowing time for them to germinate and ripen.

Example:

Lionel has been encouraged by his father to follow his trade of building – it has provided the family with wealth. Lionel has observed that his father has not felt fulfilled working as a builder – yet, he followed his father's footsteps into that trade.

He believes he could feel more fulfilled by working as a travel agent as it would enable him to work with people and help them plan vacations, whilst enabling him to travel and widen his experience of the world. Lionel informs his father of his passion, and needs. Lionel takes steps to achieve his ideal dream by working for a travel agent.

How can you achieve your dreams?

How long do you want it to take to get from where you are now to where you want to be? That will depend on where you are now, where you want to be, and how determined you are to get there. Do not question *how* you are going to get to where you want to be, or *how long* it will take – as that may put limits on your potential. Rather ask – how can I achieve what I need? Then the creativity in your mind will kick in and provide you with ideas that you can investigate, and attract people who can help you. Remember, it is the journey that counts and not the destination – The journey has no end. Today is important.

Try the following: Imagine that you are living your ideal dream now and how it feels. Sit down in a quiet place, settle your body in stillness, sit with your back upright, breathe slowly and deeply, close your eyes gently and, in the space just above the centre of your eyebrows, watch an imaginary film of your life as it could be in the future. Do you like what you see? How it makes you feel? Are you happy and committed to follow the path it will take to get there? At this point you still have time to dream big and adjust the ideal lifestyle, as necessary, before setting goals and taking action. What will you need to change in your current circumstances to enable you to live your ideal dream? What obstacles do you perceive? You will need to create a bridge to span the gap between where you are now and where you want to be. That bridge will connect you and show you the way forward.

Will your ideal dream to manifest into reality – do not be despondent that your current lifestyle does not reflect your ideal lifestyle. That can change.

When you have accepted your dream as a reality – a bit like living the future in the present – never stop dreaming. This visualisation is an ongoing process that acts like a magnet in attracting and manifesting your vision, provided you eventually take the necessary action.

You cannot assume that everyone has the same vision as you.

What are you willing / not willing to sacrifice?

What are you willing to sacrifice to achieve your ideal dream? You may have to sacrifice nothing except for some of your time, and effort. Be realistic. If you are currently in a situation you do not want to be in and need to change your lifestyle, you may have to consider what other potential changes you may need to make. Keep an open mind and heart and be open to allow change into your lifestyle. It takes courage to let go of what is not working. Simplify your life, be happy with what you have now, and make space for the desired change to unfold. Believe in this process – allow it to transform your life.

Example:

John is working as a salesman and earns a lot of money but does not feel fulfilled. He has little time to spend pursuing a social life as he has to travel a lot.

Ideally, John would like to set up his own business. He is happy to sacrifice his travels but not his social life. He is aware he needs to continue his current employment until he has saved enough money to enable him to make the desired change. During this time, John can focus on gaining additional business skills.

What are you not willing to sacrifice to get there? Never compromise your values or your integrity. Take time to appreciate nature and savour your dreams. You may need to take time to retrain, or update your skills.

Example:

Trish left school at an early age. She was unsure of her inherent talents and her long-term life dream. She trained as a hairdresser and enjoyed meeting, and interacting with lots of people and providing a service that was needed. However, having now listed her strengths and weaknesses, she is determined she would feel more fulfilled working as a lawyer and practising law. Trish currently has two teenage children who are old enough to look after themselves at home.

Initially, Trish needs to devote time to studying law and is willing to sacrifice some time that could otherwise be spent connecting with the family. Her family wants Trish to be happy with her future and fully supports her decision. During this initial training time, Trish will be at home in the evenings and within reach to supervise the children's studies. At this point in time Trish is not willing to commit to spending much time away from home – this is an issue that may arise once she becomes a qualified lawyer.

Go to Exercise Seven (at the end of this chapter) and carefully put down your answers to these two questions.

You may need to spend time reading in the library, attend relevant courses, as well as talk with your team members (refer to Chapter Eleven) before you are ready to make any major decisions or changes.

Are you truly centred, and confident that your foundation is strong and intact? Are you ready to introduce a change? Can you persevere to achieve the goal? Do you have the courage to step out of your comfort zone?

Be prepared, but do not worry if you do not know everything before you start on your new journey, as you can learn along the way and make necessary adjustments as things progress – otherwise you may never get started.

Do your homework, expect the best but be prepared for the worst to happen, so that whatever happens along the way you will not be disappointed. You need to regularly review your progress, and make adjustments, as your life journey progresses and circumstances change.

Example:

Paul, who is twenty years of age, wants to retire at age thirty-five, using property investment as a vehicle for him to create wealth. He created a Plan that could allow that dream to manifest, provided he maintains his current employment for some time.

He also needs to create a backup plan in case he is unable to continue his current employment for some reason. He may need to consider retiring later than planned, or creating additional income.

Attitude of gratitude

Remember that everything is as it should be today – you have created it. Be grateful for all – everyone and everything – you have in your life now. Thank everyone who has helped you get to where you are now, even if they are not your favourite people. You cannot change the past or the present but you can create a different future for yourself. You can change your perception of what has happened in the past, accept it, have no regrets, and move forwards, with hope in your heart.

You can do anything you want within reason. Give yourself permission to ask for and receive help – now is the time to build your resources for the future. You are not an island, and help is always available when you ask for it. Make sure you ask people who are qualified to help. If you are used to giving more than you receive you need to allow yourself to accept help in whatever form it is offered without questioning the motive of the donor.

Example:

Daniel had realised a loss in his business due to him relying on a person he believed could be trusted and knowledgeable. In hindsight, Daniel concluded this person possessed little integrity and was not as knowledgeable as he had anticipated.

Daniel recognized that he needed to let go of the past, being a wiser person after this unfortunate experience, and plan for a future based on a stronger foundation. He reviewed his team members' capabilities, and made plans to recruit a few more experienced professionals who could help him rebuild and grow his business.

Each night before you go to sleep make quiet time to be thankful for all you have today, and believe your dream will manifest in due course when the timing is right. Continue to focus your mind on it and allow success to happen. Allow time for the seeds you have planted to ripen. Have patience. Never give up. Persevere.

Be grateful for all the natural miracles in your world – your right to freedom, wellness, family and friends, home, and your will to transform your life and continue to evolve. Spend time in nature, study the effects of the seasons – nothing changes this eternal process. It is a miracle.

Believe in yourself

Believe you can achieve whatever you need by focusing your mind on the desired outcome. Do not allow anyone to sow seeds of doubt in your mind. You are responsible for your own happiness.

Visualisation

Visualisation means being able to completely focus your mind on your ideal dream, and imagine you are already living that dream. Experience how it would make you feel, and believe that it will manifest. It is like living the future in the present – in your mind and in your heart. Meditation can help you to experience this outcome. Patience will help you to allow the process to unfold. This process can enable you to visualize more than one dream and help you to prioritise your dreams – decide which one is the most important to you – before setting your goals and focusing on your action plan, as explained in Chapter Ten.

Example:

Don has recently graduated from university and has three main dreams – building a business, getting married and starting a family, and travelling to America. He needs to determine which dream is a priority. By applying the concept of visualization to each of his main dreams, and prioritising his needs, this process can help him determine which dream to focus on first.

Believe you have what you need, now

Believe you have what you need now. Live your dream – imagine you have already achieved it. Doesn't it feel good? Repeat this process at the end of each day and you will never be disappointed. One day your dream will become reality if you believe in it and positively focus on it. Your mind will be focused on success and prosperity, and all else will follow.

Example:

Angela always wanted to build a successful business from operating a gift shop. She visualized owning a shop in a location near to the coast and country where she could incorporate a healthy lifestyle when not at work. With that in mind she felt happy.

Angela made a list of tasks she needed to complete before her ideal plan could become a reality – including:

- *choosing a business name*
- *preparing a budget*
- *determining how her business could be unique*
- *considering how she could best market her products*
- *listing the benefits her products could provide to the community; and*
- *starting to look for a suitable property to lease in a commercial environment*

Spend time living your dream. Make sure it is the dream you want to live for the rest of your life. Is it large enough to demand your all? Does it make you feel excited? Does it provide room for your future growth? Does it impose any limitations? Does it fulfil all your needs and desires in life? Open your mind and your heart to allow this processing time to become a part of your life – make sure it is your real passion before proceeding further. Take time to allow this process to feel real. Enjoy. Believe. Remember, changes and or modifications can be made along the way as circumstances change.

Reflect on where you are at, and what you have now. Be present. Your dream needs to be anchored and grounded. You need first to feel balanced and connected in your present life before you can manifest your dreams. You need to be sure you are firmly grounded – like the roots of a tree – before introducing change.

Are you excited? Are you happy? When you are ready, proceed to Chapter Three.

My purpose in life:

My main dream and purpose in life has always been to:

- *attain financial freedom so I can choose to do whatever I want, when I want, with whom I want; and to attain harmony in all other areas of life;*
- *empower others to attain financial freedom, and harmony in all other areas of life so they can live life fully.*

Total freedom means having harmony in all areas of life. One of my favourite songs is "Born Free". Follow the lyrics for a moment.

Born free, as free as the wind blows
As free as the grass grows
Born free to follow your heart

Live free and beauty surrounds you
The world still astounds you
Each time you look at a star

Stay free, where no walls divide you
You're free as the roaring tide
So there's no need to hide

Born free, and life is worth living
But only worth living
'Cause you're born free

(Stay free, where no walls divide you)
You're free as the roaring tide
So there's no need to hide

Born free, and life is worth living
But only worth living
'Cause you're born free

(**Songwriters**, Don Black and John Barry, and
sung by Andy Williams)

I was young when this song came out, and it became a metaphor for my life.

Maximizing the use of my inherent talents to provide a unique service to others, spending time with like-minded friends, and family, continuing the learning process, and being spiritually connected makes me feel fulfilled. The world is my oyster – there are no boundaries.

Generally, with increased awareness, I realise that each area of life can provide untold blessings as well as opening up the heart to receive endless bounties and discoveries. However, the main focus must be on health, as without optimal health I will be unable to manifest my dream.

My main dream remains the same. I have recently reviewed and updated my Life Plan, keeping comparisons from the past to enable me to track changes and progress, or lack of progress, and make the necessary adjustments. It is essential to always stay present, and grounded, especially during hardships encountered. Financial hardship, caused mainly by the global financial crisis, became the start of a deeper inner journey of awareness that helped me realise there is much more to life than financial success. In fact, financial freedom will come automatically by exchange of energies and time, by providing services needed by others. Money, by itself, cannot manifest creativity and peace of mind.

Included in my main dream is my hope to develop a wellness centre, a space for others to benefit from expansion of abilities and growth, in a safe environment, that can enhance their well-being and capacity to live my life fully.

How to achieve my dream?

The path to achieving my dream lies in visualizing that I am living my dream now, feeling it within my heart, and allowing it to manifest. I understand the need to be patient and enjoy each day of the endless journey.

In the meantime, I am celebrating my strengths whilst reviewing the foundations in each area of life and rebuilding those that require strengthening. I need to list my achievements, what I can offer, and how I can communicate that with the world.

I need to:

+ design a business card
+ prepare a financial budget
+ devise a brand name
+ outline a strategy, and list potential services and products
+ expand my existing network
+ form a team of advisors
+ update my knowledge and skills
+ become an entrepreneur / consider how best to market and provide the services and products
+ consider the need for a website; and
+ become an author / mentor / speaker

What will make me feel fulfilled?

Ongoing connection with friends and family, taking time to stay in touch, and feeling connected with the universe will make me feel fulfilled; being grateful that I can empower others to manifest their dreams, and witness their growth.

What am I willing / not willing to sacrifice?

I have always been willing to sacrifice my time to improve my knowledge, fitness, deepen my communication with friends, and allow time for what I have learnt and experienced to assimilate into my total being. I recognize the need to focus on rebuilding those foundations in areas where they have become weakened over time – in particular, the financial and physical areas – and at the same time focus on the other areas to ensure they are all harmonious. I need time out each day to meditate and stay focused.

I have never been willing to compromise my integrity nor my values in life, which has meant sometimes walking away from unfavourable situations and disharmonious relationships. Also, I need to sacrifice time-wasters – such as watching too much TV, and energy-wasters – such as spending time with people who are too needy and hard to please. I am not willing to sacrifice peace of mind. I am not willing to compromise my yogic lifestyle of harmony and simplicity.

Attitude of gratitude:

In the process of overcoming breast cancer I studied Reiki, I have studied contemporary medicines, alternative natural healing methods, and how the mind affects the wellness of the body. I sleep well on most nights, and am happy to be alive. I consult with both allopathic and contemporary health practitioners and recognize the need to integrate remedies of both into my life, as necessary. Both practitioners are happy with this arrangement. Mindful eating provides the foundation for ongoing wellness, together with regular practices of Yoga.

I enjoy spending time with like-minded friends, and family, and continue to be inspired by nature, allowing intuition to guide me. I go with the flow and thank the Universe for all my daily blessings – shelter, food, health, water, friends, and family. The more I feel and appreciate what I have, the deeper I feel the connection with the Divine self – peace within. I am happy and feel blessed both for the many setbacks – call them blessings disguised as learning opportunities – and for the abundant opportunities in life. I believe in myself and my yogic lifestyle.

There are times when I feel sad and weary and, miraculously, they pass. I keep my mind focused on successful outcomes, the will to live, and empower others. It helps to witness such states and their potential cause, from a distance.

Belief in myself:

A few of the friends I knew, before I adopted a simpler lifestyle, are no longer in touch. That is partly because they have a rigid daily routine, know what they want to achieve and by what date. They have no time to appreciate their inherent talents and enjoy life, in the present. Hence, rather than achieving freedom, they may impose many limitations on themselves. I accept that is their choice.

I enjoy beautiful things. My hobbies include – creating works of art, for example, designing and making semi-precious bead necklaces that provide differing natural earth energies, colours, and light. Many miracles can be observed and experienced in nature. I created a Zen garden in my back yard. Knitting has always been a past-time – I find it calming and meditative. Time stands still when I am engrossed with such activities.

My journey is a constant and eternal learning experience, inner growth, and clutter-clearing – to enable change and evolvement to replace old patterns with new patterns.

I believe there is no such thing as failure – only learning experiences. The more times I fail, the more I learn, and the more determined I become to ensure whatever I try next suits my current needs. However, I need to take time out to analyse the reason for the failure, and ensure the same situation is avoided in future.

A simpler lifestyle, mindfully maximising use of my inherent talents with passion, provides premium time, and abundance in daily life. My close friends and family are priceless assets.

Visualisation:

I visualize living my ideal life at the end of five, ten, fifteen … years. It feels good. I believe that will become reality in time.

Believe I have what I need now:

Whatever I need is achievable, each day, one day at a time. Change can happen only over time. Seeds are sown, they need time to germinate, and time to ripen – the cycle of nature. I believe I will achieve my goal, and in the meantime I can enjoy the journey, focusing on today.

Space for you to write in:

Preparation, peace of mind and an open heart are keys for building the foundation for success. Are you happy with your Blueprint for success?

Exercise Six
Why Success / What Will It Mean?

What will success mean to you? What will you be able to do that you cannot do now? How will you feel? Be true to yourself and take time to complete this exercise. It will form the foundation of your focus to move forward.

Being successful will mean to you:	How will you feel?
•	
•	
•	
•	
•	
•	
•	
•	
•	
•	
•	
•	

Signature...............................

Name: ....

Date: ....

Exercise Seven
What Are You Willing / Not Willing to Sacrifice?

List below what you are willing to sacrifice to achieve your dreams:

_____

_____

_____

_____

_____

_____

List below what you are not willing to sacrifice to achieve your dreams:

_____

_____

_____

_____

_____

_____

_____

_____

Signature.....................................

Name: ....

Date: ....

Chapter Three
Understanding Harmony

Mathematics expresses values that reflect the cosmos, including orderliness, balance, harmony, logic, and abstract beauty.

– Deepak Chopra

Beauty is the product of harmony between the mind and the senses.

– Johanr Christoph Friedrich von Schiller

The ultimate truth is so simple. It is nothing more than being in the pristine state. That is all that need be said.

– Sri Ramana Maharshi

Always aim at complete harmony of thought and word and deed. Always aim at purifying your thoughts and everything will be well.

– Mahatma Gandhi

When anger arises, think of the consequences.   – Confucius

A man is what he thinks about all day long.

– Ralph Waldo Emerson

If you are not getting as much from life as you want to, then examine the state of your enthusiasm.

– Norman Vincent Peale

I invent nothing; I rediscover.

– Auguste Rodin

Every child is an artist. The problem is how to remain an artist once he grows up.   – Pablo Picasso

The happiness of man in this life does not consist in the absence but in the mastery of his passions.

– Alfred Lord Tennyson

It's a funny thing about life; if you refuse to accept anything but the best, you very often get it.

– Somerset Maugham

The aim of life is self-development. To realise one's nature perfectly – that is what each of us is here for.

– Oscar Wilde

Imagination is more important than knowledge.

– Albert Einstein

Be really whole and things will come to you.

– Lao Tzu

- Definition of Harmony

- Why you need Harmony

- Discovering Harmony

- Who are you?

- What do you want in life?

- How can you achieve what you want?

Definition of Harmony

Various dictionaries, define harmony as:

+ An agreeable combination of component parts
+ A fitting or joining from the root
+ The just adaptation of parts to each other to form a complete, symmetrical, or pleasing whole
+ Musical concord; agreement, peace, and friendship

Life is all about achieving and maintaining happiness and harmony, so you can feel joyful and fulfilled. It is not a destination. Harmony comes from within. It was usually there at birth and its presence just needs to be unveiled and discovered. It is a journey of discovering the Source of the Divine energy, which is stored and resonates within you. Without this connection, there will be chaos and imbalance. This connection is the key that will enable you to discover your inherent talents, your Gold within; and enable you to experience harmony in each and all areas of life.

Harmony is about wellness. It includes having an abundance mentality, and the awareness to appreciate and give thanks each day for these blessings in your life. By appreciating what you have, even though it may be less than ideal in the long-term, you will automatically attract more. It creates a positive vibration, resulting in balance, and wholeness within. It is not about buying something, or allowing outside entertainment to dominate your life. Happiness can be experienced by mastering and embracing the passions of life and appreciating them, rather than suppressing any of them. However, if you focus on what you do not have, you will attract a greater lack – based on what is in your thoughts. The Law of Attraction is ever present.

Example:

David, a partner in a law firm, died at an early age and was angry that he had been unable to witness the success of his sons. His focus had always been on material successes and his image in the business world. This affected his body and soul, and manifested illness; alternatively, if he had been grateful for the opportunities he had and the experiences in his life, and cultivated compassion for those who were less fortunate, or experiencing grief, he could have created a harmonious energy within and experienced a feeling of peace and a state of wellness.

Ayurveda is an ancient Hindu science and philosophy, based on the Vedas, which can bring peace to the body and mind. It encompasses a traditional healing system that is aligned to the whole of life through the five elements – ether, wind, fire, water, and earth. Ayurveda medicine focuses mainly on nutrition, and prevention of disease by treatments using Himalayan herbs as well as massage and aromatic oils. Depending on your body type (constitution) – vata, pitta, or kapha – and current state of physical and mental health, any imbalance in yourself can be determined and treated naturally with herbs to allow a harmonic state to return.

Traditional Chinese Medicine ("TCM") has a similar concept with more of a focus on the meridians – energy channels – within the body that link to the organs within the body. Herbs, acupressure, and acupuncture are remedies used to remove blockages or disharmonies, allowing harmony to be restored.

These ancient teachings are now being recognised more, and integrated together with allopathic healing techniques in the treatment of imbalances within the body, mind, and soul – resulting in harmonious being. Generally, the ancient teachings aim to find the cause of the illness and then restore wellness; whereas allopathic methods, on their own, aim at alleviating pain without necessarily discovering the underlying cause of the disharmony within. The ancient methods also aim to prevent illness and maintain well-being.

Feng Shui means wind and water, and is an ancient Chinese system that teaches people how to understand the way they react with their environment. Electromagnetic energy, known as "chi", connects you to the world around you. This energy is an emotional field that runs inside the body, through centres known as "chakras", and flows out along paths known as "meridians". Developing a knowledge of Feng Shui provides you with the means to draw in the power around you and live life to the full, with harmony and control. It is like going with the flow of the river, rather than battling upstream against the current. The energy connects your thoughts, emotions, and ideas to every cell in the body, affects the mind and the heart, links the physical and emotional beings, and is dispersed out into the space you occupy. Feng Shui can be used as a tool to enable you to understand yourself with greater awareness so you can experience and benefit from a greater harmony within your surroundings.

Chinese philosophy maintains that harmonious living is created by:

+ Luck
+ Destiny
+ Feng Shui
+ Virtues
+ Education

in that order.

In Chinese philosophy, the absolute principle underlying the universe combines the principles of yin – the feminine aspect – and yang – the masculine aspect – in harmony with the natural order, the intuitive knowing of life. The Tao philosophy focuses on the harmony of the mind and body, and being in the flow of the Universe.

Yoga focuses on establishing a union with the Divine self. The discipline of practising Yoga on a regular, ongoing basis can provide you with an integrated harmony that emanates in health and vitality, including:

+ Fearlessness
+ Control of the senses
+ Compassion for all beings
+ Modesty
+ Selflessness

+ Courage in adversity
+ Sound judgement

+ Wisdom
+ Peaceful mind
+ Gentleness
+ Humility
+ Purity of the body and mind

+ Prosperity
+ Happiness

Both practicality and spirituality must be present in life for harmony to exist. When you become more aware of the harmony within, which can be achieved through meditation, peace of mind can be experienced and creativity emerges. Creativity enables you to make natural, intuitive, decisions based on heart-felt needs – rather than erratic decisions, based on illogical reactions, that will require time and effort to correct in the future. This does not mean that you need to renounce material wealth – you can have both materiality and spirituality at the same time – they need to be interdependent. You need to renounce any attachment to material wealth, which could result in greed.

There can be no harmony where there is clutter, a blockage that fills space that could otherwise accommodate harmonious energy. Hence, clutter-clearing needs to be an ongoing process in your life. Clutter exists in many forms – physical (belongings), emotional (feelings), and mental (thoughts). Once the clutter in the mind is cleared, harmony can be restored in each of the other areas.

Beauty encompasses harmony between the mind or body and the senses, as can be witnessed, for example, in a smiling face.

The heart is the ultimate centre of self where opposite energies are woven together with love. This process leads to connection and wholeness, enabling you to embrace living and experiencing life to the full. Primordial opposites include:

+ Male and female
+ Spirit and matter

Each energy needs to be equally included and neither renounced.

Harmony is a synchronicity, of energy in all areas of life, where every aspect is in balance. If any one of the following six areas of your life lacks harmony, your equilibrium in life will be out of balance and you may feel as though your life is in turmoil:

+ Physical
+ Mental
+ Familial / Social
+ Vocational
+ Financial
+ Spiritual

Each of the above areas needs a strong foundation and this aspect will be analysed and considered in detail in the following chapters.

Mastery is an act of passion, achieved by disciplining the senses to have a greater experience. Realising the truth, and reaching enlightenment, you can experience whatever happens, in a state of harmony and freedom, without experiencing the highs and lows of elation or depression. Having a passionless mind with an attitude of worship towards your partner results in harmony.

Why you need Harmony

Your main reason for being alive is to enjoy life fully and be happy. It is best if you have wellness, and abundance. Most of you came into this world that way. What happened to you between then and now? Your mind was influenced by fear and other people, and by adverse experiences, creating obstacles that led to illness, lack of abundance, and misery.

Example:

Philip's mum was sick and he always felt that she would pass away whilst he was young — hence he feared that he would be deserted instead of feeling unconditional love and knowing that all would be well whatever the outcome. He always felt the need to possess something he did not have, rather than feeling happy and grateful for being alive. He lived in fear, rather than with joy. Philip had not yet discovered his Gold within.

Only when harmony exists in all areas of your life can you feel fulfilled and truly happy. If any area is lacking in harmony, there will be an imbalance of some kind within yourself. You need to spend time on self-development, and discovery to experience the beauty in life, and the harmony between the mind and the senses. When you purify your thoughts, deeds and actions, all will be well.

Example:

Julie is a successful business person, has a young family, and a loving partner. She fears that she will become sick and be unable to cope with all her responsibilities. She feels unhappy as she has no foundation in place in the wellness area of her life. Julie needs to take time out to review her lifestyle and mindfully focus on establishing a daily wellness routine.

The world is in turmoil. It is resonating disharmony that forces change for everyone, due to: wars, drug-related outcomes, fatal accidents, illness, poverty, homelessness, terrorism, floods, bush fires, to name a few. Generally, you spend more money and energy, yet derive less happiness; you have more conveniences, yet have less available time; you learn how to make a living, but not how to live a life; outer space was conquered but not inner space; there are deep profits, but shallow relationships.

The world is being forced to change by events caused by a lack of connection between materialism – the outer world, and the Divine self – the inner world. The world is crying out for peace and equilibrium – change is inevitable. Hopefully you will *choose* to change, rather than be forced to change by events over which you have control.

Review your lifestyle, focus your mind on what you really need, take time to remove the unwanted weeds, plant the seeds of positive change in fertile ground, be patient while the seeds grow, and you will start to experience positive changes in your life. You need to be careful what you allow into your bodies and minds, how you spend your time, and protect your inborn talents.

If you focus your thoughts on, for example, fear, and imagine you will be unable to achieve success, fear will trigger doubt and a lack of self-confidence.

Example:

David spends a lot of time with Julian who has a negative outlook on life. He feels drained of energy. David needs to search for like-minded, positive thinking, friends and choose them carefully – so he has a strong support group. They need to resonate with what he believes and needs, otherwise he may never be able to attain harmony and peace within.

Find a trusted mentor, a role model, someone you admire who has harmony in his or her life, someone with whom you can talk about how you might attain your harmony, with whom you can discuss what is not working, and who can motivate you to keep moving in the right direction. A mentor will share experiences of how they have evolved in life, and how you can avoid pitfalls they may have encountered. You may need a different mentor for each area of your life. No man is an island – you need to be willing to listen to others and accept constructive advice from qualified people.

Read books to learn about how to attain and maintain harmony. Everyone is different so you need to be the one to choose your books. The books will provide the knowledge but you need to integrate and synchronise what you read with what you need to experience; gradually introduce changes, and believe that over time new habits will form to replace old outdated habits. Persevere, with patience and determination, and you can witness the change you need to manifest your ideal dream. You are the master of your destiny – do not allow others to dissuade you. Otherwise you will live the life of others, and never feel fulfilled or happy.

Be patient – understand that Rome was not built in one day.

Discovering Harmony

Firstly, you need to question what is working and what is not working in each area of your life. What is working is likely harmonious. What is not working will require some focus and development. To eradicate a bad habit, you need to focus your mind on the opposite virtue, to remove the old habit and allow time for the new habit to replace it.

Example:

Tony lost his financial assets during a global economic crisis, and his job was made redundant. Naturally, he was devastated and deflated. Instead of focusing on this unfortunate debilitating financial loss, Tony needs to turn this outcome into an opportunity, and be thankful for the other areas in his life that are harmonious. He needs to accept what has happened and consider ways in which he can start to rebuild financial freedom, visualise that he now has what he needs and take action to achieve it. He could sell whatever is no longer useful to generate additional income.

By staying positive, having faith, and focusing on abundance you will feel relaxed and have peace of mind, which will allow your mind to attract what you need. If you focus on what you do not have that will continue to be the status quo and nothing will change, or things could become worse than they already are.

Before you were born there was a vibratory energy resonating in your body, which was likely to have been positive. That is why babies usually appear to be happy. They live for the moment with enthusiasm. Some of them may appear to be unhappy, which could mean that in a prior life their non-physical element had suffered a traumatic experience, or they may be experiencing temporary discomfort. You need to rediscover the state of harmony in each area of your life.

My Mum used to say – *everyone is different*. You need to know who you are, taking into account your family history and circumstances, to be able to fully consider what area of your life is not in harmony and needs some attention.

Who are you?

As you were growing up, negative influences were probably imposed on your initial harmonious state by your parents, teachers, and others. This may have been unintentional, they were doing their best in their given circumstances. Parents, peers, teachers, loved ones – all have different backgrounds, ways of thinking, beliefs, and thought patterns. In any case, that initial state of perfect harmony was temporarily lost. The good news is that the harmonious state can be rediscovered. You need to follow your own thoughts back to their conception. This process can help you to discover what happened to change the initial state of harmony, and determine the path you need to follow to re-connect with your inner truth.

Recognising and observing patterns is the beginning of wisdom, insight into the big picture. Illusions are shattered, dreams are integrated, and clarity begins. Knowing your archetypal influence clarifies your purpose in life, and enables you to attract the circumstances you need to fulfil your purpose in life.

Example:

Joe has experienced an interesting and successful career in business, which his father felt was the most appropriate career for him. Over time, Joe has realized that he does not feel fulfilled each day and feels there must be something more to life.

After spending most of his life sitting at a desk, Joe now feels the need to experience the beauty of nature and give thanks for the miracles that are all around. He decides to study photography as that will enable him to travel the world, under-water, above the clouds, on mountains, in cities, and wherever he feels the need to be. Joe writes books to share his experiences with others and donates part of the proceeds from the sale of the book to a charity of his choice. He is now living life with passion, and having fun. He enjoys spending more time with his partner, family, and friends.

There are deeper levels of consciousness than those available through the basic life energy. Dreams link the conscious and unconscious mind states, the upper chakras with the lower chakras, and can become powerful teachers. Hence, you need to write down your dreams in a journal for future reference. Intuition is the unconscious recognition of patterns that enhance psychic ability, rather than analytical reasoning. By finding your own light you can break free of unwanted established patterns. It is important to use the energy of instinct consciously and harmoniously for reflection, as a gateway to self- knowledge and expression. Symbols, such as mandalas, force the mind into clarity – an emergence of personal vision. You may begin to see more deeply into people and situations around you and create your own vision – a new way of being, to unveil something that has been hidden from you until now.

The heart chakra acts as a conduit between the mind and body. It can be recognised and released when it is working harmoniously. It allows the mind to witness experiences in the body. Relationships can have stability, mutual respect, and freedom. Nature seeks balance. Until then stored tensions and unresolved emotional transactions act as a veil. Areas in which the heart integrates balance are:

+ Reaching out and taking in: experiencing fear and grief. You need to establish boundaries, in which you can reach out safely to others

+ Attachment and freedom: longing and fear of commitment. You need to establish a balance in the soul, between freedom and commitment, expansion and constriction when you respect freedom of self and another – then you can make a commitment based on interdependence rather than dependence.

You need to come to terms with:

+ Grief – acknowledge it, accept it, express it
+ Compassion for yourself and others – stop identifying with your past disappointments – the past cannot be changed but you can change the way you perceive it
+ Anger – focus on empathy and compassion
+ Devotion to the Divine self – relax and allow an ego-less surrender, knowing all will be well
+ Rejection – reconnect to the Divine self to overcome this limiting fear

A feeling of rigidity or tightness in the chest can indicate some blockage in the heart due, for example, to parental rejection. You need to reach beyond yourself and connect with others to enable this blockage to be dissolved. A deficient energy in the heart chakra can also result from withdrawal due to a divorce, or dwelling on a past relationship, that you have been unable to move on from, even though it ended a long time ago, causing you to be stuck in anger and betrayal. Hence the heart stays closed and you have trouble giving empathy to yourself as well as others; lack compassion; and remain critical and judgemental – all of which keep channels for expression and reception closed, and projects this hurt to the person you love.

The practice of deep abdominal breathing can provide a natural balance for taking in and giving out. Most people have never learnt how to breathe properly by using the full extent of their lungs. Try lying on the floor on your back, or sitting on a chair, with a straight spine and place the hands on the abdomen – when breathing in feel the abdomen expand and when fully breathing out – feel the abdomen deflate. You can practice this way of breathing until your mind feels calmer, and your body feels more relaxed.

Example:

Paul feels guilty that he did not spend enough time with his ex-spouse, who divorced him five years ago. He fears the same result will happen in any future relationship he enters into. By recognising his fear, he chose to find a solution to enable him to regain his self-confidence. Paul attended a meditation class where he was introduced to the practice of deep abdominal breathing, which he practised regularly at home and after a period of two weeks his mind felt much calmer. Paul overcame his fear and joined a few social activities knowing that in time he would connect with another partner.

Healing a broken heart enables the mind, body, and another individual to be reunited into an integrated whole, whereby you can:

+ see things anew
+ expand horizons
+ gain a deeper connection with yourself and another
+ celebrate the temple within; and
+ express intimacy

This exhilarating cleansing experience, and feeling of wholeness can deepen your own divinity, excite you to take better care of your body, and to clean the clutter from your house.

Firstly, you need to know yourself, honour that aspect of yourself that lives within another, and love yourself before you can openly offer love to someone else. That can result in a feeling of liberation joy, and happiness.

Imagine your ideal person – how would they speak to you. What would they do for you? Let your feelings permeate your body with nourishment. How would it feel? Fantasy helps reprogram the heart chakra. The purpose is to get the self to expand beyond its limited ego state into a wider sense of connection with all life.

You need to balance intimacy with autonomy and monitor your boundaries. Recognise this state of being, versus the state of doing. Relationship furthers the evolution of individual souls and collective souls of our planet. By enjoying this state of inclusiveness and connectedness you can relax and feel free.

What do you want in life?

There are two ways to feel – good or bad. The choice is yours. If you choose to feel good, each day will be easy and harmonious. If you choose to feel unhappy, each day will be difficult and unpleasant. You need to put positive thoughts in your mind – make your mind your friend.

Has the choice you once made for your lifestyle outgrown its purpose? Is it time to transform it to something new? Are you willing to make mistakes, be responsible, learn from them, and correct them? Transition from the past to the future is powerful. Balance / harmony / moderation is the underlying foundation of longevity in all beings. It is important not to feel stuck or disheartened.

You need to love yourself, and allow others to take care of their own life needs – as only they can understand their individual needs. The only person you can change is you, so that needs to be your primary focus. You need to have compassion for yourself and others, and not judge anyone. Act respectfully and responsibly towards yourself, and spend your time wisely. Learn to enjoy your own company, honour your limits so you experience minimum stress, and speak your truth so you maintain your integrity. Have patience. You can find and befriend people who treat you the way you expect to be treated.

Always focus on your needs, and be patient. Relax and allow time for positive change to naturally take place – within the space you are creating by removing old habits.

Vision propels you forward to a goal that is constantly changing and evolving, as directed by the vision. It is an essential part of the healing process and evolvement.

What is your vision, your mountain, your paradise? Forget your age, present circumstances, and other excuses. Go for it.

How can you achieve what you want?

You need to regularly spend quality time to be alone to discover what is not working for you, and then revise your daily actions and / or change your belief system and reconnect with your harmonious state. Observe how you reacted to situations that arose during the day and determine what you could do differently the next time – how to improve the outcome.

Find a book that is uplifting and discover how you can achieve more harmony in your life. A few suggestions are listed in the Resources section at the end of the book. Be compassionate with yourself and others. Love yourself and others unconditionally.

Adapt to new circumstances without having unrealistic expectations. Have faith that you can cope with life's changing circumstances. Be grateful for what you have now and simplify your life. Witness your own needs.

Imagine change, and you can create and experience change. Adopt an image, symbol, or sign to sharpen your reality, your goal for the future, which draws its needs from the present.

Follow your dream. Never give up. Your vision will enable you to consciously formulate the path to the future, and liberate yourself from and grips of the past. Your unique path in life needs to be determined based on your temperament. Allow for a complete transformation to be assimilated, little by little.

In the meantime, celebrate what you have and allow yourself to have fun each day. Progress at your own speed to suit your lifestyle, there is no need to compare yourself with others.

Consider the sculptor who, when asked what he was doing, replied – "building a cathedral", rather than "chipping away at a block of stone".

My definition of Harmony:

As a child, I received a new bicycle for a birthday. I had asked for a bike because it would enable me to travel faster, and further afield, than by walking. How did I learn to ride it? I visualized myself riding it along country lanes with the wind blowing through my hair. I felt elated. After a few trial runs with Mum holding onto the bike, I could balance and ride it alone. Of course, I fell off a few times, which made me more determined to try again and succeed. Mum was my helper / mentor at that time.

Mum thought it would be good for me to learn to swim. Although she was a proficient swimmer she decided to sign me up for lessons with an instructor. The teacher thought that if she pushed me into the pool I would automatically swim (is that bullying?). I panicked and did not enjoy the experience, and never went near the water again until much later in life when I wanted to learn to swim, with confidence, and now I enjoy the experience. The circumstances and the timing must be right for the harmony to manifest.

Mum also thought that attending elocution class would be good for me. The issue was I always forgot the words when asked to speak before an audience, especially for exams, I did not enjoy this experience and chose not to continue attending those classes, much to Mum's disappointment and embarrassment. I pretended to be fast asleep in bed when it was time to leave home for the class. There was no harmony here! Later in life I learned to overcome this fear of public speaking by attending a course and professional speaker workshops. Although now I am naturally nervous before speaking to an audience I enjoy sharing my knowledge with, and showing my experiences to, audiences. Getting to know more about other people, their hopes, fears, and needs, is a privilege. I had to overcome my initial fear, to gain connection with the audiences. Harmony is like building a communication bridge, to become connected.

Why I need Harmony:

I need harmony to enable me to enjoy life fully, with joy; to feel connected with others; to understand how things work with ease and without restriction; to conserve my energy flow and experience ease in every day routines, instead of fighting against the flow and sensing difficulties.

Did you ever try to get a wooden swing to work so that it moved to and fro without much effort? It took a lot of practice for me to learn this technique. When I could swing to and fro without too much effort I felt a great sense of freedom and connection – harmony with nature, and a feeling of happiness.

Riding a horse, and working together to attain a co-ordinated rhythm provides excellent training in leadership skills. I never learnt how to persuade the horse to jump over the water jump – they dug their feet into the ground and stopped dead in their tracks, leaving me to catapult over their head and into the water – maybe they sensed my fear. Horses are sensitive, regal and intelligent animals that demand respect. They can also provide a sense of tranquillity to those who need to be healed from trauma, as they are gentle and caring creatures.

~ ~ ~

Going with the flow, living in the NOW is harmony. Otherwise, it is easy to impose limitations on what can be achieved each day. During my recent sabbatical I discovered that it is not only the knowledge that is important, but more the experience of living each day with awareness and mindfulness – integrating the knowledge into experiences of everyday life. Karma yoga is meditation in action – when actions are guided by divine grace from within. Practising meditation each day allows this harmonic state to deepen. The whole of life can become a meditation.

I feel a strong connection with, and appreciation of, nature – the flowers, trees, birds, and animals, and experience the miracle of life's natural harmony. Observing natural events enables me to feel the eternity and flow of the seasons. I take time to listen to the birds singing when I awake – it happens every day, irrespective of the weather conditions. I aim to start each day with a session connecting with and appreciating the simple pleasures in life the universe offers. I listen to the silence that allows the trees and plants to grow at their own pace, in whatever environment they live.

I feel happier doing less and actually have more, now I have cleared a lot of clutter from my life – physical, emotional, and mental – which is an ongoing process. Every movement, when done with mindfulness and joy feels like a connection with the Divine, and belonging to a world of infinity and greatness.

Discovering Harmony:

After I discovered the immensity of Yoga and experienced the heart's deep involvement in life, before which the head ruled everything I did, I felt lighter and more joyful. It took a while for me to recognize and verbalise my deep feelings and able to communicate them to others, thereby creating a closer bond with, and deeper understanding of, other human beings.

It is important to feel connected to a much larger universe than the immediate surroundings. Recognition of my feelings strengthens the practice of listening and acknowledging that each person has a different perception and experience of life. This, in turn, deepens my empathy and compassion for others.

I discovered that without harmony in each area of life energy was wasted, and I became easily tired and unable to live life fully with joy. There is a need to conserve energy within – this concept can be compared with maintaining and running a car economically and efficiently. However, the energy needs to be used effectively or else the internal pressure finds a way to escape to alleviate internal stress – in my case through a series of debilitating nose bleeds.

The process of reviewing each area of life to detect disharmony and work on bringing that area back into balance is ongoing. I need to prioritise which area needs to be focused on each day. Eating mindfully is the main area that needs a special focus as there is no diet plan that works every day. I need to listen to my body's needs to determine what will be most nutritious for each meal. It is fun to plan nutritious meals based on the body's needs – time well spent. By keeping a food journal my knowledge increases. Learning which herbs enhance and enrich each dish is a whole new world, and ongoing project.

Who am I?

Realising that I am an eternal divine being with a mortal body and mind helps me to balance my daily routine by allowing time for meditation and mindfulness in completing all the tasks I undertake each day. This process enables me to tackle daily projects with peace of mind, appreciate the world of beauty, and personal relationships.

What do I want in life?

My need is for simplicity – optimum health, peace of mind, like-minded friends, financial freedom, and time to empower others so they can become aware of and experience harmony in each area of life, and live life fully without boundaries and regret.

I have learnt that happiness comes from internal peace and not from outside achievements. Hence, whatever projects I undertake from now on need to enable me to feel joyful, without stress. Self-mastery is ongoing and the most important asset, from which all else can grow. With a calm mind I can visualise how to manifest my dreams.

How can I achieve what I want?

I chose Yoga as the tool that can most effectively enable me to attain harmony in each area of life and share my experience with others, as it encompasses the whole of life and is an expansive science.

I aim to live each day fully, believing in myself, and having compassion for others. I need to spend time alone when necessary to recharge my batteries. Each night, before going to sleep, I review the day and consider whether any actions or thoughts could be improved upon for the next time. I visualize the tasks that need to be done the following day as though I have completed them successfully and effortlessly, and let them go to allow intuition to play its part. Whenever I feel that things are not going as planned I take time out to appreciate and be grateful for the goodness and blessings in my life, and consider my thoughts and reactions, before returning to my daily routines.

Each day, I learn more about my body's capacity and needs, so it can be well-maintained and fit for living life fully.

After living in the Yoga centre for five years, I now need time to assimilate these experiences into my new surroundings, to integrate and synchronise the two worlds. I am fortunate to have good neighbours, including Kate, with whom I shared a room for two years at the Yoga centre.

At a time when most other people of a similar age group are considering retirement, I am embracing a new, exciting adventure in life, with a bigger heart, and deeper awareness: and my heart needs to be physically strengthened to be able to cope.

The process of completing this book has provided the opportunity to relive and show my life experiences to you with an expanded awareness. It has helped me redefine my ideal dream, and express my innate artistic ability, whilst sharing the knowledge gained during my extensive career. I have always wanted to build my own house and learn to fly an aeroplane — those dreams are on my bucket list!

Space for you to write in:

Read on to analyse the six component parts of life's Harmony.

Chapter Four
Physical Harmony

Health is the first prerequisite of all attainments in life. The attainment of health is not only an individual human aspiration, but also a basic human right.

– World Health Organisation

To keep the body in good health is a duty. ... Otherwise we shall not be able to keep our mind strong and clear.

– Buddha

The first wealth is health.

– Ralph Waldo Emerson

The greatest wealth is health.

– Virgil

Very few people know what real health is because most are occupied with killing themselves ... the body must be in an intimate relationship with the mind.

– Albert Szent-Gyorgyi

To me good health is more than just exercise and diet. It's really a point of view and a mental attitude you have about yourself.

– Albert Schweitzer

I have decided to stick with love. Hate is too great a burden to bear.

– Martin Luther King Jr

Our physical body possesses a wisdom which we who inherit the body lack. We give it orders which make no sense.

– Henry Miller

Use your health, even to the point of wearing it out. That is what it is for. Spend all you have before you die; do not outlive yourself.

– George Bernard Shaw

The part can never be well unless the whole is well.

– Plato

Yoga teaches us to cure what need not be endured and endure what cannot be cured.

– BKS Iyengar

- Health
- Preventing Stress
- Heart
- Energy
- Food
- Wellness
- Exercise
- Rejuvenation

Health

You need harmony in your physical body, mind and soul. This foundation is the most important aspect in your tapestry of life, your personal jigsaw puzzle. If any part of your body – your blueprint – is unwell, it will affect the whole energy of your being, and you will feel miserable.

The foundation to achieving physical harmony is to gain a depth of knowledge of the blueprint of the body, and understand how each part of the physical body interacts with, and is affected by the mind and the soul. This blueprint is a miracle – it is the same for each and every body. However, everyone is different and you need to understand the current state of your body so you can become aware of and address any areas of disharmony.

You need to protect your body from danger at all times – do not take it for granted – so it can enable you to live life fully. You need to respect its capabilities that can vary from day to day, to prevent stress, and maintain a healthy body. You need to conserve energy to ensure your body can cope with daily activities.

When you were born, subject to genetic imbalance that may have been inherited – and can usually be managed – your physical and mental health was pure, and unfettered by influences from the outside world. In that state, children can be likened to artists who are creating a beautiful tapestry in life – their smiles radiate happiness and a passion for living. Trauma to the body can upset your overall harmony. The cause of any un-wellness needs to be determined and healed. You need to reconnect with that initial harmonious state by focusing on optimal health – to allow abundance in each area of life to be enjoyed to the full. Yoga is a tool that can help to provide this healing process, and there are other tools.

Birth is a miracle. You were born with a physical body that you inherited from your parents. The first experience in life, after spending about nine months in the protected environment of your mother's womb, affects your well-being. Sometimes the experience is welcoming (being embraced by your mother) and sometimes it can be traumatic – such as when the baby is lifted into the air by its feet and patted on the backside, with a view to allowing the blood to circulate properly and the lungs to function. Birthing under water can provide a more natural, and less traumatic, birthing experience. Premature birthing can cause trauma to the lungs.

The physical body has a limited lifespan – it is the vehicle that enables you to live your life. It is your servant. It provides the vehicle from which success and harmony in each of the other areas of life can be fully experienced.

Life is like a tapestry, or jigsaw puzzle – each piece affects the whole, and if any piece is missing the whole is not complete. Your body is like a temple, and needs to be revered and treated with utmost care and respect. It is up to you to learn how your physical body works, internally and externally, and always maintain it in good working order, to enable you to live life fully each day. Without optimum health, life cannot be lived fully, and harmony cannot be enjoyed in each of the other areas of life.

The state of your physical body is affected by the state of your mind. Whatever you think you become.

Most diseases are psychosomatic – caused by negative emotions or states of mind, which weaken the immune system and allow disease to enter the body. If you experience any of these harmful states, you need to focus on introducing the opposite positive state into your life.

These negative states need to be changed to positive states for you to experience wellness rather than disease.

Examples – substitute:

- hope for fear – visualize successfully completing a special project and work towards allowing that successful experience into your life
- cheerfulness for anger – accept that all is at it should be for now, you created it, and smile knowing you can change the future
- forgiveness for hatred – accept that everyone's perceptions differ, and forgive yourself and others for any misunderstanding, and never take anything personally
- humility for pride – play fairly, be grateful for your lot in life and treat others as you expect to be treated
- kindness for cruelty – if someone treats you unfairly do not allow their ways to influence your integrity
- unconditional love for self-love – see the Divine in everyone, and act from a state of abundance, rather than being needy
- listening and learning to combat ignorance – make sure you understand the overall situation and do not jump to any conclusions before you have all the facts

- self-esteem for instability – be sure of your strengths and weaknesses with confidence and do not compare yourself with others
- gratefulness for greed – understand the difference between what you want, or wish, and what you really need, and live within your means

The state of mind affects the functioning of the various glands.

Examples:

The thymus gland regulates the immune system. Examples of states that can cause a weakened immune system, include:
- *grief, which often precedes disease, such as cancer*
- *A Type A personality that is more prone to stress and heart disease*
- *any kind of prolonged stress depresses the immune system and lowers resistance to infection, resulting in disorders, such as – hypertension, heart disease, stroke, bowel disease, stomach ulcers, asthma, migraine, arthritis, and cancer*
- *The endocrine glands secrete chemical hormones into the bloodstream*
- *The pituitary gland co-ordinates the glandular system with the nervous system and relays messages to all the endocrine glands – regulating the body temperature by toning up the blood vessels and stimulating the kidneys*
- *The adrenal glands govern sudden bursts of energy and heat, and stimulate the fight and flight response mechanisms. Over-stimulated adrenal glands maintain the body and mind in a state of perpetual alarm, resulting in depression or anxiety – as human beings are unable to flee from problems or physically battle adversities, and thus face continued and unrelenting stress from which they are unable to respond with physical activity.*

Defects in the secretion of digestive enzymes into the small intestine by the pancreas can cause diabetes.

When you learn to understand the functions of the various internal structures in the body, you can focus on healing any imbalances in conjunction with your medical practitioner, who may be grateful that you are taking an interest in the management of your well-being.

The foundation of wellness includes discovering where you fit into your family ancestry. Who were your parents, grandparents and ancestors? What was the condition of their health? What were their occupations and circumstances during their lifespan? Once this information is available, you can question – and begin to understand – the cause of certain of your illnesses, and consider choosing a natural remedy rather than merely accepting and treating the symptoms of the illness with medication that may produce undesirable side-effects that require additional medication. It is wise to mindfully question the real need for medication that is prescribed to ensure there will be minimal side effects.

Example:

Betty was diagnosed with breast cancer and was treated with chemotherapy and radiation therapy. Five years later she was given the all-clear by the surgeon. The physical aspect was cured. However, Betty recognised that the mental and spiritual causes of the cancer could remain within the body and the cause of the cancer still needed to be determined and dealt with or else, without adopting a change in lifestyle, the cancer could recur.

Betty discovered that her grandmother had breast cancer at an early age, after which she became depressed. She decided to spend regular time practising suitable Yoga asanas and meditation to allow her body to fully recover from her condition, and her mind to remain in a state of quietness, to minimise the risk of the cancer recurring.

Some people believe that they automatically inherit their physical ailments from their ancestors, which is not always true. Even though this may be a fact, such ailments can often be cured. For example, certain disease can be a result of the eating patterns of our ancestors, and once this is recognized, you can change your eating habits. Your thought pattern may believe such conditions are hereditary and cannot be cured but by changing the thought pattern to one of wellness you may be able to improve the current condition of your physical body.

Example:

Keith has arthritis in his knees but also in other joints and he believes that condition was inherited from his mother. This may be true but Keith could choose to cure his condition by changing his thought / belief pattern. Instead of blindly accepting that his condition was inherited from his mother and is incurable, he could imagine that his body is now well and enjoy the feeling of wellness and, possibly, the disease could heal.

Currently, Keith chooses to have cortisone injections that result in undesirable side-effects that, in turn, require additional healing treatment. He needs to believe the condition can be cured to allow the healing process to take place. In addition, he could consider the healing effects of natural foods and herbs, and suitable Yoga asanas but says he is currently too busy to deal with this potential change. Keith needs to realise that health needs to come first in planning daily routines so the functions of the body can maintain their effectiveness.

Combining holistic and allopathic approaches to wellness, after obtaining a diagnosis of the cause of your un-wellness, and seeking a second and third opinion, before combining the best of both approaches, can enable wellness to be restored using the most appropriate healing solution for your ailment. Always keep an open mind and heart. Conduct your own research so you are fully informed, and then allow the healing process to proceed calmly.

The physical and mental states of your body and mind also affect the Soul. The Spirit lives on and is usually automatically incarnated into a new physical body, lifetime after lifetime. Different levels of spiritual progression may reincarnate. All souls do not originate from the same place or have the same evolutionary progression. Spiritual disconnection from the soul often results in disease and disharmony within the physical body.

Preventing Stress

How do you prevent stress? What type of body do you have? Are you doubting the capacity of the body to serve you well? What type of food does your body need? What type of exercise does your body need? There is so much to consider and learn!

You need to honour the needs of your physical body, learn to love it, just as it is. It is the temple of your soul. The more you understand about your anatomy, the more meaningful life's process will become.

When you compare yourself with others, you are bound to cause stress – you are denying the beauty of your uniqueness. Go and take a look at yourself in the mirror. What do you see? Do you admire the miracle of who you are? Or, do you focus on the wrinkles that show you have endured life well; or, the sagging muscles that could be tightened by practising Yoga, walking, or some other beneficial exercise? Or, the bulge around the midriff that could benefit from following a mindful eating regime?

Examples:

- *Stella took a look in the mirror one day and saw a bulging midriff. She had some spare funds, and decided to undergo surgery to remove the excess fat. Unless she changes her thoughts about her body image, this may be the start of other "needs" to change her outer appearance, rather than focusing on building her self-esteem. This is an example of changing the packaging, rather than the contents.*
- *Denise took a look in the mirror one day and realised that her face contained a few more wrinkles than she would like. She chose to focus on getting a shorter hair-cut that would accentuate her beautiful large eyes, and greet each day with an attitude of gratitude. Over time, the wrinkles lost any importance as they were natural. Denise chose to accept and love her body, and was grateful for her beautiful eyes and peaceful mind.*

There is no need to fear your body – better to get to know it well, and focus on maintaining it in optimum working order. When you feel well, you become aligned with your reason for living. The world is your oyster.

When you recognise that everyone has imperfections, and build your self-esteem, based on your uniqueness, you can express that uniqueness.

Trying to be someone else robs you of your true identity. There is no need to hide – better to accept and celebrate the real you.

You need to seriously consider the potential ongoing after-effects of cosmetic surgery before agreeing to enter into it. What are the potential side-effects? How could it affect your body? Is it worth it? Is it really necessary? Remember, as the physical body ages its structure will change – and that needs to be factored in. Your natural beauty can be more important than a look you do not need.

Sound and communication through mantra chanting can release tensions and provide a connection with the Divine Self.

Heart

The heart is the bridge that connects the body, and mind – it is where the soul resides. The heart is like a temple within the body, and needs to be understood and treated with respect, so it can function well. Like the engine of a car – once it stops, the body stops. Any pain you are experiencing in the heart region needs to be discussed with your doctor.

Just as important as the physical body is the non-physical body as it affects the state of the physical body. Your vibrational energy within was resonating long before your physical birth, and getting in touch with your Source can enable you to focus your thoughts on wellness. The heart energy connects the heart to the lungs, and the thymus gland. All other energy channels in the body need to be functioning harmoniously to allow a healthy heart to be maintained.

Heart irregularities are common and can be caused and affected by stress, negative thoughts, both conscious and subconscious, and shallow breathing.

It is important you consult with your doctor to determine the cause of any heart irregularity or dysfunction before concluding what the most effective remedy might be. Sometimes a doctor may be unaware of the cause of the condition and prescribe medication that, seemingly, could have undesirable side effects that result in additional dis-ease without addressing the real cause of the heart irregularity. Natural medicines, such as herbs, may provide a more effective remedy by treating the cause of the illness, rather than just providing temporary pain relief. Depending on the type of irregularity, you may need a combination of both allopathic and naturopathic remedies. You need to be fully informed about the condition, the cause of the irregularity, and all potential remedies, and side-effects of each remedy. Certain medications may be less toxic than others. If you are in any doubt about medication that has been prescribed, it may be advisable to seek a second opinion.

Healing can mean restoring balance to the heart's organism. The practice of certain Yoga asanas, for example Shavasana, Yoga Nidra, and Nadi Shodhana may be beneficial for people experiencing heart malfunction.

Understanding how to breathe correctly, which enables the lungs to be used to their full capacity and the heart kept purified, is one of the most important practices you can incorporate into your lifestyle. You can experience this process by lying on the floor, or sitting in a chair, with your spine straight. Settle your body, and breathing naturally through the nose, allow the cool air to enter the nostrils – feeling the cold air flowing in on inhalation, and the warmer air flowing out on exhalation. When you breathe through the nose, the cold air becomes warm before it is ingested by the lungs (in the tropics the hot air from outside is warm on inhalation and cooler on exhalation and the nose acts as a thermostat, cooling down the air before its entry into the lungs). Also, by breathing through the nose and not the mouth, the nostrils act as a filter and purify the air intake. If you breathe through the mouth, these beneficial processes cannot happen. Breathing through the mouth, especially in cold weather, can cause a chill or worse.

See above where I spoke about the breath. Breathing correctly balances the sympathetic and parasympathetic nervous systems, providing harmony within the body and mind, and influencing the activity of the heart. Correct breathing can restore the cells in the body to their normal condition. Generally, only one sixth of your full lung capacity is used when breathing.

Proper breathing is one of the primary keys to opening the healing channel – the circulatory system that burns up toxins, releases stored emotions, changes the body structure, and changes consciousness. Most intellectual activity leads to shallow breathing, slower metabolism, lower physical energy levels, and lethargy. Involuntarily, the breath contracts when you are afraid. You can combat fear by deepening the breath and easing tension in the whole body.

Example:

During the course of practising mindful breathing, Jackie and her friend Simone, discussed the concept of correct breathing. Simone mentioned that she had always practised "reverse breathing" – drawing in the abdomen on inhalation, and pressing it out on exhalation.

Jackie discovered she also had always practised reverse breathing. Both of them decided to practice breathing correctly and felt much better, as the lungs could then be used to their maximum capacity. The abdominal muscles became stronger, the digestion improved, the diaphragm developed, and the heart function benefited.

Energy

It is important that you have a basic understanding of how energy flows throughout the body, and how any energy blockage can be removed and the balance of energy restored. Energy is the bridge to wellness.

Learning how to conserve your energy is important – so you can always feel energized, and have a real passion for life, rather than experiencing a lack of energy, and depression.

The practice of Yoga can help restore the harmonic flow of energy throughout the body and it is worthwhile investing time to have a program tailored to your individual needs by a qualified yoga instructor. Tai Chi and other healing principles can also help to restore harmonic flow of energy. Regular practice is required to maintain the harmonic flow of energy. This can prevent blockages, which may arise from daily life experiences.

Breath forms the gateway between the mind and body. The whole system of yoga is built on breathing techniques (Pranayama) designed to nourish psychic and spiritual pathways in the body – major nadis and acupuncture meridians. When practised in conjunction with appropriate meditation practices you can gain maximum benefit.

Regular relaxation in Shavasana – lying on your back on the floor, or sitting in a chair – can refresh the whole body with new vital energy, when practised mindfully together with natural breathing, followed by deep abdominal breathing. Overtaxed nerves can be revitalized, muscle tensions eased, and blood pressure and pulse rates lowered. Excess energy produced by cells can be conserved and accumulated for future needs. Batteries can be recharged. Disturbing emotional worries can be dissolved from the mind. Ailments, such as chronic headaches and asthma may be completely relieved. In the state of deep relaxation, muscular reflexes respond more rapidly to stimuli, and every task can be performed more efficiently and with less effort.

Deep breathing can vitalise energy in every part of the body, eliminating anxiety, and negative emotions. Yawning often signifies a state of anxiety. Insufficient oxygen can result in a low metabolism and low energy. Many people rarely maximise their lung capacity, resulting in shallow breathing, and a build-up of toxins within the body. The brain requires more oxygen than the rest of the organs to prevent a slowing down of the thinking processes and death of brain cells.

Benefits of deep breathing include:

+ less wear and tear on the body
+ less work for the heart
+ lower blood pressure
+ relaxation of body tensions
+ quietening of the nerves

The blood is oxygenated from the breath in the lungs. The oxygen is carried to every cell in the body. Reduced oxygen damages the health. A well-developed deep breathing program can do wonders for your health.

It is important that you do not over- breathe as that state can be harmful.

Improper breathing can result in:

+ build-up of stress causing extreme inner tensions
+ tense muscles
+ irregular breathing
+ fist clenching
+ increase in blood pressure
+ heart palpitations

Yoga breathing practices can purify and stimulate the human body in every way, and specifically can result in:

+ improving and stimulating metabolism
+ harmonising glandular secretions
+ burning up fat
+ making joints more flexible
+ stimulating circulation, improving digestion
+ rejuvenating organs and systems of the body

Example:

Frances felt tired after a day at work, even though he spent an hour in the gym each day. He was concerned that if he became sick he would be unable to provide for his young family. He became depressed, and decided to review his lifestyle with a view to making changes as necessary.

Frances became aware that his mind was focused on making money rather than focusing on work that could be more suited to his inherent strengths. At his current job, he spends three hours commuting each day and most of the time sitting down at a desk. Frances realized that he would be happier working nearer to home in a job that would include more physical activity and interaction with people. He chose to focus on real estate sales and applied to work with a local real estate agent. The result was he could maintain closer contact with his family and the local community, spend more time walking and meditating, and felt much happier and less stressed.

Food

What you eat and drink, and when, it plays a major part in the state of your health. You need to mindfully consider the daily requirements of your body. Never compare your own needs with the needs of others as their needs will likely be different. Question how your existing eating habits impact on the state of your health – this can vary from day to day and from season to season, and determining what your body needs are at any one time.

Much is said about the potential benefits of various diets. None of them necessarily promotes mindful eating, and they often can limit real benefits as they are designed to cut down on time spent mastering food preparation, nutrition, and eating habits.

Although certain diets can be generally beneficial to everybody, it is necessary that you understand what your body type specifically needs, each day, to provide nourishment and maintain it in optimum working capacity. Without this understanding you may unintentionally limit the effectiveness of food on the digestive process. This understanding comes from mindfully listening to the body's needs, and observing the way the food you eat affects your energy levels. It includes understanding how the body's internal organs function individually and harmonise overall within the body; and how the body's energies circulate and are inter-communicative. It involves much more than merely following a routine diet that may appear to work but may also put limitations on you meeting your body's nutritional needs, and on maximizing the energy for your body type.

You need to understand why you feel hungry and, if it is due to emotional upset that condition needs to be addressed, rather than eating what may be inappropriate food at that time. What you need to eat can vary from time to time as your body becomes more purified, and for the seasons of the year. A physician can diagnose whether the body is deficient in any mineral or vitamin, and it is wise not to rely on self-diagnosis, so that any deficiency can be properly remedied.

Generally, you need to cut down on sugar and salt intake, and anything else that may impact on your cholesterol level. Many advertisements proclaim the general benefits to be gained from taking vitamin supplements, which, if taken without first consulting with a qualified medical practitioner, may be more detrimental than beneficial. Most likely, the medical practitioner will request you to undergo a series of routine blood tests and focus on an eating plan that consists of natural foods, with supplements only if, and when, required. At certain times, the body may require a remedy to address a lack of essential minerals.

Junk foods – processed foods provide no benefit to the body, as well as depleting the energy within. Wholesome foods – including raw, lightly-boiled or steamed vegetables, and pulses – are more easily digestible, and produce less toxins in the body, thus leaving the body and mind calmer and more alert. This process can be compared to the engine of a car – when the engine is regularly maintained and fed with good oil, the car can run effectively; whereas, if the car engine is not regularly maintained and, or, is fed with contaminated oil it will become clogged up and may eventually break down.

You need to maintain a staple of basic foods in your pantry to include, for example, fresh vegetables and fruit, and other natural foods, herbs and herbal teas. Also, list all foods that are appropriate for your constitution.

A good way to build a foundation for mindful eating is to keep a food diary, and list all the foods you eat and the drinks you take at the end of each day. Compare your current eating patterns with recommended eating regimes to suit your body's specific needs, monitor your progress, and introduce changes that may be needed as you go. By following this regime, you can feel more in control of your own diet, feel much fitter and able to think more clearly.

During long periods of meditation the body may require less food intake, and a cooling diet to counter dynamic heat produced. The amount of exercise undertaken can also impact on the amount of food required for each meal. At the end of each day your body and mind need to feel light and at peace. If there is a feeling of unease you need to consider how this could have arisen and modify the eating plan. Once you establish this habit you can begin to enjoy the eating process and feel more energetic.

Illness can be cured and wellness maintained by eating only the foods your body needs. It is beneficial to become aware of the healing aspects that certain herbs contain, for example: black pepper can relieve a cold, ginger aids digestion, and turmeric is an antiseptic. You need to be aware of allergies – intolerance to certain foods that can cause indigestion or have more serious effects.

Mindfulness is the key to living a conscious life, paying attention to your body's daily needs, and eating slowly in quiet surroundings, at regular times each day, to allow proper digestion of the food within the body. It ensures that each food item is prepared without any stress and is cooked naturally. When food is cooked within a stressful environment, that energy is absorbed by the food, and the body. Mindfulness is a state of being in the "now", a state of observation, being a witness of what you are eating and how the food tastes. It enables you to witness old experiences, observe your reactions, and discover the underlying truth. Once mastered and established, it is an enjoyable and rewarding experience.

The holistic science of Ayurveda is based on three different body types – Doshas, which determine your constitution. Each body type resonates to a specific energy and requires a mix of food that ensures the internal organs and systems can function most effectively and harmoniously, depending on the current balance of the Dosha. The three body types are Kapha, Pitta, and Vata. Ayurveda practice aims to harmonise imbalance of body functions by means of cleansing, herbs and massage. Your body balance can change daily and seasonally and it is important to understand the foods, and other conditions that can affect the balance of each Dosha. In addition to the requirements of your body type you also need to be aware of the specific food requirements and, or allergies applicable to your blood type.

Traditional Chinese Medicine focuses on the harmonious flow of energy (Chi) throughout the body and, depending on which of the five elements – wood, fire, earth, metal, water – are out of balance at any one time, the appropriate food intake and herbal remedies required can be planned, monitored, and adjusted as necessary.

Traditional treatments aim to prevent disharmony or imbalance within the body, establish the cause and consider effective natural remedies, rather than only easing the apparent symptoms.

If you eat whilst you are upset, you can poison your body. The best appetiser is laughter.

Wellness

All disease, whether caused by a germ, injury, or stress, is the result of an "imbalance" that fragments the organism and destroys its natural resonating capacity. To be able to completely heal someone they need first to come into balance within their own energy.

By following a holistic system of healing and preventative health care, including – relaxation, exercise, meditation, and proper diet – the entire being can be maintained in perfect harmony.

The word "wellness" can be substituted for the word "illness", allowing more focus to be given to that state of positive being – a more upbeat way of living. Health equals wealth – without good health we are unable to fully enjoy financial wealth and live life fully. Health encompasses the body, mind, and spirit.

By disbelieving the reality of sickness, even when you are ill, and focusing on a feeling of wellness, what is not recognized can disappear from the body and allow wellness to be naturally restored within. The key to healing lies within, rather than coming from outside sources. Happiness is a natural state – within ourselves is where the secrets lie.

The body needs both internal and external cleanliness, including:

+ natural foods and fluids
+ adequate peaceful sleep
+ natural and comfortable clothing and shoes
+ adequate sunshine and water
+ cheerfulness

Regular practice of Yoga asanas can benefit the body and mind by:

+ exercising all the muscles, preventing atrophy by inducing relaxation and conserving energy
+ balancing hormone secretions and controlling emotions so that mental composure can be ultimately attained
+ balancing glandular systems
+ relaxing and toning muscles and the nervous system; stimulating circulation; stretching stiff ligaments and tendons
+ making joints more flexible
+ massaging internal organs
+ calming and focusing the mind

+ restoring flexibility to the spine and preventing painful stiffening
+ lubricating and exercising the joints, restoring free and natural movement – you may hear a cracking sound that can be caused by the breaking up of calcium deposits in the joints
+ regaining agility and flexibility of the body
+ twisting and stretching asanas stretch the blood vessels, increasing elasticity, preventing stiffening and destruction by harmful toxins
+ certain asanas can assist in clearing the veins and reducing any swelling; and toning up the entire system, giving internal organs a complete massage, and improving circulation of blood to the stomach and liver

Regular practice of Meditation, one of the most effective techniques for self-mastery, quietens the central nervous system, and can slow down the heart rate, lower blood pressure, and slow down breathing. It focuses the mind's capacity to pay attention and ignore distractions. It can enhance physical health, and well-being, resulting in greater productivity at work, better concentration, increased creativity, peaceful sleep, and greater personal satisfaction. The various meditation techniques include:

+ controlled breathing
+ gazing at an image, flame, mandala, or other symbol
+ mantra chanting
+ observing the witness
+ following one's thoughts
+ focusing on a concept or problem
+ listening to sounds of music
+ guided visualisations – including witnessing energy moving up and down the spinal, or frontal energy passage of the body
+ relaxing, being receptive
+ receptive guided meditations
+ Yoga Nidra, (a deep relaxing meditation, practised with awareness, conducted by a qualified instructor)

Meditation can allow the body and mind to become quiet and peaceful, so you can reflect on where you are now, assimilate what you have learned, and question whether the status quo still supports your current or ideal lifestyle. In a deeper state of consciousness, old habits can be erased, and space made available for new more appropriate habits to be stored within.

Good sleeping patterns need to be in place to ensure you are best able to cope with daily living demands. If you experience irregular sleep, you need to discuss this condition with your medical practitioner. The cause needs to be ascertained, and dealt with appropriately. Irregular sleep can result in tiredness during the day and have other harmful side-effects. Meditation (not medication!) can help you to sleep well – for example you could include a session in the evening before you go to bed, instead of watching TV programs, especially those that include violence of any kind.

Recent scientific research uncovered by top-notch medical doctors provides facts concerning the beneficial effects of herbal alternatives, compared with conventional drugs. This research is ongoing. By becoming fully informed of all the facts you can understand the effects of conventional drugs and their herbal alternatives, the benefits to be gained from Yoga practices, and the most effective remedies.

Your immune system needs to be kept healthy. Disharmony in the physical and magnetic realms of the body paves the way for invasion of the body by disease, via a weakened immune system. Living in the present, rather than the past or the future, can help maintain your immune system by conserving energy. For example, desire can be a toxin that needs to be released by replacing it with contentment; allow yourself to rise in love, rather than to fall in love – then there can be less fear.

Boredom can result in un-wellness. The antidote is to take an active and lively interest in all around you throughout the day; learn the Truth that lies behind all things; lose yourself in the study and art of gaining new knowledge and experience; and lookout for opportunities to use this new knowledge for the advantage of yourself and fellow travellers. Change can take time. It is never too late to start – one small step is all it takes to start the ball rolling.

Regular eye check-ups need to form a part of your regular medical routines. The gift of sight allows an image to be internalized and seen by the brain from images reflected through the lenses in the eyes. The health of the eyes and the brain are inter-connected.

As your body and mind become more purified – your intuitiveness can allow information to be retrieved from the future, and enable you to experience how a future event feels to make it more of a reality now – time can be transcended.

The liver is the most important organ for nourishment, as well as overall health. It also governs longevity, and is directly impacted by the mind.

Exercise

Exercise is important and the type of exercise beneficial to your fitness condition and constitution needs to be determined based on your current health condition and lifestyle needs. Your priorities may differ from those of others, depending on your constitution, circumstances, and beliefs.

I recently came across a man aged ninety six, who was physically and mentally in good health, and he attributed his radiant condition to be the outcome of focusing on work, diet, and exercise – in that order.

Although your body needs an exercise program tailored to its specific needs, it is important that during the process of exercising the body, the mind is peaceful and not under any type of stress. Otherwise the exercise could be more harmful than beneficial. You need to let the body move naturally, from the heart, not from the head; perform each exercise with mindful breathing, so it incorporates meditation; and be aware of how your energy is being used. Consider whether it can be better conserved.

Examples:

- *Ann benefits from daily power-walking. She enjoys her forays into the bush and finds this exercise meditative.*
- *Wendy suffers from leg and ankle issues, caused by lymphedema, and benefits from swimming, and water aerobics. These exercises prevent undue stress to her knee and ankle joints.*

Various exercise programs may be available in the workplace, provided by gymnasiums, and other community outlets.

Dancing is an excellent form of exercise, and also promotes social interaction. Walking up the stairs rather than catching an elevator can provide benefit to strengthening the leg muscles, cardiovascular system, and bones.

Maybe, you could cycle to work instead of catching the bus or train. Or, you could consider walking to work instead of driving the car or catching the bus. None of these pursuits are expensive.

Any pursuit needs to be practised regularly for there to be any real, lasting benefit. You need to remember to be active as, whatever you do not use you lose. When you are unwell, you can gain benefit from visualising various exercise movements, which may produce some relief and help aid recovery.

The condition of your body may change from day to day, for various reasons, and you need to take care not to overuse any part of it – to prevent injuries and stress.

Rejuvenation

You need to take time out, on a regular basis as required, to allow your mind and body time to completely rest and relax at a retreat, or other place that provides a safe and peaceful environment. Consider how you might benefit from a walk along the beach, listening to the waves; or from climbing a mountain and enjoying the view from a higher place; or from a walk in the bush.

Real rest is secured in meditation not sleep. Regular meditation practice can allow the mind to attain a peaceful and tranquil state. When the mind is cheerful the body is healthy.

The tool of Yoga provides practices that, when incorporated into your daily lifestyle routine, can enable the entire body to become purified, bad habits from the past eliminated and replaced by good habits. Regular practice of Antar Mouna (silence), facilitated by a qualified Yoga teacher, can help to provide this cleansing and rejuvenating process – as explained in Chapter Nine. By disengaging from habitual responses and allowing the mind to be quiet, freeing the self from anger, judgement, fears and desires – your body can become free of energy blockages.

By accepting and releasing the past, forgiving yourself and others – negative energy and feelings can be erased from the body – you can feel lighter as though a burden has been removed.

Aim to adopt a simpler lifestyle – allow time to study humanity and the laws of the Universe. Life can be, and is meant to be, an adventure where body, mind, and soul are in harmony. You need to remove toxic noise and relationships from your environment, including watching mindless TV programs, spending time in noisy surroundings, and spending time with argumentative people. Silent mantra chanting can cleanse the mind and bring a state of peace and tranquillity.

Rest and relaxation of the body and mind can aid recovery from illness. A closer union between the personality and the soul may result in harmony and peace, allowing space and providing distance from difficulties encountered, and stresses of the outside world.

Breath is the subtle link between the body and soul. The mind is the transmission station through which the Divine self can work to harmonise this link.

You need to continually work at clearing or releasing clutter from all areas of your life. By letting go you can gain more harmony in everyday life, and be guided by your intuition.

Examples of clutter:

- *Physical – stuff you no longer need can be sold or donated*
- *Grievances from the past – can be reduced by focusing on hopes for the future*
- *Old wounds or painful relationships – can be accepted and replaced by unconditional love of yourself and others*
- *Pain – pay attention to emotional and psychological pain, examine the cause, and consider whether you need to seek and accept professional help to enable healing to take place*
- *Negative memories – those that need to be recognized and removed from the mind to allow space for happiness in your life*

Once the mind is cleared of clutter, the other areas will automatically follow.

Allow the body to heal – and feel the body repairing itself. Healing is an adventure inside the self:

- Physical
- Mental
- Emotional
- Spiritual

Celebrate your strengths. Recognise and realise your weaknesses and the gaps of inadequacy in each area of your life, and then create action plans to bridge those gaps. Be aware of your shadow side – it needs to be harmonized with your strengths. The universe is a mass of light, and the essence of creation always includes both light and shadow.

Make sure you have a community of loving friends, and family, based on shared interests and emotional nurturing, and not out of neediness.

You need to examine your relationships with others, to ensure you are not expending too much of your energy when you need to conserve it to allow yourself to heal; consider whether you have unrealistic expectations that you need to address; expand the way you define yourself. Are you limiting your passion, based on your current role in life? Can you feel a unity with mankind? Do you see the Divine in everyone?

Appreciating how small you are in comparison to the Universe can be felt by witnessing, observing and experiencing natural miracles, such as the stars in the night sky, the formation of a rainbow, the vivid colours and hues of a sunset, the changing of the four seasons. It is important you understand these natural phenomena, take time to be grateful for your life, and make appropriate changes in your lifestyle when necessary to allow natural harmony to return.

Yoga can bring union among human beings and nature. It can enable you to evolve from an animal state of gross awareness, to a subtler state so that basic instincts are no longer driving you. It can help you to develop a brotherhood, and equal mindedness, so that you can work together for the good of the world.

You need to use three forms of perception in all areas of your life to enhance your healing powers:

+ Resolve problems
+ Understand conflicts in relationships
+ Appreciate blessings that come into your life

Life changes externally as you change internally and become more aware. Talents you never knew existed may emerge. Be courageous and allow change to happen. Life is an adventure to be enjoyed – an exciting process. You cannot turn back the clock and relive your previous lifestyle.

Examples of the benefits of change – you may:

- *heal, when your perception of reality changes*
- *experience deeper intuitive skills*
- *decide to create something new for yourself, regardless of your age*
- *discover new ambitions, or a new identity*
- *desire to adopt a different lifestyle*

You can:

- *feel a sense of liberation, a need for more contact with nature, and to spend more time on your own*
- *experience a higher level of mastery and satisfaction, by uncovering the perceived difficulties that can mask the potential for greater joys and fulfilment*

- *observe patterns of strength and weakness that have always influenced you, compare alternatives to each weakness, and make new choices utilising your strengths*

Your victim mentality can weaken and your victor mentality can become stronger and shine through. Have faith that what may seem impossible is possible – provided you believe.

Learn to say "No". Set boundaries and use your time in the most effective way. Reclaim your energy that is currently being wasted reflecting on past events. Allow empty space to "do" nothing, to allow new ideas and feelings to surface.

Example:

Max was informed by his employer that his services were no longer required. He felt that he had been unfairly dismissed, and after seeking legal advice decided to sue his employer. His lawyer won the case. However, the legal costs to represent Max amounted to more than the compensation granted by his ex-employer. Max could have chosen to conserve his energy and funds by letting go of the past and seeking a more suitable job.

You need to:

+ focus on the cycles of nature, reducing excesses and increasing insufficiencies; learn to accept change with equanimity; aim not to isolate yourself from reality and your needs
+ review and balance the energy at each of the main chakras and focus on balancing the overall energies

Examples – if you:

- *experience a feeling of lack, replace the feeling with gratitude*
- *are feeling a sensation of greed, give away something*
- *feel a lack of self-esteem or inadequacy, replace that with self-respect, self-esteem, and integrity*
- *experience a victim mentality, replace it with empathy and respect*
- *feel defensive or dishonest – practice right speech, and purification*
- *experience self-doubt and compare yourself with others – have compassion for others, and release these limitations*
- *focus on the past – accept what no longer works for you, let it go and focus on your blessings and goals*
- *misuse your power – increase your self-awareness, detach, and discover gold in all your experiences*

Harmonise thoughts, words, and deeds. Mindfully, sow a thought, and reap an action; sow a habit, and reap a character; sow a character and reap your destiny. Allow space and time for change to manifest, and transformation to take place.

All things are possible when you have hope. You need to make sure you use your health fully – it is your birth right.

Health:

As mentioned, Dad passed away when I was sixteen. He had a pain in his abdomen, which did not indicate any irregularity on the x-ray. He always kept a supply of Rennies in his coat pocket, which was an indication he could have suffered from indigestion. The only time he ate at home was at the weekends. On reflection, maybe he could have suffered a lot of stress in his job and did not take time to eat a healthy diet, as most of his food was eaten from cafes on the way to work and back home. He always did everything within his means to provide for his family, and help less fortunate people, but apparently may not have cared enough to monitor his own health.

~ ~ ~

I often used to cycle to high school instead of catching two buses. It was quicker, healthier, and more enjoyable. When I started work, I either walked or cycled, rather than catching an overcrowded bus. The exercise was also meditative. At weekends, I frequently caught a train to remote locations in the countryside – for example, the moors, or Yorkshire Dales, and walked for hours staying at youth hostels overnight. I enjoyed being out in the open air and was rarely sick. When I moved away from home to pursue my career, I missed these natural pleasures in life.

When I lived in London, the doctor recommended I attend Weight Watchers to address my overweight condition. I informed him that, if I did not lose thirty pounds in weight within four weeks, I would attend the classes. During that four-week period, I visualised a mini-vacuum cleaner working its way around the inside of my body, sucking out excess fat from the cells, and ate only when I was hungry. I did not have much exercise during that time, other than walking to and from work. After four weeks, I returned to see the doctor, and discovered my body had lost thirty pounds in weight, so I did not have to attend the Weight Watcher sessions. My body never regained any weight for many years.

~ ~ ~

I am fortunate to have a far-distant cousin, Doug, who provided me with a copy of the family tree of Dad's ancestry that he had spent much time preparing.

Dad never spoke about his elder brother, Josiah, who died in combat at war at the age of twenty-one and is buried in the cemetery at Dar es Salaam, Tanzania. This must have been a traumatic loss for Dad.

The missing link was Mum's ancestry. Until recently I was unable to obtain details relating to her background from anyone in the family. From what little I knew she was partly Welsh, and I thought she could have been an orphan, as she never talked about any of her direct relatives. Recently, I attended a genealogy session at the local neighbourhood house and the teacher helped me piece together Mum's history — she was one of six children — now I have a photo of her mum for my records. I wonder why Mum never discussed or introduced me to her brothers and sisters. It pays to do the necessary research to check the facts, and not rely on assumptions, or hearsay. Although I have a photo of each grandmother, unfortunately I have none of either grandfather. I shall continue to do more research to ascertain if any additional information is available.

I recall that Mum had "heavy legs" — she did a lot of walking and never complained about her legs, so I never realised that anything was unusual. Although I recall that from an early age I was never able to wear fashionable high boots because the calves of my legs were too wide to fit into the boots. I later learnt that I have primary lymphedema — it is hereditary, mainly caused by poor circulation. Excess fluid in the lymph vessels causes blockages in the vessels, making them unable to carry away lymph fluid from the tissues, which results in swelling of the limbs. I attend the local lymph clinic to ensure it is properly managed. I wear compression garments, attend aqua aerobic classes, and walk as much as possible.

~ ~ ~

A few years after I chose to move on from Philip, my partner of fourteen years in Singapore, I was diagnosed with breast cancer — this was the biggest emotional upheaval in my life. I could not believe it could happen to me — and underwent the necessary lumpectomy surgery. I was blessed with a wonderful surgeon, whom I knew from the social club that we both frequented, and he was horrified to learn that I was his patient. I jokingly said that the right breast was bigger than the left one so now it could become the same size — he was not amused. I was dazed after the surgery, and shocked at the realisation of what had happened, yet I was grateful to be alive, and gave thanks to the Universe for this second chance in life. I underwent chemotherapy and radiation treatment, accepting it as part of my daily routine, and read a book whilst I waited. Due to my cheerful and positive disposition, I was chosen to mentor other breast cancer patients through their recovery period. I drank pints of carrot juice, whilst my friends drank their pints of beer, and thought my body may turn orange but it never did. I attended courses on self-motivation I studied Reiki I with Marianne Williamson (famous author), and have never looked back. I attended classes to learn how to design jewellery, which I found meditative, and still enjoy. Peace of mind was my focus. I asked the surgeon what could have caused the cancer and was told it was likely due to a combination of diet, stress, and hormone replacement therapy.

I questioned what was stressful in my life, and concluded I needed to focus more time and energy on my health and lifestyle; to reconnect with a country that has four seasons, and more countryside. It was approaching winter in the Western Hemisphere, so I chose to remain in the Southern Hemisphere and planned to move to Australia.

Preventing Stress:

I decided to change my lifestyle. I chose to feel well each day, and appreciate the many blessings in my life. Up to that time, I had taken good health for granted. It was time to realise that stress is toxic and consider how I could reduce the stress in my life, and eliminate the stored toxins.

I became interested in Yoga and attended Iyengar classes at the weekends. Although I felt lonely at first in my new home, I enjoyed living in the natural surroundings of the bush and exploring the Yarra Valley in my free time. I was fortunate to have friendly and supportive neighbours.

I focused my time working, studying, travelling, becoming a citizen of Australia, and changing jobs, as necessary. Sadly, one-by-one, my neighbours passed away. They had introduced me to the Salvation Army, which they had always attended. During difficult time the Salvos provided much-needed support and guidance, especially during job redundancies and related financial difficulties.

~ ~ ~

On my travels, I met an Indian student, whose grandfather had lived to the age of one-hundred-and-two. He was a vegetarian, spent time meditating, loved his family, and lived at home until he passed away. He lived a harmonious and full life.

After the latest job redundancy, I chose to spend time living in a Yoga Ashram. This opportunity enabled me to gain a deeper understanding of the inter-relatedness between the physical, mental, and spiritual awareness, experience how they work and integrate together. During this solitude, I immersed myself in the library to gain more in-depth knowledge and experience of the ancient cultures of India, and experience and study the science of Yoga. With that knowledge, and experience, a new phase of life emerged: a strong desire to feel and experience a deeper sense of connection with the true meaning of life. This knowledge is based on ancient, scientific truth that is available for everyone to discover for themselves, no matter what religion, if any, they pursue.

This time out of the rat-race, leading a simpler way of life, provided time for me to distance myself from the problems I had faced in the outside world. I feel privileged to have benefited from this feeling of becoming reconnected with the inner self and benefit from the peace within. Due to regular eating habits, and a vegetarian diet, my body lost twenty kilograms in weight, and lost its pear-shape. Lack of stress from the outside world, also helped.

Heart:

During the course of my yogic studies, the allopathic doctor diagnosed an irregular pulse, advised me I had atrial fibrillation, and referred me to see a cardiologist who prescribed warfarin, which is a blood thinner and did not address the irregularity I had. I nearly freaked out. After conducting my own research and becoming aware of the potential side effects I challenged this path. I immediately started to practice specific recommended yoga asanas and breathing techniques, and worked with a Chinese medical practitioner with a view to determining the cause of the condition, and incorporated natural healing processes into my daily regime. He advised that the current condition may have been caused by a build-up of toxins in the body over time, causing energy blockages, and that once these toxins were removed the body could possibly be purified and the irregular pulse could become regular. Although the cancer had been removed from my body, when I lived in Singapore, I realised that the cause still needed to be removed from the mind to enable the body to be completely healed. The cardiologist was shocked that, after only three months, the condition had improved. I had an in-depth discussion with him, and he wanted to know what I had been doing. I informed him of the Yoga practices and provided him with a copy of the Yoga book. He reluctantly signed me out but cautioned me to undergo regular medical check-ups with the allopathic doctor.

I continue with the herbal treatment and acupuncture, which has been accepted by the allopathic doctor, with whom I continue to consult and undergo regular routine blood tests. Fortunately, following the recent move from the Ashram to a nearby small town, I have a new allopathic doctor who immediately prescribed Digoxin, a derivative of the Foxglove, to help align the heartbeat within the upper and lower chambers of the left ventricle. Finally, the irregular pulse – atrial fibrillation – is being properly managed. This outcome is in line with recommendations of the Chinese doctor, and I am confident and happy, that the way ahead can result in an improved overall health outcome, with regular monitoring. I feel fortunate to have met my new doctor. Just think, for two years the condition was not being managed properly and, fortunately, it did not worsen during that time. Since then, the condition has improved significantly.

Unfortunately, I have experienced several chronic nose bleeds. The allopathic doctor is of the view that the nose-bleed was probably caused by seasonal climatic changes. In any case, this outcome led to there being a shortage of iron in my body, so I had to take iron tablets to rectify that condition. Also, in conjunction with a visit to the lymph clinic, it was determined that I needed to take diuretics as there was an excess of fluid in my body — in addition to the water retention caused by the regular lymph condition. So, I had to take diuretics to regularise this condition. All is now rectified and more or less in balance. Blood tests are normal and my cholesterol is low.

I hope that eventually the pulse will become regular and the debilitating nose bleeds will cease.

Energy:

Physical harmony provides the prime foundation, without which the other areas of life cannot be fully enjoyed. I still need to lose more weight so there can be less stress on my heart and lymphatic system, and my energy can be used more efficiently and conserved.

I aim to go to bed early each evening, with a quiet mind, to enable me to rise early in the morning, which is the time when my mind and body are ready and best able to start coping with the needs of the day ahead.

Food:

When living in the Ashram, I had adapted to cooking for up to one hundred people on a regular basis, and after leaving the Ashram I found that cooking for one person provided a real challenge. Hence, I attended a talk on Mindful Eating at the local library. No specific diet was recommended. I started to maintain a food diary and made a list of foods that could provide the staple basis for preparing meals at home, and result in supplying optimum energy for my body. It will take time to get the balance right, and I learn something new each day. I also need to be aware of the daily calorie intake so my body can begin to lose some weight.

Wellness:

When I left the Ashram, I had few belongings other than those in storage. Once I found permanent accommodation, I arranged for my belongings to be delivered from storage, in two separate batches – furniture first, followed later by books and paperwork. The first two years were devoted intermittently to sorting through each item and selling or donating items that were no longer appropriate to my new living environment. Clearing the paper clutter is the biggest challenge and ongoing, and will take longer to sort through as I also need to devote time to other projects. Allocating time, prioritising different projects, and imposing boundaries so I do not take on more than I can effectively cope with provides new challenges.

I practice my own yoga program that focuses on enhancing the flow of blood in my legs (lymphatic system), whilst becoming aware of practices that can strengthen the heart's capacity in the long-term. Each day I make time for meditation and relaxation and maintain awareness of the need to breathe correctly to maintain peace of mind.

Exercise:

Due to the lymphedema and heart condition, I need to be careful not to overstrain my body's capacity, to enable it to focus on removing toxins, so it can become stronger over time. Walking and aerobic exercise work well for these conditions. I build exercises into my housework and that process makes it more tolerable and enjoyable.

Rejuvenation:

Each week, I take a day out of my routine schedule to explore a new place, try a new activity, and meet up with friends. It is important to take a regular break and spend time alone to appreciate the abundance I now have, relax doing nothing except allowing the mind to be still. During this quiet time, my mind is free to be creative, and I enjoy making bead necklaces — most of which are donated as presents or sold.

There also needs to be space during the day for reading, listening to music, meeting with friends, and living life fully; time to reflect, time to dream, time to plan and introduce changes. I spend time appreciating where I am at today, reflecting on experiences in the past and learning from setbacks encountered to turn them into blessings, and allowing the future to present itself.

I feel like a caterpillar, in the process of turning into a butterfly. During the course of my travels, I appreciate how far I have come in this new phase of life when I witness the stresses of those people less fortunate than me. Life is beautiful and the transition process is ongoing.

~ ~ ~

Physical harmony is the most important foundation to establish. I need to heed the seasons of nature and take time out to allow the body and mind to rejuvenate so they can cope with the next phase of my life. It is a time to rejoice and appreciate the miracle of life.

Space for you to write in:

Treat your body like a temple, so it can provide the energy you need to enjoy your life to the full.

Physical Harmony

Chapter Five
Mental Harmony

The mind can be made steady by focusing on the activities of the senses.
— Rishi Patanjali

Real learning comes about when the competitive spirit has ceased.
— J Krishnamurti

Come from a state of peace and you'll find that you can deal with anything.
— Michael A Singer

A great hallmark of mental wellness is the ability to be in the present moment, fully and with no thoughts of being elsewhere.
— Wayne Dyer

The intuitive mind is a sacred gift, and the rational mind is a faithful servant. We have created a society that honours the servant and has forgotten the gift.
— Albert Einstein

The centre that I cannot find is known to my unconscious mind.
— W H Auden

The thing always happens that you really believe in; and the belief in a thing makes it happen.
— Frank Lloyd Wright

The energy of the mind is the essence of life.
— Aristotle

Change your thoughts and you change the world.
— Norman Vincent Peale

Did you ever observe to whom accidents happen? Chance favours only the prepared mind.
— Louis Pasteur

Habit has made you the person you are.
— William George Plunkett

Progress is impossible without change; and those who cannot change their minds cannot change anything.
— George Bernard Shaw

- Peace of mind
- Being positive
- Control your thoughts
- Choose your heroes wisely

Peace of mind

You need to master the mind and make it your friend. A calm, peaceful state of mind provides the foundation for mental harmony. You need to protect your mind from harmful influences and substances. A calm and peaceful mind can be manifested through regular practice of meditation, which can purify the mind. Various practices of meditation are outlined in Chapter Nine.

Only with peace of mind, can you feel calm and happy, and able to make rational decisions. With a one-pointed focus of the mind, and detachment from everyday issues, you can integrate change calmly, and deal with unfavourable situations, acting mindfully, with enlightenment and without regret.

In a disturbed mental state, your mental energy is scattered and unfocused, and you may make mistakes that can result in situations becoming chaotic; or make radical decisions which you may later regret. Under no circumstances should you make any decisions when you feel angry – you need to allow time for the mind to become peaceful first. It is better to do nothing than to act irrationally. This state can be likened to a boat with no master, or anchor, which is tossed around by the sea, with no destination in sight.

Over time, with practice, all the impurities and disturbances in the mind can disappear. This process is like cleaning a hard drive of a computer.

Before you can make friends with the mind you need to understand how it works. Whatever you will your mind to do, it can be achieved. What do you desire most in life, and what lifestyle do you want to live? Be specific. This is the most important question you can ever answer. It is the reason for your being. Review your current lifestyle. Is it ideal? Your habits have made you the way you are today. You may be happy, in which case you may need to make no change. If not, you need to consider what will make you happy and take steps to change your thoughts.

You need to recognize your inherent temperament, and talents; allow cosmic intervention – a higher intelligence – to direct you to choose the most effective way in which you can activate your unique talents for the benefit of mankind, and become completely receptive to receiving this Divine direction.

Example:

If you desire optimum health and energy, with unlimited abundance, to be able to do what you want when you want, to spend time with wonderful people who are stimulating, uplifting, and exciting, and to empower others to manifest the same abundance for themselves – you first need to experience how that would make you feel. How different could your lifestyle become?

This desire need not focus only on having a lot of money, although that could be important to you, it needs to focus on adopting a fulfilling lifestyle. No limitations need be imposed. How can you achieve that desired state? What do you need to do differently from what you have been doing in the past to adopt a new lifestyle of your choice? Listen to your intuition.

Imagine that you are now living your ideal lifestyle. What is the biggest difference – and how can you build a bridge to enable the ideal to become reality? Recognising that you may need to make changes to your current lifestyle is the start of your new journey in life. You have started to make progress. Are you ready to change some of your existing habits?

Live in the present, with a focused mind, be grateful for what you have today, knowing that all is well and as it should be for now.

Being positive

You need to feed your mind with positive thoughts, not negative thoughts, as you will always get what you ask for. For example:

+ visualize an abundance of all you need to feel fulfilled, rather than focusing on what you do not have
+ focus on those things that will fill your life with joy, rather than waste your time with doubts or fear
+ clear the mental clutter, to allow space for the positives to kick in
+ mindfully question each moment of every day, to find ways to make more efficient use of your time. You need to use your time wisely

Examples:

- *Question the need to watch television as, although there may be one or two stimulating programs available, the news, advertisements, and certain serials can fill your mind with negative influences including fear and horror, which can be detrimental to you getting a good night's sleep. Maybe, you could use the time more wisely to focus your mind on doing more positive things, for example – reading, listening to music or dancing. The choice is yours.*

  Apart from taking up a lot of time that could otherwise be spent more productively, watching too many TV programs can detach the focus of your mind from the Divine self. Hence you can soon feel disconnected from reality and need to spend time to refocus the mind before connecting with more creative pursuits.

- *The effect of spending a lot of time in a noisy environment can affect your hearing capacity in the long-term. The World Health Organisation recently proclaimed that cell phone radiation may cause brain tumours; and using cell phones for half-an-hour per day may increase the risk of a brain tumour by 40%.*

Regular yoga practice, including controlled breathing, and mantra chanting, can help you to maintain a peaceful state of mind and gain enlightenment by removing the veils and obstacles that currently block the underlying truth. They can also improve your posture and the flexibility of your body. Or, you may find other ways of calming the mind that work for you. In any case, purification of the mind is the goal.

You may need to let go of unsuitable habits, to allow time for more suitable habits to develop and replace them; let go of the past, enjoy the present, and embrace the future. The practice of Antar Mouna – silence (as summarized in Chapter Nine) can help the mind focus on positive outcomes, and a state of calmness, and allow space for new beneficial habits to manifest.

You may need to review your past and re-run certain events in your mind. Focus the mind on the space just above the eyebrows – to witness what happened that you could have done differently with hindsight – this is a useful exercise as it helps you to better understand your past motives. You may no longer have the same motives, but if you do – you can question whether they are still beneficial in your life.

Example:

Some years ago, Max was disappointed when Nan, a friend he would have liked to get to know better, felt he was intruding in her lifestyle. In retrospect, the real issue was that Nan was emotionally unavailable – even though she had been divorced for ten years she had not let go of that relationship, and hence was unable to love Max and accept him in her life. She did not specifically tell Max about her unavailability, which became apparent during various incidents – Max felt that Nan was hiding her true feelings – was not being open and truthful. He felt unappreciated, and experienced a lack of self-esteem. He did not question the initial lack of harmony and ask Nan if she needed space to deal with this situation.

Subsequently Max met Donna, and they share several strong ethical values. He is hesitant to get to know her in case he is disappointed again. He decides to tell Donna he would like to become friends but clarifies that he needs to be sure she is available, and ready to give and receive unconditional love. Donna is happy to become friends with Max and respects, and appreciates his initial concern, honesty, and openness. They develop a deep and trusting friendship over time.

The world is nothing but a projection of your mind. If you correct your vision you can see the truth. Discovering the truth is your goal.

The mind needs always to be focused on positive outcomes, so you can remain open to new concepts and ideas, and higher ways of thinking. You need to let go of fixed perceptions, and rigid judgement, and never jump to conclusions without checking the real facts, otherwise your conclusions could be totally unfounded, and incorrect, based on your reactions and perceptions, rather than the truth.

Whenever you feel that things are not going your way, or not making sense, take time out to observe your reactions. Do not doubt your decisions and plans, or make changes based on your initial reactions. Once these perceptions have surfaced, been accepted, challenged, dealt with, and let go there will be space in your mind for more positive thoughts to develop – in line with the needs of your ideal lifestyle.

Control your thoughts

There are three states of mind:

- *Tamasic*: where the mind is closed and unable to conceive the whole picture due to ignorance and insensitivity. The vision is narrow, illogical, unreasonable, fanatical and blind and consequently mistakes in reasoning are made with carelessness and dullness. This state of mind controls the fatty tissue in the body.
- *Rajasic*: where the mind is biased and skews the whole picture, based on needs of the ego, leading to attachment, greed and selfishness – worship of power and wealth. This state of mind controls the muscle tissue in the body.
- *Sattvic*: where the mind sees the whole picture as one, unity in diversity and the cause behind the various effects. This vision leads to unconditional love and selfless service, sharing and caring, joy, happiness, and wisdom. Also, the body functions with vigour, and vitality – the results of mindful eating. This state of mind controls the nervous tissue in the human body.

These states of mind are established at birth. There is also a fourth state – *Turya* – where the mind is as one with the Divine self and contains none of the above limitations. Attainment of this state requires a surrender to a higher consciousness. In this state of mind, you can dis-identify with the mind, resulting in freedom. Regular practice of yoga can lead to this equanimity of mind. Yoga is the middle path that focuses on moderation in everything. A calm and pure mind, free of turbulence, together with a purity of heart, can lead to peace and harmony within.

Others see you through their mind's eye – whatever state is controlling them. Hence, you need to understand that others may have limitations or see things differently than you, and be patient and clarify they understood what is in your mind by asking relevant questions. You need to vibrate with people on their wavelength, and have compassion, to really get to know them. Otherwise, you need to stay away and not judge them for appearing to be different.

Example:

Prue met Tim for lunch and they were discussing their feelings about how the mind could be limited by people watching the same television programs each week. Prue felt that in such a state – being mindlessly entertained – the mind is unable to think creatively and people may believe that the outcomes portrayed by the program are normal. Tim initially felt that despite this potential outcome of watching the program, watching the television could provide the viewer with a feeling of connectedness, rather than a feeling of loneliness that may otherwise exist – meaning that watching a program that may limit the mind could be preferable to a person feeling lonely.

Prue recognized the need for a person to take time out but felt that instead of watching a program that could limit the mind's creativity the time could be spent more creatively, and the mind stay focused and grow from the experience, for example, by gardening. In such case the person may be alone, but not lonely. Tim agreed that by mindlessly watching a television program a person may forego the opportunity to grow.

Time is precious. It is a universal truth that your thoughts control the outcome of each day. Take some time at the end of each day to quieten your mind, and write in your journal, your actions and thoughts of the day, your experiences, how you felt, and your reactions. Consider, in hindsight, whether any outcome could have been different or more beneficial. With that in mind you can make plans for tomorrow to include changes that may be needed to result in different outcomes. Without going through this process there can be no progress. Never become disheartened if at first you may not succeed. Keep on trying and never give up.

Your thoughts can affect others, no matter where they are located, and – when focused – your minds can connect throughout the universe. Your thoughts are powerful and need to be used for the benefit of mankind.

Choose your heroes wisely

Look around you and see how this mental harmony works by studying successful people, their lifestyles and beliefs. What are their life values? What is their vision? How did they achieve success? What difficulties did they encounter, overcome, and how?

Who are your heroes? Who do you want as a role model?

You need to be sure that your heroes have the same moral principles, social values and integrity that you aspire to. Question their mission and vision of life. Take time to get to know their personality, before becoming comfortable that your potential hero meets your expectations. Be aware that just because someone has achieved financial freedom may not mean they have sound moral standards, are fair, and truthful.

If you choose heroes who are not qualified to inspire you, you may become disillusioned in your pursuit of happiness. Choose wisely, so you can be inspired, and stay on track.

You can learn from your heroes. You will find they worked hard, with devotion and determination, stayed on track – adapted to unforeseen circumstances along the way, and never gave up. They remained persistent in pursuit of their vision, amid inevitable trials and tribulations. You may want to pin-up a photo of your heroes in your room so you can be constantly inspired by them – that can help you keep your mind focused for your success.

Some of you may have distant heroes. Others may have heroes within your local communities, or families.

Example:

Robert Kiyosaki had two dads, one who worked for an employer all his life (his real dad) and who never attained financial freedom; and one who was self-employed and financially independent (his financial hero). He observed the lifestyles of both individuals and chose to be inspired by the one who had attained financial freedom, which was his goal.

Peace of mind:

The more time I spend meditating, including mindfulness of action in every moment of the day, my mind is quiet and more focused on the task in hand. I feel happy and content with what I have and where I am today, knowing that whatever I need will materialize in due course. There is minimum stress in my life. This means that mental clutter has been cleared from my mind. I feel at one with the divine being within, and from this state I can work through my projects with a feeling of abundance. Intuition and creativity emerge naturally and new ideas present themselves that make daily life more interesting and fulfilling. I have goals and aspirations, and devote time to progressing and monitoring them, without anxiety or doubt.

From time to time, when I find my mind roaming, I breathe deeply and allow it to refocus. I realise I may need to take time out during such times, and that is OK.

Being positive:

During the process of clarifying my current needs, I recognised what had happened in the past, accepted what had happened, released it, and have no regrets about anything. This process of distancing from past events took time to master. In a few instances, I was deeply disappointed at what had happened. I was particularly distressed when my financial foundation was traumatically rocked by the global economic downturn. By accepting the disappointing outcomes as part of my life experience and treating them as lessons learnt, my mind became calm, and detached from them, and I was able to focus on resolving them from a state of tranquillity. In planning my current and future needs, I am prepared not to repeat the same patterns. These experiences have, in fact, become a blessing in disguise that impel me to start anew with a clear mind, to pursue greater outcomes both for myself and others.

Although I do not know exactly where the future journey will take me – unlike in the past where I had planned all events carefully and made sure they happened, which was sometimes like being in a pressure-cooker – limiting, and counter-productive – I am confident that my needs can be met with abundance. I expect the best to happen, and regularly monitor my progress. I can witness my motives, mindfully heed my intuition, and adjust outcomes to embrace current ongoing needs and conditions.

By realising that each setback has provided an opportunity to overcome events that may not have been best suited to my lifestyle, there is a space and mental energy available to focus on current and potential projects with a calm and renewed mind-set.

I have surrendered my mind to a higher consciousness.

Controlling my thoughts:

My mind is focused on fairness – treating others as I would like to be treated, without judgement and without bias, good living and moral principles, and honesty. I appeal to others' sense of integrity, and have learnt from experience that not everyone has integrity. Sometimes, it is necessary to walk away from a bad outcome, and focus on more positive outcomes – that way my energy can be preserved and disappointment avoided.

Although I do have doubts from time to time – I recognize that state as my dark side – I have faith that state will pass. I refocus on my current needs and give thanks for all my blessings each day. I maintain a wider vision and my heart is pure.

It is easy to over-react to accusations made by others. Under such circumstances I aim not to take the inference of my own perception personally, and realise that the other person may not perceive my actions from my perspective but only from their own limited perspective, and I aim to be non-judgemental. Thoughts are powerful and need to be controlled and mastered by the mind.

Moving from my home town in the north of England, travelling across the world and working in and with different cultures, living in Singapore and having to embrace a new culture and the different expectations of the communities there; choosing a new country, Australia, in which to live and work, moving and resettling – new country, new home, new job, new studies, surviving breast cancer – was quite a daunting and challenging experience at times. There were occasions when I had to remain calm in the midst of controversies and adversities that arose. I realized later that my spiritual connection and foundation needed to be strengthened for me to regain, maintain, and fully experience mental harmony. This was a monumental journey.

No matter how busy I was each day, I needed to make time to connect with the Divine at the beginning and the end of the day, so that my mind remained calm throughout the day and I could cope with all situations encountered, to avoid an uncontrolled roller-coaster ride feeling, and weather the storms. Sometimes, due to pressures of work, my lifestyle lacked this balance and total harmony.

Recently, when there had been many changes within a short time-span, it was disappointing to feel out of control. Although I felt calm, the constant changes took their toll, and I felt as though I had lost my "mojo". Fortunately, I have a few dear friends who provided understanding and the encouragement needed for me to weather the storm, and reach calmer waters. I always believe that "it too shall pass".

During my life I always aim to maintain my sense of humour, which helps me realise I am just a small piece of the global jigsaw, or tapestry. I try to laugh at myself and situations, rather than at other people; to laugh with others, even if they do not understand my intention.

I am happy with my world of adventure and discovery, and feel a deeper sense of gratitude, and connection with the natural laws of nature.

Choosing my heroes:

As far as I know, my heroes each have integrity, are fearless, and believe in fairness, and equality. They never compromise their integrity for the sake of winning, and are persistent in pursuing their ideal. Without exception, it can be said that great failures make great men / women – the tougher the failures they encountered, the more resilient they became. Their success only shows as the tip of the ice-berg. My heroes include:

Mahatma Gandhi: *never allowed violence to come between his ideal and its outcome. He was the greatest advocate of non-violent protest, and persevered with his ideal in mind no matter what adversity arose. He unconditionally loved his neighbours and strove to attain peace whilst learning in the process. He became the head of the Indian Congress Party, and achieved independence for India against the might of the British Empire. He was a democrat and not a dictator, who died thinking that he had failed, that his message of non-violence was unheard.*

Helen Keller: *deprived of sight, hearing, and the ability to speak at the age of two, she later learned how to read, write, and speak and became the author of several articles, books, and biographies.*

Julius Tahija: *made a huge contribution to the development of Indonesia through his tireless focus and effort on improving post-war conditions of both the local communities and transnational companies. I learnt a lot from the tenacity of this man.*

Lee Kuan Yew: *former Prime Minister of Singapore transformed Singapore from a backwater port into one of the most affluent societies in the world. Most of the citizens own their own homes and this Island Nation is always in surplus funds despite its limited natural resources. He also grew a capable team to succeed him.*

The Dalai Lama: *radiates peace and harmony, no matter what circumstances he encounters.*

Margaret Thatcher: *first woman in European history to be elected Prime Minister, and became known as the Iron Lady.*

Lee Iacocca: *achieved success as a business leader, with Ford and Chrysler corporations. Lee has a big-picture mentality, an analytical mind, and is brutally honest, yet fair.*

Sir Edmund Hillary: *once gave a talk, which I attended, at my local library about his conquest of Mt Everest. I later learnt, that although his initial goal was to climb Mt Everest, his real focus became discovering himself, and funding education projects for under-privileged children. He was a member of the social club I joined in London.*

Bill Gates: *started Microsoft with a friend in 1975, after dropping out of college. He liked to hire people who had made mistakes as it showed they took calculated risks. Together with his wife, Melinda, he set up a foundation to provide funding for disadvantaged people, and has empowered other financially successful people to adopt this philanthropic path.*

Stephen Hawking: *a former British professor, who was affected by progressively incurable motor neuron disease that left his limbs and voice box paralysed. At the age of twenty-one he was given two and a half years to live. Despite his severe disabilities, he remained courageous, committed, and indomitable in staying on course to make the world a better place. He advocated that compassion is a virtue that needs to be nurtured, especially in the current climate of apparent hopelessness in daily life.*

~ ~ ~

My heroes give me hope when I am in a predicament that I need to resolve – I visualise what they might have done if faced with similar circumstances, as well as quietening my mind, before making any decision.

~ ~ ~

The foundation for mental harmony is to focus on positive thoughts and visualise the outcome of the ideal dream. Having sown the seeds, meditation and reflection can provide space and time for the seeds to germinate and ripen, and for the dreams to synchronise into reality.

Space for you to write in:

The past is history – it cannot be changed; today is a present – a blessing; tomorrow is waiting for you to create – there are no boundaries. By living in the present, with peace of mind, you can create miracles.

Celebrate Your Gold Within

Chapter Six
Familial / Social Harmony

Begin with your family in the beautiful land of life.   – Albert Einstein

Family is not an important thing, it's everything.

                                                    – Michael Andrew (J) Fox

Every man needs a house to live in, but a supportive family is what builds a home.

                                                    – Anthony Liccione

A family is a place where minds come in contact with one another.

                                                    – Buddha

I sustain myself with the love of family.   – Maya Angelou

It didn't matter how big our house was; it mattered that there was love in it.

                                                    – Peter Buffett

*To put the world right in order, we must first put our nation in order; to put our nation in
order, we must first put the family in order; to put the family in order, we must first cultivate
our personal life; we must first set our hearts right.*

                                                    – Confucius

All that I am or ever hope to be, I owe to my angel Mother.

                                                    – Abraham Lincoln

The most important thing a father can do for his children is to love their mother.

                                                    – Henry Ward Beecher

*I believe that love is the greatest thing in the world; that it alone can overcome hate; that
right can and will triumph over might.*

                                                    – John Davison Rockefeller, Sr.

As we grow as unique persons, we learn to respect the uniqueness of others.

                                                    – Robert Harold Schuller

Knowing your darkness is the best method for dealing with the darkness of other people.

                                                    – Carl Gustav Jung

*Adversity draws men together and produces beauty and harmony in life's relationships, just
as the cold of winter produces ice-flowers on the window panes, which vanish with warmth.*

                                                    – Soren Kierkegaard

We are all born for love. It is the principle of existence, and its only end

                                                    – Benjamin Disraeli

*Love does not consist in gazing at each other, but in looking outward together in the same
direction.*

                                                    – Antoine De Saint-Exupery

You have to balance love and individuality and actually sacrifice a portion of each.

                                                    – David Herbert Lawrence

*One day there will be no borders, no boundaries, no flags and no countries and the only
passport will be the heart.*   – Carlos Santana

- Family – Your most important asset
- Friends / Community
- Communication. Commitment

Family – Your most important asset

The foundation for a functional family life is, in my view, individuals with the same ethics, and more similarities than differences, who agree to respect and cherish each other and share their love for each other, no matter what trials and tribulations they endure, enriching their and their children's lives.

The family unit forms the cornerstone of society where harmony needs to be present for family members to experience wellness, feel respected, and connected within the family unit, and within the world outside. It is the place where the different personalities can evolve in a non-threatening environment.

Should you have no natural family, which is quite common – due to death, fatal accidents, or other causes – or have left a dysfunctional one, you may need to "adopt" a mum, dad, sister, brother, or whoever you feel the need of in your life

The family home is not merely a building, a house. A home is a place of self-discovery, a sanctuary, and a place where the family resides. I love the following quotation from John Howard Payne – "Mid pleasures and places though we may roam, be it ever so humble, there's no place like home". The size of the house is irrelevant.

You need to understand your origins, parental influence, and that of role models who have played a part in your evolvement, and consider the benefits you have acquired. You may need to re-evaluate beliefs, restrictions, and expectations that were placed on you, and determine whether they are still relevant.

The duty of a parent is to act as agent in the birthing of a soul and to care for its personality during the first few years of its existence on earth; to nurture the child in its physical and mental growth, and provide protection during the formative years, whilst allowing the soul freedom to guide the child in gaining knowledge and experience that will form the basis of the child's evolution and independence. They need encouragement and freedom to discover who they are in the home. In that environment, family members can achieve for themselves what might otherwise be impossible. By understanding their unique personality, strengths and weaknesses, and special needs as they grow into adults, parents can give them a head start in life.

The process of evolution can enable a human being to progress from a basic level of thinking, feeling, and functioning to a spiritual realisation where there is harmony within and inherent / inborn talents can be freely expressed in the world.

Different aspects of personalities can determine:

- What aspects of sensations and perceptions are most meaningful
- What the most significant memories are
- What in particular drives thinking patterns
- What favourite emotions are
- What the most likely behaviour patterns are

An exercise that can be practised with members of the family, to help understand which part of their chakra (energy) systems may be out of balance, is to give each person a large blank sheet of paper and a pencil. Either sitting on the floor, or on a chair around a table, each person closes their eyes; then, using their feelings, and not their thoughts, they each draw a picture of them-self on the paper. It is interesting to witness which part of their body is missing in the drawing – which can indicate which chakra may be out of balance; and the relevant healing can take place to remove the blockage. Blockages in the chakras often occur from feelings of fear, anger or pain. There are several different methods of diagnosing the state of the chakras.

The more depth family members understand about the evolution of the personality, and different dimensions of reality, the more they can appreciate the different personalities of themselves, and thus accept themselves and each other without having unrealistic expectations. Within the same family each person can have a different personality and be at a different stage of evolution. Whatever their level of evolution, each can celebrate their gold within.

The outside world is full of stress, and the home needs to provide a safe place to return to. I remember reading once, that before Captain Scott of the Antarctic died, he had lots of time to reflect on the values of life. Apparently the last words that he wrote were, "For God's sake, look after our people". He realised that what really matters to man is family.

Family members need a set of guidelines based on truth, reason, mutual respect, non-violence – physical, emotional, and verbal – fairness, and acceptable behaviour. They need to understand that behavioural boundaries are designed for their benefit, safety, and protection so they can face the outside world with confidence.

Parenting can be difficult, sometimes challenging, yet rewarding. It is a learning experience for each family member that continues throughout life. Freedom comes with discipline. Confidence comes through self-mastery.

It is important to spend regular quality time together when family members are free to discuss issues that may be of concern to them, when it is important to listen without judgement and offer suggestions based on truth and respect for them, to enable them to make, and respect, their own conclusions; and become independent, so they are prepared for whatever challenges they face in life outside the home. They can agree to differ with others' conclusions, as long as they show respect.

The home can provide a practice ground. Without discussion, there is no place for the child's truth to be honoured, and communication and reasoning skills to be learned. Children have questions, feelings, and ideas that need to be communicated to, and discussed with, caring adults — they need to have life issues truthfully explained to them. During conversation, by witnessing a sense of timing and grace in their activities and body movements, a child can learn the ability, and gain the confidence, to effectively speak, listen and respond. Thus, they can live creatively, with mindfulness, rather than as creatures of habit. Otherwise, they may turn to outside sources or repress their feelings, which could be harmful to their development.

Issues relating to internet availability and the pros and cons of social media need to be included on the discussion agenda, so everyone is aware of the need to protect their identity and also to minimise harmful effects that can be caused by electronic devices. Family members could choose, and agree, which TV programs would be beneficial for them to watch to encourage them to take a mindful approach to TV time. They need to feel grounded so they know what to do in case of uncertainties and challenges. Time spent in discussion can create bridges to understanding, and enable blocked anger to be recognized and released in a safe and effective way.

A family that plays together stays together — playing games, such as table tennis, cards, and cricket, with the family can build self-esteem within the family. Encourage family members to read books as they can provide a new world of adventure to be experienced in the safety of the home — horizons can be broadened and compassion gained.

Example:

David and Tina, your two young children, expressed an interest in learning to swim. You are concerned that swimming may not be safe for them. Rather than convey your fear to them you could accompany them to swimming lessons to ensure they receive proper instruction and guidance from a qualified teacher to alleviate your fear and enable David and Tina to benefit from learning to swim.

Unconditional love is the unifying force that can strengthen self-esteem. Strength lies in unity and harmony within and only when you have that harmony are you able to effectively give to others. Hugs can create harmony at home, as well as elsewhere. They contain the three meridians – Chinese healing channels – that correspond to the heart, lungs, and pericardium. The hands are very sensitive extensions of the body and mind.

Example:

Children do not feel appreciated if they are told by their parents that they can have a lolly, only if they eat the rest of their food (or something to that effect) – that is conditional love not unconditional love. Parents need to take the time to explain the reason why wholesome, unprocessed, food needs to be eaten three times a day at set meal times – because they need nourishment to enable them to cope well with their school activities, and maintain a healthy body. Children need to know the why behind the rule so they are mindful and do not blindly accept what they are told.

Lack of harmony at home, happens from time to time, when family members need to meet to ascertain the most appropriate way to deal with this issue. The main criterion is that everyone concerned first understands the cause of the disharmony and addresses that to find the best solution. If anyone appears to be withdrawn, it is wise to seek the reason why – without jumping to unfounded conclusions.

The whole family's ethics need to be understood and respected so that when different behaviour is experienced outside the home family members know what is expected of them and do not compromise their standards. For example: arguments need to be avoided and instead channelled into meaningful and respectful discussion; the other person needs to be given the benefit of the doubt until proven otherwise; not to take remarks personally – usually they are not meant that way.

Example:

When outside the home children need to treat their surroundings with the same respect as they would do in their home environment.

Children need to understand that not all people they will meet outside their home environment are trustworthy, that they must not speak to anyone they do not know – to protect their own safety. Children are naturally friendly and inquisitive and need to be protected from potential dangerous encounters.

Where partners separate, due to irreconcilable differences, both parents need to ensure the children understand that they are not the cause of their parents' disharmony, otherwise they could unfairly suffer mental and emotional stress.

Children need to be made aware that people from different cultures and living environments may have a different understanding about certain concepts of life – for example, the types of food they eat and the way in which they eat – and need to appreciate there may not be a right or wrong way to behave in such instances. Everyone needs to be treated as an equal and given respect for differing ethnic customs.

There will come a time when children have formed their own career aspirations, blueprint in life, and need to move on to pursue their calling. They need time to experiment, and evolve. Likewise, parents need time to experiment and evolve. Their formative years, foundation, is the most important part of children's lives and they need to be able to look back on them with fond memories, respect, and gratitude. They will remember the material gifts they received but cherish and value how much time was devoted to them during those years.

They need to understand and feel that they are loved unconditionally and home is always there for them no matter what happens in their lives. Love is the greatest gift.

Friends / Community

Everyone in the world has the same basic needs in life – food, shelter, love, education, water – even though they may have different circumstances and, or, originate from different backgrounds, or have different approaches to learning: for example: homeless people, refugees, and people with disabilities and other disadvantages, as well as your neighbours and friends. Everyone is entitled to fairness and justice.

Friends

Friends are an invaluable asset. Before you can make friends with others, you need to make friends with yourself. You need to know your strengths and weaknesses – your inherent talents – and uniqueness. You need to approach friendship with a strong emotional foundation, without a needy motive, so you can radiate love and understanding to the friendship, and respect the uniqueness of others. You need to be ready to accept new friends and be available for them. You do not always need to be physically present with them as long as they are in your thoughts, and know you are available in case they need your help. They need to feel understood and supported, and so do you. They need your unconditional love, and you need theirs.

This appreciation and learning is ongoing, and it embraces both the light side and the dark sides of the personality. Unconditional love consists of looking outward in the same direction – not gazing into each other's eyes – as well as communicating your needs, thoughts and feelings, and sharing experiences. You need to get to know each other, your different backgrounds, and experiences in life. If someone has suffered a loss in their life, they need time to accept and process the loss – grieving time, and trust themselves again. Without that understanding the friendship may never progress, for example – if one person is not willing to allow the other person the time out they need for themselves. Trust needs to be established for both parties to feel safe. There is a compromise to be made.

You need to be a friend to gain a friend. The foundation of friendship is giving of your self and allowing yourself to receive from others. This means getting to know someone well, understand their needs in life, and respecting them. It can take time to get to know someone well. Making new friends is like building a new foundation. Building friendships with like-minded people is time well spent. Friendship cannot be taken for granted, it is earned over time. Good friends provide a support group in your life, during both good and difficult times. Understanding others, and making friends, can take a long time and it is worthwhile to allow room for each party to grow without having unreasonable expectations.

Some friends are in your life for a reason, some for a season, and some can be forever friends. Treasure your friends.

You need to stay in contact and communicate with friends to make sure they are well and happy. Sometimes you may not hear from a friend if they are experiencing illness or some other kind of life issue, which may have left them feeling depressed. They need you to stay in contact even if it takes a while for them to recover – you may be one of their only life lines. On the other hand, one of your friends may need some space to focus more time on a particular aspect of their life – you could let them know you want to be sure they are OK and look forward to hearing from them once they have dealt with the issue. They need to know they are supported, and you need to respect their needs. You must not perceive that they do not care and write them off or think badly of them, or speculate, assume, or imagine why they have not stayed in touch. You need to be patient and not take this distancing personally. When they are ready, they will resurface.

Example:

Sue has been experiencing a state of mental depression and Jen has not heard from her for over one week. Jen would like to catch up for a chat. Sue does not answer phone calls or respond to e-mails, neither did she come to the door when Jen tried to visit her. Fortunately, Jen did not give up on Sue and she decided she would buy a bunch of flowers and attach them to the door handle of Sue's home. Before she could do that Sue called and suggested they meet for coffee and a chat.

Community

As a citizen, it is your duty to make a positive difference in the community, country, and world in which you live. The world is your home and needs to be treated with respect. By making some contribution you can be sure that the community is also aware of your needs and can function for the good of everyone. The contribution can be worldly duties – your daily job – or else some other kind of responsibility for a much larger family. You need to contribute to the community to feel fulfilled.

In the current global conditions, it is more important than ever before to be community – minded. Everyone needs to give and receive support, to feel a part of the community in which they live – everyone is interrelated and interdependent. It stands to reason that if you make some contribution to the community in which you live you will feel more connected with that community.

Being in a state of harmony within your community can make a positive difference in someone's day. Smile to those people you meet today and feel how much lighter you feel, and witness how your smile may bring a smile to the face of others – how wonderful is that. The more you give the more you receive and the more connected and integrated you can feel within the community. Otherwise, you could feel isolated. It can seem easier to feel included in community life in a country or rural environment than in an urban environment.

Everyone has different interests, responsibilities, and amounts of free time. Community events are usually listed in the local newspaper. You can choose which group to attend and contact them to register your interest, and become involved. Some groups meet during the day and some meet in the evenings. Some groups may benefit from administrative support in case you are unable to attend all the functions and events but would like to help in other ways.

How can you add value to the community, to the world?

Example:

Liz was born in a city where she attended drama school in her spare time. She recently moved to a country town to settle with her young family and noticed an advert for auditions for a play. She attended the audition and discussed this with Bill, her partner, who supported her taking part in the play and during rehearsals he agreed to look after the children. Liz met a few like-minded people, helped provide entertainment to the local community, and quickly settled into her new surroundings.

The whole world is your home. It means thinking favourably of others and doing well without expecting any reward. Every good act is charity and the best form of giving is imparting wisdom, rather than donating money. Sharing with others the knowledge and experience you have gained can purify the heart. You will always receive more than you give and your heart will expand.

Example:

Peter noticed that a young family from overseas recently moved into his neighbourhood. He imagined how he might feel if he moved to live in an overseas location – he could imagine feeling rather lost. Peter decided to invite the family to his home to share a meal and explain the various activities available within the community, and gave them a copy of the latest community newsletter. The family appreciated this gesture and immediately felt welcome in their new environment.

You need to be aware that there are a lot of angry people in the world who try to vent their anger onto others, rather than addressing the underlying cause of their anger and changing that negative trait to a positive outcome. This can result in an act of bullying, which cannot not be tolerated under any circumstances as it can undermine a person's self-esteem. The relevant community group needs to be kept informed of such occurrences so the perpetrators can be properly monitored and counselled.

Example:

John works for a not-for-profit group as a team leader. He is instructing his team members how to do a job. Penny, a person with higher authority, who is unfamiliar with the job, arrives on the scene and shouts at John accusing him of gossiping with the members of the team. The team members become upset and John feels humiliated. He needs to get the job completed in the allotted time and get his team back under control.

This was an act of verbal bullying, and John needs to report the facts of the incident to his supervisor who is on leave. In the meantime, John could take no action; confront Penny with the real facts and let her know how her behaviour had upset his team members' morale; or he could report the unwarranted behaviour to the highest authority who always supports Penny. He chose to report the incident to a person in higher authority but also decided to hand in his notice as this type of incident had happened in the past and John was unable to tolerate this type of behaviour any longer.

In fact, Penny had jumped to a conclusion without being aware of the reason why John was having a discussion with his team. She is a bully and needs to be told that her behaviour is unacceptable. When the issue was investigated, it turned out that she has some personal issues at home that she is projecting onto people at work. Penny was asked to take one month's leave and sort out her personal issues, before returning for duty.

Communication

Communication is the gateway between the inner and outer worlds. Through mindful communication you shape your future – through vibrations and symbols, listening and responding at the same time. It is also a gateway between the mind and body, and a bottleneck for the passage of energy. Purification is a vibrational refinement that takes place at the fifth chakra level of the throat as you rid the body of toxins and authentically work through issues pertaining to the lower chakras. A resonant, rhythmical voice that speaks truthfully, clearly, and concisely is the sign of a healthy fifth chakra. A balance in the fifth chakra energy enhances the ability to listen and respond, with no need to deny or hide feelings, and have the courage to differ, even in the face of opposition. You need to learn to say "no", whenever that is necessary, to protect your boundaries.

Due to work assignments and other commitments you cannot always be physically present with your family, friends and community. You can still communicate through your mind so they can feel your presence, or you can communicate via e-mail, whichever way works best. It is important to communicate, to play your part in the game of life. In return, you too will feel more supported and connected.

It is OK to express your feelings of appreciation, fear, happiness, sadness, compassion, disappointment to others, as appropriate. That way the other person is aware of your current state of mind, and feelings which may otherwise be suppressed and cause confusion or resentment, or even result in ill health. Both parties can benefit from listening and learning, and developing compassion.

When you constrict your emotions, you restrict and suppress expression. You need to let it all out, express the emotions, and experience a state of internal peace. Connect the body, breath, and voice with confidence and without fear. If you express yourself before establishing the truth, the result may be confusing and harmful to you. Question how your communication can become more direct and effective. Choose your words thoughtfully.

Acknowledge the other person's problems without feeling the need to fix the problem. Allow the person time to be heard, then ask questions to clarify your understanding and repeat your understanding to ensure it is the truth, instead of jumping to unfounded conclusions. Let there be no misunderstanding.

Witness the way you are reacting to circumstances and consider whether there could have been a more appropriate outcome.

Example:

Joy over-reacted to something David said to her without clarifying the facts. By Joy raising questions instead of jumping to conclusions without having full knowledge of the content and context of the comment made by David the disharmony could have been avoided.

Observe how other people are acting and whether they may need help.

Example:

At the local yoga class Bill notices that Anna seems unable to cope with most of the practices and she advised the teacher who spoke to Anna to find out whether she had any problem. It turned out that Anna was feeling depressed and in need of counselling, which the teacher diplomatically suggested and helped Anna to find the most appropriate counselling service provider.

Someone could be perceived as having no feelings and aloof, whereas in fact their feelings may merely be hidden, due to an emotional wound or traumatic experience in the past that they have not been able to come to terms with. You may also experience this yourself from time to time. You need to recognize the inner child, feel empathy for the inner child, release anger, fear, or longing and move on. By removing guilt the hidden feelings can be unblocked. It helps to channel the blocking emotions into appropriate activities to allow those emotions to be released and replaced by positive feelings.

Examples:

- *Anger – physical work performed with mindfulness can help to restore peace of mind*
- *Fear – heightened awareness of the fear and coming to terms with it by taking appropriate action can help eradicate the fear and restore confidence*
- *Longing – creative activities can help to release creativity and restore a feeling of contentment and well-being*

You only know what is inside someone's thoughts when they choose to tell you. If you are unable to get a point across to someone – you may have misunderstood their point of view and need to seek further clarification, by asking them to repeat their understanding. If you choose not to take that time you may miss knowing the truth and potential opportunities. In certain cultures, it is first necessary to take time to establish a sincere friendship between various business parties before potential business opportunities can be discussed. If time is not adequate for this procedure to take place, you may be wasting your time, and preventing potential opportunities from becoming reality.

It is always best to clarify facts stated to ensure you have heard and correctly understood the true meaning of the facts – that they were not based on hearsay or gossip, or unwarranted assumption or perception. It is also wise to communicate how you felt to the other person and not allow yourself to become angry. You may decide to withdraw from a conversation to rethink the facts from a distance, and return later to discuss them after gaining clarity. Take time to review all aspects of the impact your decision will have on each person – put yourself in their shoes – before taking the most appropriate action. Whatever you do – never argue as that can create animosity. Never make a decision when you are angry, as you may live to regret it.

It is important to learn how to receive constructive feedback as well as how to give constructive feedback – in both instances each party can benefit. The tone of voice of the person providing the feedback needs to be supportive. The person receiving the feedback needs to carefully listen, accept, clarify as necessary, and appreciate the feedback so they can gain self-confidence and improve their performance going forward. It is important for the person receiving the feedback not to take it personally.

Example:

Tony had to teach yoga to a class of beginners and was being assessed by one of the yoga teachers. After the end of the class the teacher informed Tony that he had not correctly followed the required procedures and had demonstrated one of the asanas, which was not allowed. Due to the teacher's tone of voice Tony felt unsupported.

You need to cultivate emotional balance within, so you have more to give and share with others. Negative experiences can teach you to deny and withhold the truth, living a lie that does not resonate with your own being. Vibration needs to be expressed, or it is stored as stress in the body, blocking the throat chakra and separating you from the chorus of life. Wearing a tight neck-tie can choke the individuality of a person. Disconnection from the core self, by hiding from shame, or fear, isolates you from the world. Various kinds of music can heal certain emotional states.

Having broken free of established patterns, you need to allow creativity into your life – make something that did not exist before – build a gateway between the past and future. Never feel the need to justify yourself when challenged. Communication comes in forms other than what you say verbally – in body language, facial and tonal expression, and movement. Spoken words form only a small percentage of what you communicate. Spend some time discovering the meaning behind various body-language postures and actions – what is effective and what is inappropriate, to understand whether your communication style is effective or whether it could be improved in any way.

Before you speak, you need to have in mind exactly what you want to convey, the effect it could have on others, and ensure the message comes from the heart. It may be more effective to first summarise the message in the form of a letter or e-mail, to give the recipient time to consider the overall facts in their true context, so they will be prepared for a meaningful discussion.

Balanced mindful communication, punctuating your verbal expressions, using well-chosen words, with pauses to allow time for the message to be heard and understood, indicates to the listener that you have taken time to explain the message you wish to portray. Allow time to listen to the response that is provided, and clarify anything that is unclear. Be sure you are actively engaged in the conversation, not merely delivering a message to the other party. Communicate from the heart by looking into the recipient's eyes – that way they know you have nothing to hide. Silence also forms a part of the communication process – it can unify energies within, and emphasize the meaning of important issues being discussed.

Communication – listening, clarifying, and responding appropriately, takes time to master and is worth your effort and investment of time. Have compassion for the person who may have upset you but remember the experience. You need to bear this in mind for future reference.

Commitment

You need to recognize the fruits of your individuality – your inborn talents that may currently be latent, your unlimited potential, which is your unique power that can be unleashed to benefit the community.

Consider how you can best add value in your community. If, currently, you do not have available time, maybe you can donate to a worthy cause that could benefit from your donation – you need to be sure what percentage of the amount you donate will reach the cause you have chosen to donate to – certain organisations have high administrative costs.

If you are self-employed, consider what policies are in place to enhance employee training, fitness and welfare, and charitable affiliation. A business that makes nothing but money lacks community integrity, its direction can become focused on lack, rather than abundance, and in the long-term employee turnover may be high and the business will fail to develop and expand.

For as long as you breathe the free air of the earth, you are obliged to give service to the community in whatever way you choose. If you are financially secure, have surplus funds, or want to make difference for a worthy cause and you can help raise funds, you may consider setting up a charitable foundation, whereby, should something happen to you in the future, the entity could continue to function and the financial support would continue.

Example:

Bill Gates and his wife, Melinda, have opted for this route, as have others.

Activities that you could donate time to, depending on your circumstances, and time available, include:

- Walking the neighbour's dog if the neighbour is sick or too busy
- Pet sitting if a neighbour is away for some time
- Comforting someone who is crying
- Collecting groceries for a neighbour if they are unable to go out
- Baby-sitting to allow parents to take a break
- Volunteering at Riding for the Disabled
- Volunteering at RSPCA
- Volunteering at the Salvation Army, or other group, activities
- Helping an older or younger person to cross the road if they need the help
- If a person in the street looks lost or ill, asking them if they need help – do not pass them by
- Helping the neighbours with gardening, or other duties
- Volunteering at the local wild life animal shelter
- Raising funds for a charity by getting sponsored to cycle, walk, or participate in some other event

You may experience a greater feeling of connection and belonging by becoming a volunteer with a non-for profit organization.

You do not necessarily need spare funds available to help less fortunate people or people in need. You can use some of your available time to raise funds for whatever cause you believe in.

Example:

In 2011, Pat Farmer ran 21,000 kilometres from the North Pole to the South Pole through Canada, the United States, Central America, and South America. It took him one year to complete the run, averaging 65 kilometres each day through blizzards, deserts, -40 degree temperatures, wild animals, armed bandits and militia, whilst suffering dehydration, stress injuries and pain. Pat endured this epic journey so that people in impoverished and devastated communities all over the world could benefit from the funds raised. He sold his family home to raise funds for this venture. He wrote a book to document his daily experiences that was published and sold – with proceeds being donated to the Red Cross.

The community can be wider than your immediate area. For example, you may choose to volunteer with an organisation that requires help with their overseas projects. Such a commitment could make a huge difference to the lives of people in less developed countries. It would also open your eyes to the conditions in which other people live whilst you help to improve those conditions, and be an enriching life-changing experience.

It is your duty to live for the sake of others; sacrifice is the law of life. Should you choose only to receive – that is like being a thief. There needs to be a balance of giving and receiving for harmony to exist. Opening your heart and developing compassion, connection, and understanding with the community, naturally urges you to help in whatever capacity you can. You cannot advance alone while others need help, as you are all one, and you need to request and accept help when you need it.

Family – My most important asset:

I was fortunate to have a caring mum who stayed home full time throughout my formative years and beyond. Mum was a quiet person who seemed contented at home. We played cards and other board games when my homework was complete, and she taught me how to knit.

Dad was away at work during weekdays and I dearly missed not spending more time with him, although the time we spent together was quality time, and we had a close bond. We often played table tennis on the polished wooden dining room table. Each weekend we spent time together at meal times, around the dining table whenever possible, and without the interference of television. The home environment was usually peaceful except when I chose to rebel by wanting to stay up late to see my dad during the week when he arrived home late after work.

During my childhood, I experienced a lot of alone time at home and adapted to that by listening to music, cycling, and reading books. I also took care of the garden, which I enjoyed as it allowed a certain amount of creativity. I did not do much housework as Mum seemed happy to do that herself. The only pets in the house were Sandy, my brother's dog, who enjoyed chewing the mail and died of a seizure; Monty a talking budgie, who loved to work his way along the top of newspapers, as they were being read, chewing them as he progressed; and a tortoise that mysteriously disappeared. I found no joy in playing with dolls, and enjoyed collecting toy cars that I could race with those of the neighbours. I guess I was a tomboy at heart.

Sadly, neither of my parents felt the need to connect with my teachers, as they considered this would be seen as interfering with the teachers' role. Hence this important liaison was missing throughout my school life.

One of the areas on which Mum and I strongly disagreed was based on the "class system" endemic in the UK at that time. A school friend of mine, Gladys, lived a few streets away from in what Mum considered to be a "lower class" neighbourhood. I met Gladys around the corner and we walked to school together. Mum did not encourage this as Gladys came from a family that did not have the "same background" and her mum worked as a house-cleaner. I did not understand this logic and chose to accept that Mum was entitled to her own beliefs but I chose to accept everyone as spiritual equals. This topic raised its ugly head on many future occasions.

I always felt safe at home, and my parents usually allowed me to play and travel with others – they trusted that I would be safe. Every year we took an annual two-week holiday together as a family, usually to Llandudno in North Wales. Two large trunks of clothes were packed – we took the train to Liverpool and a steamer, either the St Trillo, a turbine vessel, or the St Tudno, a steel paddle steamer, to Llandudno for the rest of the journey. I loved the travel experiences. I learned a lot – carried with me some I-Spy books on trains and other topics, avidly observed the engines of the trains and boats; and carried a notebook with me to record new words of the Welsh language that I learned as I chatted to the various shop keepers.

Mum and Dad allowed me to stay on the beach, where I helped run one of the donkey teams – fun and good exercise – I joined them later at a cafe up the Great Orme where we had morning tea, after which we walked back to our accommodation. Sometimes, we caught the funicular railway tram to the top of the Great Orme where there was a church – the St Trillo, overlooking the sea.

Later we visited Scotland, exploring the lochs amid the remote wild scenery, where it rained most of the time. Our home was not far from the English Lake District, and we enjoyed sailing around the various lakes and walking in that area – the scenery was more tranquil than that in Scotland and Wales, but picturesque and invigorating.

Dad offered me a cigarette when I was sixteen, allowing me to experience whether to become a regular smoker, which he was not. We were attending a social function and he seemed aware that if I was not introduced to smoking at such an event I may try it elsewhere. He understood me very well. I did not enjoy smoking and rarely touched cigarettes after that. I could not envisage allowing my lungs to be treated as an ashtray.

Whilst Dad was alive we visited Brother John's home at the weekends to spend time with his family. His lovely wife, Phyllis, was sick most of the time, never complained and always had a smile for everyone. She allowed me to play the piano, which I managed to do by ear, I could also read music for the right hand but not for the left hand. They had two sons, Philip and Brian. Sadly, at the age of thirty-five, Phyllis passed away – the children were aged ten and five. Mum and Dad enjoyed spending time with their grandchildren.

Familial / Social Harmony

Soon after Phyllis' death, Dad passed away. From time to time I "adopt" new family members, or they adopt me, but I never managed to find another real father figure – Dad was unique.

Following that tragedy, Mum and I spent two weeks at a holiday camp with John, Philip, and Brian. I taught Philip how to ride a pony, and roller-skate. John baby sat in the evenings, whilst Mum and I checked out the social events. Soon after that most of my time was spent working and studying. Mum continued to spend regular time with her grandchildren.

Mum and I took a cruise from Liverpool to the Isle of Man. I recall the sea was rough as we neared Ramsey, on the North of the island. Most of the passengers disappeared below deck but I remained in the howling wind and the rain, which was exhilarating.

I visited Philip and Brian, and their families, on my two latest visits to England and met their wives and children.

Apart from my two nephews, and their families, the only direct living relative, of whom I am aware, is Elsie, a cousin from Dad's side of the family who lives in Honiton, Devon, in England. We stay in touch on a regular basis.

Through certain life experiences encountered I have made friends who have become closer than blood ties.

After Mum died, Katy a close friend with whom I trained as an accountant, advised me that her mum would "adopt" me, which was lovely. The family loved animals – Jasper the parrot, and a Labrador dog. I enjoyed visiting their home whenever I could. Katy's mum passed away some time ago. Katy visited me in each country in which I have lived, and I stayed at her home in Scotland, where she lives with her husband Mike, and we maintain regular contact.

When I lived in Singapore, Philip, my Singaporean partner and I, had a Filipina housemaid – Mary – who lived with us. She was more a member of the family than a maid. She was efficient at her job and patient with Philip's son, Franco, who was five years old when he came to stay with us. She accompanied him to and from school and cooked all our meals, as well as doing all the housework. Mary was allowed a visa to stay in Singapore for only eight years. Despite a few major disappointments encountered in her life, she always remained cheerful. Hence, I helped to sponsor her migration to Canada where she had a few relatives and could benefit from a more democratic and fulfilling lifestyle. We stayed in touch and I am regarded as part of her family – her mum wrote a letter to thank me and let me know that I was more than a friend to the family. Now all her family is based in Canada.

Philip, worked in the hospitality industry. The early years of our family life were happy and memorable but eventually Philip spent little time at home with his son Franco, which was disappointing. We remained in the relationship for fourteen years, although it became apparent after about eight years that our life values had become worlds apart, and the differences were irreconcilable. Although I was not Franco's biological mother I felt a close spiritual bond and empathy for him – his early life had not been easy. I always hoped he would grow up to be a caring adult. After Franco left school he chose to join the Air Force – National Service was compulsory for boys who were Singapore citizens. He greatly benefited from the discipline it provided and the friends he made. Franco later became a professional photographer, music aficionado, and successful businessman. With deep sorrow, I learnt about his tragic death at age forty three. He was a passenger in a car that went out of control at very high speed. Franco is greatly missed. I never had biological children of my own – during one of the regular health check-ups with the doctor I was advised that if I had become pregnant it was possible that my body may not have survived the birthing process.

Friends / Community:

During my life in Asia, I spent most of my vacation time travelling. One of the countries I visited was Thailand. Apart from the busy cities and the ancient monuments and temples, life proceeds in the countryside at a much slower pace and with less hustle and bustle. It was there, near to the border with Laos, where I experienced and realized that people all over the world share the same basic needs in life – love, shelter, food, and water, regardless of their religion, race, and current circumstances.

Friends:

In Singapore I made friends with Es, who owned and managed a school. We shared a hotel room in Singapore and witnessed the handover of Hong Kong to PRC. Due to our hectic career schedules, it took a while for us to become friends, but now the friendship is strong. She encouraged me to study and practice yoga. Neither of us lost our sense of humour, despite trying experiences we have each encountered.

When I first arrived in Australia, I stayed in a granny flat next door to James, one of my ex-colleagues from Singapore, and his wife Marjorie, with whom I had become good friends in Singapore. The flat belonged to a young family who lived in the main house. That was my first family experience in Melbourne and helped me settle into life in Australia.

Verena was my main friend in Adelaide. During a visit to the cathedral one New Year's Eve I was inspired to spread the message in this book to the world.

During my time at the yoga centre, I met several spiritual brothers and sisters with whom I share much in common. It is a blessing and a privilege to be part of that community and have that bond. We remain in contact, via the extensive yoga family network.

Community:

From my experiences at an early age attending Sunday school at a local church, I felt compassion for both abused children and their parents who, in turn, had experienced violence in the process of growing up.

During my teenage years, I spent a lot of time organizing youth group activities at the local church with my first boyfriend, David, who I had known since our primary school days. It was a strong social group and everyone had fun. That community spirit was grounding when we were growing up. The main activity I recall was dancing.

I sponsored several children through World Vision and enjoyed hearing about their family life and progress at school. They were much loved in their home environment and it was a privilege to be able to help them with their educational needs. When they reached a certain age and no longer needed help for their education, I felt sad as there was then no way to track their progress in life and remain in contact.

When I started work, I joined the local students' society and took part in their activities – in particular, I was on the Careers group sub-committee that met with high school students to advise them what they could expect from a career in Chartered Accountancy. As we received no career advice at secondary school, I found sharing my knowledge and experience with the students a rewarding experience.

I was privileged to spend a day in the life of the Karan hill tribe in Northern Thailand. The whole family lived in a small wooden hut with no internal walls. They were happy to share what little they had with me, including allowing me to sleep on the floor of their hut for the night. My back will never forget the close feeling of nature – the morning dew seeping through the floorboards. The nearby river was their only source of water, and their bathroom. Usually, children in those regions need to leave home to attend schools elsewhere. In cases of extreme poverty, the community may require help from people more fortunate than themselves. Getting to and from such remote places is not always easy – I travelled with some of the locals – you can go by organized tours.

At The Tanglin Club in Singapore, I was elected to serve as a member on the Food and Beverage Committee, which I found interesting and educational. One of the functions was to plan menus, and as the club hosted many international events I learnt a lot about the different foods, and enjoyed participating as a committee member. I also wrote travel articles for the monthly members' magazine when I travelled to Malaysia, Thailand, and Indonesia, and illustrated them with photographs that I took.

I became a member of one of one of the Rotary Clubs in Singapore and was asked to give a presentation on taxation in the Asia Pacific region to its members. I also became a member of Zonta International and participated in various projects relating to women's needs in the community. I enjoyed sharing my knowledge and donating my time to these groups. They provided an international community with a philanthropic vision and their members were dedicated to making a difference in their communities.

During my work assignments in Indonesia, I was always looked after by Bob, the US accountant, whose wife Nuri was Indonesian. Although I spoke very little Indonesian, and she spoke very little English, we communicated by using sign language and often ended up in fits of laughter. I stayed with them at their beach house in South Java, from where we could see the volcano Krakatoa. We particularly enjoyed eating the local fruit durian – many people do not enjoy this fruit as it has a pungent smell, but it tastes divine. Bob's daughter lived in Seattle, and when I visited Seattle we all met for a meal. Sadly, I lost contact with them when Bob passed away.

I enjoyed my time working in Indonesia, despite the unrest within the country. Together with the wife of the managing director of my client, I visited a site in Java where brass and copper gongs were made and witnessed the gong that I bought being moulded, and tuned – it is very special, as the art of gong-making is disappearing. It is now located in my living room.

Whilst I lived in Singapore, following the separation from my long-time partner Philip, I travelled with another friend throughout Thailand and Indonesia during one of my vacations – whilst we were travelling there was a great harmony as we benefited from each other's company to share the experiences and survive some harsh living conditions. The experiences of travelling on local transport were unforgettable and enriching. When it came to sharing a home, there was no harmony as we each had different life values and expectations, so we went our separate ways. That was a friendship that lasted for only a season.

Communication:

Communication has always been an important part of my life. During my early years I recall being unable to openly express my feelings and that may have made me appear to be aloof. However, I was actively listening and attentive, and focusing on my inner development.

Mum's attempt to introduce me to elocution failed as I did not understand the reason for learning by rote and repeating what I had learned to an examiner of whom I had no knowledge and with whom I had no connection. During my career in Adelaide, Australia, I joined Professional Speakers Australia and attended their Academy training program when I learnt from prominent speakers how to convey a message to an audience with maximum impact and maintain their attention. I also attended a workshop facilitated by one of their members who was trained at the National Institute of Dramatic Art. His role was to ensure that people like me, whose career training and experience was gained mainly from books, learned to become more spontaneous in presenting their message to an audience. It was fun – a true awakening of reaching out and engaging with an audience in a more effective and alive way, by encouraging interaction; rather than delivering a message without any knowledge of whether or not it had been effectively received. I learnt a lot, and continued to gain more experience and training in professional speaking whilst I lived in Adelaide.

I communicated with pen pals – wrote letters and stayed in touch, which was a good way of making friends with people at a distance. It provided a base of compatible friends away from home, some of whom I visited during my travels.

During the course of my work, I spent time listening to client needs and providing them with written advice based on facts provided and legal research that enabled me to conclude how best their requirements could be achieved. I was also required to review legal documents and provide written reports for boards of directors to advise on the correctness of client tax exposure in audited accounts.

The only regret I have is that I was unable to see Mum more often after I had left home and before she passed away. We communicated weekly by mail. I had planned to visit four years after my last visit and she advised she could not cope with that. I realised later that she may not be well but this was not communicated to me either by my brother or her family doctor and which I discovered only after her death when I questioned why I had not been kept informed.

During my travels throughout Asia, even when I was unable to speak the local language it was possible to communicate by using sign language and laughing when the message was not understood at first. In addition to the hectic work schedule, I decided to learn Mandarin but managed to progress only as far as the intermediate level – I would have needed to spend many hours learning more vocabulary to link together sentences, there is no grammar. So, I chose to study Bahasa Indonesia, similar to Bahasa Malay, which was interesting. Although there was not much opportunity to practice that language – most indigenous people spoke in dialect – I could sometimes understand what was being said by the Malays in Singapore and Malaysia.

If all else failed, and I did not speak the local language well, I waited for action to take place – especially when I was going through customs in Malaysia, Thailand and Indonesia and my passport mysteriously disappeared. In the end the officials had to comply and return my passport and let me through Customs. I never provided the bribes they wanted.

When I lived in Adelaide, I was prompted to convey my message to the world – to inspire everyone to live their life fully with no limitations, and hence the birth of this book. I am hoping that it will sell widely so that many people can gain hope to celebrate their life, their gold within, without limitation.

Commitment:

After I had been living in Australia for a few years, James and his wife Marjorie bought a new apartment nearer to Melbourne. Once my work travels commenced I was unable to visit them so often but always met them when I returned to Melbourne. Sadly, James was diagnosed with cancer, and needed to move into a high-care facility in an age-care nursing home. He remained cheerful throughout his life there. Eventually, Marjorie decided to move to the same age-care centre so she could be nearer to James and spend more time with him – she had her own room there, and regularly led the choir and played the piano. When I returned to work in Melbourne I often visited Marjorie and we played cards and Scrabble at the weekends. James passed away four years before Marjorie, who had suffered with diabetes from a very young age. I recall the last time I visited her – she was resting and unable to recognize me but must have heard my voice, as on my way home I heard her voice say my name. She was a beautiful soul, who sacrificed her life in England to be with her husband in Singapore and Australia, and maintained contact with all her friends worldwide who she loved dearly.

I was horrified by the way James and Marjorie's children dealt with their parents' in later years. It seemed that they rarely visited them and waited to inherit their financial wealth, encouraging Marjorie to spend as little of her monetary funds as possible after James had passed away.

In Adelaide, Australia, I was invited to join the Council of the Experimental Arts Foundation that enabled me to get to know a different sector of the community and work with their committee, in a financial advisory capacity. My main role became to help the Director set financial goals and achieve the Council's financial needs, so he could present the Council's financial plan to the local bank manager and obtain funding from the bank. I had a lot of fun working in a different environment – it provided a challenge, and I broadened my horizons. I had to allow time to get to know the committee members, who each had an artistic background, and their roles in the financial area of the Council, before providing any advice – so they accepted me as one of them and did not feel threatened by my presence.

During the time I lived in the ashram, and isolated from the outside world for a period of five years, I lost contact with some of my friends. When I left the ashram I had to reconnect with some of my old friends and make new friends – a whole new world came into being as I had gained a deeper appreciation of life.

Having familial and social harmony provides the foundation from which I can operate in the outside world, without being affected adversely by negative influences. The more I feel connected, within and without, there can be a greater scope for experiencing potential opportunities and fully participating in all that life has to offer.

I appreciate, and aim to protect, my precious assets and spend time building and maintaining new networks on an ongoing basis.

Space for you to write in:

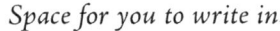

Be thankful for the time you spend with your family and friends - your most precious assets; and the opportunity to make a positive difference in the world community.

Celebrate Your Gold Within

Chapter Seven
Vocational Harmony

Your work is to discover your life and with all your heart to give yourself to it.
— Buddha

Choose a job you love, and you will never have to work a day in your life.
— Confucius

Lack of money is the root of all evil.
— George Bernard Shaw

Try not to be a man of success, but rather, try to become a man of value.
— Albert Einstein

The cause of success must be the individual, and nowhere else.
— Wallace Delois Wattles

Never attribute to malevolence what is merely due to incompetence.
— Arthur Charles Clarke

Nothing will strengthen a man more than the confidence shown in him.
— Johann Wolfgang von Goethe

Every man has a right to be valued by his best moment.
— Ralph Waldo Emerson

Not only is there an art in knowing a thing, but also a certain art of teaching it.
— Cicero

I know the price of success: dedication, hard work, and an unrelenting devotion to the things you want to see happen.
— Frank Lloyd Wright

You must be the change you want to see in the world.
— Mahatma Gandhi

- What is your motivation?
- What is your passion?
- How can you make a difference?
- Coping with change

What is your motivation?

You certainly need enough money to provide for your real needs in life, but money must not be the main motivation for you to be working. Your work, whether it be as an employer, employee, or entrepreneur, needs to include a passion that comes from utilizing your inherent talents, otherwise you will feel unhappy and unfulfilled, and become unwell. Wellness is a prerequisite to enjoying all other areas of life, and it cannot be compromised.

It is likely that you spend at least fifty per cent of your waking time at your day job or vocation. Therefore, it is important that you enjoy it, that it motivates you to get out of bed in the morning. If you find that your current job or vocation is stressful, maybe it is not the right one for you. If you experience stress in your work life you could become sick and you need to avoid that at all costs. Otherwise, you may need to spend time recuperating, instead of enjoying your free time.

What may have suited your needs earlier in your life may not suit your current or future needs – your passion can change depending on your evolvement and / or changed needs in life. If your current job or vocation does not provide satisfaction, and motivation, then you need to consider a different way of spending that portion of your time. Your well-being is more important than financial wealth. When you are doing the type of work you enjoy – with passion – financial wealth will follow in abundance. You can feel more fulfilled.

You need to discover or rediscover your inherent talents and how best you can use these to make a unique contribution in the world – to perform the work for which you were created, or else there can be no harmony. You need to build a strong foundation, based on your core values, your uniqueness, your potential, and your vision. Question whether your current circumstances meet those criteria and, if not, reconsider the potential alternatives that could enable you to feel fulfilled.

Refer to Exercises Two and Three, at the end of Chapter One to review your strengths and weaknesses again.

You may benefit from consulting with a careers adviser if you have any doubts about choosing your ideal vocation. It is important you are happy with your choice and your decision. Otherwise, you may end up living someone else's life and become unhappy.

What is your passion?

When you enjoy, and are passionate about, what you are doing, you will always have time to experience a harmonious life with minimal stress. That is the way things are meant to be. Happiness attracts wellness, abundance, and an excitement to live life fully.

Are you a leader or a follower? Do you enjoy being employed and under the direction of an employer, or do you prefer to work for yourself and employ other people if necessary? If you enjoy teamwork that environment can be present in your own your own business, as well as in your capacity as an employee. Answering this question will help you decide what mode of working will be fulfilling and suitable for you. Only you can decide this.

Working for others may impose limitations on your creative skills. Or, you may find that a routine job does not allow you to use your leadership skills. You may decide that you do not enjoy working for other people and choose to start your own business. There is no right or wrong thing to do. You may find that commuting to work each day takes up too much time that you could otherwise spend with your family or close friends. It is your choice, based on your needs and constitution.

Examples:

- *Belinda currently works for a major city accounting firm which requires her to commute from her home each day. She enjoys her work but finds that spending three hours of commuting time each day detracts from her need to spend more time with her two young children. The book-keeping duties she performs could be provided from home, and after discussion with her boss it is agreed she does not need to be present in the office every day of the week but can work in the city office on a Monday to report on her client work progress and obtain new work assignments. This arrangement works well for both parties.*

- *Steve works for a major engineering company and finds the work to be quite routine. He has saved a substantial amount of money and believes he would be happier providing unique engineering services to a wider base of clients, which would allow him to experience greater client contact and develop his business skills. Steve discussed his plan with his boss and they agree that the services Steve will provide will not create a conflict of interest. Steve sets up an office in his home and, together with his accountant, decided on a business name and the most appropriate operating structure, and develops a strategy for marketing his services.*

You may discover that working for yourself as an entrepreneur demands too much time to enable you to grow your business as well as providing the principle services, in which case you may need to consider employing additional help, or changing your role to that of a consultant to a wider range of clients. You may need to consider employing an accountant to keep your business records in order and help you develop some new business strategies.

Working for yourself may mean that you will not have a regular income stream for some time so you need to take this into account when considering when is the best time to make a change from being employed. You will need to determine how the services you intend to provide are unique and what brand name will best help you market them. How will you market them? You may need to attend training programs to learn new skills – for example, computer skills.

When reviewing your strengths and weaknesses, and where you would like to be in five, ten, and twenty years' time, consider what changes you need to plan for now to bridge the gap between where you currently are and where you want to be. You may need to update your studies, or learn new skills. It is never too late to make a change, but it will take courage, and needs planning. You need to factor in time for the change to take place, so you can monitor your progress.

Example:

When Colin left school, he attended university and graduated with an arts degree. He had worked in a library, a museum, and travelled the world. Now back in his home town, he has decided that he wants to trade in antiques that will allow him to develop business skills, continue learning more about history, and share his knowledge and experiences with others. He started by working for an antique dealer to gain a general appreciation for the trade and later intends to set up a business of his own.

Timing is important as you need to ensure that you are in a position – financially, mentally, and physically – to start a new adventure and survive, before you make any change. Also, you need to gain the support of those you love and care for so they are aware of your new plans and can provide you with emotional support. You may need to factor in some time to further anticipate what your ideal lifestyle will mean to you, before making any change.

Whatever you enjoy, and decide to do, remember that each job you undertake needs to be done as efficiently as possible, with mindfulness, and without stress. This will enable you, and everyone involved, to conserve their energy and fully live their life with happiness and without limitation.

You need to be in harmony with your real purpose in life.

How can you make a difference?

Some people always say they have no time to fit new experiences into their lives. This may indicate they have a mentality of lack, rather than one of abundance. Or, it may mean they are stuck in a rut – like being on a round-about they are unable to jump off.

Take control of your time and plan time out of your busy routine to dream about your ideal future. What is stopping you from being there now, making a change? What obstacles are in the way? How can you overcome those hurdles? By expanding your way of thinking, and taking appropriate actions, you can change your lifestyle. Something worthwhile attaining will not happen overnight.

Examples:

- *Andrew has a mortgage to pay, a family to support, and needs to maintain the monthly level of income he currently earns. His job has become routine and lacks challenge. Andrew feels it is limiting his need to grow. He decides to review his strengths and weaknesses, and consider what lifestyle he needs to feel fulfilled.*

  Andrew decides to continue working at his current job with this new mind-set and hope for the future, to allow the time he needs to manifest the change process.

- *Jane works in the general store in the town where she was born. Although she did well at school she had to stay at home to care for her mum who was sick when her friends went to universities elsewhere. Recently, her mum passed away and Jane now wants to travel in China and Japan for a year before deciding what she would like to do in the future. She contacts one of her friends who works in Beijing and arranges to stay there whilst she plans the rest of her trip, and her ideal lifestyle.*

There is no satisfaction in being stuck in a role that no longer motivates you or you no longer enjoy, not only can it adversely affect your health, but it can also be detrimental to the productivity of your employer's business. It can even adversely affect your relationships with your family and close friends. You need to recognize the mismatch, and plan an alternative strategy so you can enjoy the future in a place that is more suitable, where you can best use your inherent talents and creativity. Time is precious, and needs to be used wisely.

Question whether you can renounce an unsuitable lesser-paid role when you could perform a more suitable more highly-paid role – when you are in a state of wisdom rather than in a state of confusion, despondency, fear, or attachment. Quieten your mind before coming to any conclusions. Change will take courage. Consider if the more highly-paid role could change your lifestyle. Does it suit your needs? If not, why not? Why settle for a lesser-paid role that could lack challenge and growth potential?

You can experience success only after recognising and releasing (not suppressing) the disharmony within, and taking time out to review your real needs in life, changing your daily routine and embracing harmony. It is not based on other people's beliefs, thoughts, or actions – it is chosen by you. Change can be stressful but not as stressful as accepting a lack of harmony in your life. It can also lead to a new adventure, be exciting, and invigorating.

Example:

Wendy has been working in a law firm for the past ten years. Her careers adviser had told her that it was a career that she would enjoy, based on her talents. When she was growing up at home her parents did not encourage her to express her feelings and hence they were not naturally recognized. Wendy knew in her heart that being a lawyer was not what she wanted to do for the rest of her life. She enjoyed working with people and was good at languages. So, she decided to change her job and work as a travel adviser and translator. Now she is happy.

When you are leading a work team, you need to lead by example – extract work from others through kindness, service, respect, and love. Treat others as you would like to be treated. Bear in mind that a worthy leader has the desire to serve, not to dominate and dictate. You need to be there for your team to consult with when they need help, to provide encouragement and constructive feedback. Help them to succeed and contribute to the team dynamics. Show confidence in them. It is your role to get the job done as efficiently as possible within the allocated time-frame. Regularly monitor progress, and address issues to ensure this happens. Respect your team, their strengths and weaknesses. Check in with each team member regularly, to monitor progress and ensure the project is on track – never make any assumptions. The team needs your interaction and opportunity to clarify issues.

Because of inappropriate behaviour in the workplace or, if for some other reason, you feel despondent or depressed, you may need to seek help from a qualified counsellor. Those are not acceptable states and need to be changed to enable you to achieve your optimum potential. Never feel you are on your own when you need help – it is your responsibility to seek it.

How can you serve society in a way that others are unable to do by unleashing and using your inherent talents? What is your brand? What is your uniqueness?

Coping with change

Most of you will likely be faced with the necessity to change your job or career at some time in your life, for various reasons. Hence, you may need to work with recruiters who may be able to help you to find a new job. Remember, it is easier to find a new job whilst you still have a job.

If this happens to you, treat it as an opportunity to reconsider what you really want to do and how you want to spend about one-third of your life. Take time to reconsider your needs, whether they match the requirements of the potential role – before locking your time into a new role that may not be suitable for you.

Example:

Paul's job was made redundant during a financial economic crisis. It came as a shock at the time. The first thing Paul did was update his resume. Then he set out to find a recruiter who could best match his inherent talents and work experience with potential suitable roles.

Like teachers, recruiters can play an important role in your life. Working with recruiters may be a new experience and you need to be aware of the tips and traps. Recruiters specialise in different lines of business, so you need to become aware which ones can best promote your inherent talents and experience to meet their client's needs. Some recruiters understand the jobs they advertise and the clients they represent, others do not. Some recruiters are out to sell the jobs that come to them – they are salespeople and unless you know exactly what you are looking for and present your resume / CV to reflect that – so it fits the requirements of the specific job advertised – it is unlikely you will even be contacted to attend an interview. Sometimes, their clients are not certain of the exact job description they want to fill. You need to be aware of this as, otherwise, it can be a frustrating and demoralizing experience.

You need to develop a standard resume / CV template that can be copied and adapted to suit specific descriptions of jobs that you apply for. Likewise, you need to prepare a standard job application letter template that can be copied and adapted to suit the specific job for which you apply. The same standard resume / CV and letter will not work for every job application.

It is best to call the recruiter to discuss the potential job before sending them a copy of your resume / CV and make sure you know exactly to whom your resume / CV will be forwarded. It is important that you find, and build a relationship with, a few recruiters who are willing to get to know you and what you are looking for, who can best represent you to their clients – this process may take some time. You can learn a lot about how the recruiting process works from recruiters who are willing to share their knowledge with you, and explain how you can gain knowledge of their clients' business operations, vision statement, and staff training and welfare programs, prior to finalizing your documentation and submitting your job application.

Not all jobs are advertised through recruiters and you may also need to approach organizations direct to apply for a job. Consider which organisations you may like to work for, based on their culture and ethics, and research their web-sites to learn more about their business operations, the profiles of the leaders in the organization, and whether they have any current suitable vacancies. Even if there are no current suitable vacancies you may find the human resource person is willing to receive a copy of your resume / CV for future consideration. There is no harm in giving them a call to register your interest in working with them, establishing a communication bridge, and following up from time to time.

At all times, you need to know where your resume / CV has been sent, so keep a list on file.

Do your homework and read a few of the books written about getting a job and attending interviews – it will be time well-invested. Always be well dressed and on time for meetings, ready to answer questions, and raise your own questions.

There are several standard questions that recruiters ask and you need to research these and develop meaningful and well-thought out replies, prior to the initial meeting. Create a harmonious working relationship with the recruiter. Remain calm throughout the interview, and allow time for them to outline the scope of their services, and the job specifications available that match your background and working experience. Ensure the recruiter knows your needs and expectations, so they can represent you in the best light to their clients, Thank the recruiter for their time and stay in touch but do not call them too often.

Do not be put off by rejections – always remain positive about your future. It is a numbers game and in time you will be successful. Never give up hope. Do not allow a recruiter to put you into a job you do not want. It is your life. Do not underestimate your abilities or settle for something less than the best.

Once you have found a helpful recruiter keep them informed of your contact details and your career progression as you never know when you may need their services again, or you may want to refer your friends and / or colleagues to them. They may wish to contact you if they have suitable candidates for a potential role with your new employer.

Changing jobs can be stressful. You need to focus on maintaining your wellness through this important time of change and transition. Believe in yourself and know that you will find the best way forward. Stay in contact with family and friends, and the community during the process. Stay connected with your Divine self by including meditation sessions in your daily time schedule. Stay grounded. Look after yourself.

You may have an opportunity to participate in a career transition program. Take advantage of such an opportunity as it can provide you with an update on current trends in the market place, enable you to update your resume / CV in line with current employer / recruiter specifications, and reconsider what role will best suit your current needs. It can also rebuild your self-confidence and open new gateways to the future, and potential networking opportunities.

What is my motivation?

My initial career motivation was to gain experience working within an accounting firm, encompassing the total range of client services available, and to provide excellent services to the clients. I would have liked to become a partner in a firm of accountants. However, one of my ideals in life was to travel and experience living in a different country and culture and, when my potential marriage plan did not materialize, I decided to focus on this bigger picture by working overseas. I realized that by moving I may also sacrifice the potential to become a partner in an accounting firm. Nonetheless, my work experience overseas was challenging and interesting, and the experience was enriching and life changing, so I have no regrets.

What is my passion?

The first five years of my working life were spent within a small accounting practice in my home town, helping small businesses to meet their legal, accounting, and tax reporting requirements. This experience provided an overall appreciation of most business activities. It also provided an opportunity to observe the behaviour and motivation of my colleagues – practical training in psychology. The most important lesson I learnt, during my training within the small firm, was to go the extra mile – go beyond what the client expected, and suggest additional services that may be beneficial to the client.

One of our clients went bankrupt and then committed suicide – I shall never forget that tragic ending.

The training gained within a small accounting office environment stood me in good stead for progression through the ranks within a larger organization – an international firm of accountants in the nearby city, where I worked for five years.

The audit work in the larger environment was interesting and provided diverse experience of many different types of business organization. I vividly and fondly recall my boss, who was the senior audit manager – he was tall, immaculately dressed, always wore a smile, and had a calm temperament – he was a true leader. I thrived in the challenging environment, and was promoted soon after I joined the firm.

Being one of the first women in the UK to qualify as a Chartered Accountant meant I had to fight for my rights to establish that I was equal to the men. On one occasion, I was informed I could not be assigned to a job that would require me to work in different city and stay away from home overnight. I persuaded my boss that this was merely a work assignment and that I could manage the travel experience. Eventually, I was assigned to the audit job, together with a colleague. After that, I was sent away again – the next time on my own – and with that freedom, after work I caught a bus into the nearby town to attend a theatrical performance in the evening. I am glad to say that things have changed for the better since then – there is more gender equality nowadays, even though the pay is still not always equal. However, sexism and bullying have raised their ugly heads – fortunately I experienced neither of these traumas during my working life in the UK. After a couple of years, I decided to specialise in taxation accounting and consulting, as that provided more scope for forward planning and corporate structuring.

The partners of this firm never understood why I wanted to move and work overseas. I was young and had a spirit of adventure, no longer needed to remain in my home environment, and saw little opportunity for advancement within the firm in the long-term, mainly due to nepotism. After five years, I chose to progress my career overseas and experience living and working in a different culture.

My first overseas role was with a major international accounting firm in Brussels, Belgium, auditing multinational headquarter operations. I was good at that type of work, even though I gained little satisfaction from checking historical records. Before I started work I was required to attend seminars outside Paris, when I visited the Eiffel Tower, Palais de Versailles, and experienced some of the nightlife in Paris. One aspect I did not enjoy, was the need to rely on a translator to review transactions in Flemish. It tested my reliance on trusting others, although in this case they were also professionals working in the same firm so I relied on their ethical standards. I lived with a local family in Brussels for six months to improve my spoken French.

How can I make a difference?

During my time in Brussels – the marriage plans were aborted, and I decided to return to London to specialise in international taxation, which I found to be more challenging and creative than auditing. I joined another of the major international accounting firms. London was an expensive city to live in but I enjoyed the challenging international work.

One of my clients was a film star and I was invited to attend a board meeting in Dublin, Northern Ireland, after which I attended the opening of the Abbey Theatre. Another assignment took me to Geneva, Switzerland, where I was provided with an office to myself, overlooking the Lake, to review the tax positions of an international corporate group that was being considered for acquisition, and to provide a written report to the Board of Directors. I enjoyed that challenge, developing my investigatory, written communication, and documentation skills, but missed the lack of verbal communication, due to the secrecy surrounding this assignment.

One way I can make a difference is to share my experiences with you, and challenge you by providing hope for your endeavours. You need a mentor and I have time to steer your boat for a while and make a difference in your world.

Coping with change:

At first I felt excruciatingly lonely living in London (and subsequently in Hong Kong) – a big "cold" environment after the warmer, more communicative, environment experienced living in the North of England.

I intended to stay in London long enough to learn as much about international tax planning as was possible, before seeking another overseas work opportunity. It took me five years to master international tax law, and gain experience in its application, and after living in London for five years, it was time to reconsider working overseas. I chose to focus on the Asia Pacific Region, which was an area of prolific business growth and expansion.

Securing a job in Asia was not an easy process and required much persever-ance as, at that time, it was unusual for accountants to be assigned to overseas office locations. One or two of my bosses in the UK informed me that I would never be offered a transfer with the firm in which I worked, and they were right. I answered a newspaper advertisement, and made the opportunity happen myself. I persevered and did not accept "No" for an answer.

Hence, I was offered a job with another international accounting firm in their Hong Kong office – the interview was conducted in the Ritz Carlton Hotel in London. On the way to Hong Kong I was required to spend six weeks in the New York office, to become acquainted with my international colleagues and the firm's worldwide operating practices. I was fortunate to have a pen-pal, Warren, who met me at the airport in New York and ensured that all went well during my stay in New York, which became my favourite city. It is alive for twenty-four hours each day! When working in New York I visited many of the galleries, and particularly enjoyed the Frick Gallery that contained many paintings of William Turner, Radio City Music Hall, and spent time in the Empire State Building, which was a different experience, each time – depending on the changing weather conditions. I also managed to visit my friend Ken in Minneapolis, where I saw the statue of Hiawatha – on my way to visit the firm's offices in San Francisco and Los Angeles in California.

After that, I boarded a flight to Honolulu, where I spent a memorable evening in the hotel, before boarding a Thai Airways flight to Hong Kong, on which I appeared to be the only non-Asian passenger.

I enjoyed working with Alan, my first boss in Hong Kong, who was Australian. After eighteen months, he decided to return to Australia. Although the overall work experience was interesting, I did not enjoy living in Hong Kong as a single person. I never felt safe there — one day one of my neighbours' was attacked on her way home from work. I learned much about the local culture, and history — I was in Hong Kong at the time of Mao Zedong's death, and witnessed the many yellow chrysanthemum wreaths sombrely displayed on the ground around the outside of the Bank of China, which was closely monitored by armed guards. My boss' return to Australia became an opportune time for me to leave.

I decided to move to Singapore so I could remain longer in the Asia Pacific region, rather than relocating to the United States. My first year in Singapore was unsettling as my first job, as a tax consultant with a small company that prepared US individual income tax returns, did not pay well and the company director left to return to the United States to continue his accounting studies. After eleven months building up that company I was hired by one of the major international accounting firms.

My initial assignments were to develop a tax training manual for Singapore tax return preparation and train the local staff, set up appropriate corporate structures and obtain government grants for international corporate clients doing business within the Asia Pacific region. I was also required to establish a US tax group, to prepare individual income tax returns for US expatriates working within the Asia Pacific region, and provide a link between the audit group and our US offices in respect of US accounting standards and reporting requirements. During this time I travelled to two oil camps in Indonesia — I was there for about one year off-and-on and was well looked after by their executives. When the US tax group grew to a sizeable operation, which demanded most of my time, my corporate consulting duties lessened. I enjoyed training, and leading multi-cultural teams.

Due to a government regulation — the audit of the oil company be rotated every few years — we lost that US tax assignment. Hence, I decided to join another firm in Singapore to enable me to enhance my career experience in US taxation. During that time, I was also required to deliver tax presentations to various business organisations, and market the firm's services to potential new clients.

Following my breast cancer surgery — I was away from work on medical leave for only ten days — on the day I returned to work I was informed by my boss during lunch that my services were no longer required as my job had been made redundant. That was a huge disappointment and a shock, especially as I was at the early stages of recovery — and undergoing radiation treatment for a few more months. I asked him what he would do if he were in my situation, which provided some thinking time. An interview was arranged with that firm's Dallas office in the United States. The other alternative was to relocate to Australia with my previous employer. I chose Australia – it was summer there at the time so it was easier to continue my recovery than it would have been in a cold winter in the United States, and I considered that in the long-term Australia could provide a better lifestyle than the United States. So, I contacted my previous employer and they arranged to sponsor my Australian work visa. In fact, it was time to leave Singapore as the humidity was unhealthy, and twenty years in that climate was long enough – there are no seasons in Singapore, and most of my friends had relocated elsewhere. This adversity became an opportunity to live and work in Australia. I knew this would not be an easy ride, especially as my immune system needed strengthening after the invasive surgery.

I decided to become a citizen of Australia so I could remain here permanently. This meant that my employer was required to sponsor my permanent residency visa application. Soon after my arrival in Australia the organization was merged with another group and the culture and systems changed significantly, and became very different. From working within a small group environment in the old system, our group was swallowed into a larger one that operated with a pooling of staff. My former colleagues left the organization and I experienced a difficult time surviving in this new cultural environment, which resembled more of a takeover than a merger. I always visualized my dream of becoming an Australian citizen, and eventually was granted permanent residency, after which I left that organisation and moved on to progress my career elsewhere. A few minor insignificant roles followed in Queensland and South Australia.

Following a few job redundancies, I decided to volunteer for a not-for-profit organization where I stayed for almost five years – refer to Chapters Four and Nine.

I spent most of my working life as a servant – working for someone else. Now is the time to consider other potential options – how to live life fully with no limitations imposed by others.

~ ~ ~

Vocational harmony provides the foundation from which I can contribute my unique inherent talents, and skills, to make the outside world a better living environment, and leave a legacy for future generations. I have no plans to retire from life. I need to continually update my skills, and learn new skills to master technology changes.

Space for you to write in:

Use your time and energy wisely – they are yours to control, your Gold.

Vocational Harmony

Chapter Eight
Financial Harmony

The wise man does not lay up treasure. The more he gives to others, the more he has of his own.

— Lao Tzu

A business that makes nothing but money is a poor kind of business.

— Henry Ford

By putting the employee first, the customer effectively comes first by default, and in the end, the shareholder comes first be default as well.

— Sir Richard Branson

Possession of property ... a means to happiness not an end.

— Thomas Jefferson

The greatest good you can do for another is not to share your riches but to reveal to him his own.

— Benjamin Disraeli

Start by doing what is necessary; then do what is possible, and suddenly you are doing the impossible.

— St. Francis of Assisi

A mind stretched to a new idea never goes back to its original dimensions.

— Oliver Wendell Holmes Jr

In the middle of difficulty lies opportunity.

— Albert Einstein

There is no such thing as a problem without a gift for you in its hands.

— Richard Bach

Let me tell you the secret that has led me to my goal. My strength lies in my tenacity.

— Louis Pasteur

- Financial freedom and responsibility
- Timing
- Abundance
- Persistence

Financial freedom and responsibility

The foundation for financial freedom is financial mastery. You need to become knowledgeable about financial matters; become aware of those who offer something for nothing; and find a trustworthy financial adviser with integrity and proven success. Financial mastery can provide you with self-confidence, knowing that you are in control of your finances, and not the financial institutions or other third parties.

How good would it feel to be able to do what you like, when you like? When you have created financial freedom, you will never have to depend on anyone else for this freedom.

Financial freedom can provide you with more choices on how you can best enjoy your time and spend your wealth. For example, how would it feel to be able to spend more time with your family and loved ones, or take a long holiday as often as you like? Financially, your ideal aim is likely to be able to do what you like, whenever you like, with whom you like. Right? This means that you first need to create financial freedom, rather than just coping with daily financial survival.

Your family environment provided the initial perceptions, and experience, you had about money. It may have portrayed an abundance, or a limitation, to the amount of money available to you in your life. It may have portrayed that it was easy to generate an abundance of the flow of money that was limitless; or, it may have portrayed that money was in scarce supply, and people had to work hard just to make ends meet.

Depending on your belief, you may need to reconsider this initial belief and perception. How does it resonate with your ideal lifestyle today? Does your ideal lifestyle include abundance, using your inherent talents without limitation, to generate the energy flow of money, which − like a river − flows in and out? The more you give, the more you can receive, ad infinitum.

The Law of Attraction will manifest your belief, whatever it may be − what you believe will manifest into reality. Hence, you need to allow your thoughts to will an abundance of money in your life, to manifest your ability to give more − with that mentality, everyone can benefit.

Finances may not have been included in your school curriculum. After you left school you may have been encouraged to invest your money into a bank account, obtain a loan or credit card, or both, and that could have been the start of a road to uncontrollable debt that snowballed over time. If your debt has spiralled out of control, Financial Counselling Australia can help you get it under control.

There are people who have no credit cards, have financial freedom, and some of them own their own home. How much money do you need? What do you need it for? How can you attain financial freedom? It is never too late to start.

Review your real current needs. Could you be happier living in a smaller or less-expensive house, if this could get you started on building your financial freedom? What lifestyle would you like to have in the future? Do you need to consider making some compromises now so that you can enjoy that ideal lifestyle later? Perhaps you have some assets you no longer need that you could sell, and put the proceeds towards your future needs?

Example:

You may have household items or collectibles that you no longer need or like, which could be auctioned. You may have hobbies that could generate additional income. Review the regular expenses, such as e-mail provider costs, mobile phone costs, and question whether any of them can be reduced – including whether other providers can provide a lesser quote. Review any loan arrangements you have in place to see whether they could be paid off early or reduced. Review credit card facilities and be sure to pay off the total within the given time to prevent excessive interest being charged.

Do you have adequate insurance cover in place or, maybe the extent of the cover is excessive, in view of your current needs? You may need to review your existing policies and make changes, as appropriate.

Example:

+ life
+ health
+ home – building
+ home – contents
+ pets
+ car
+ funeral
+ income protection
+ investments

No matter whether you are a man or a woman, it is important that you plan to become financially free. You cannot expect to depend on any man, woman person, family, company, or government to take care of your financial needs. It is your responsibility. It is unrealistic to give your power away to anyone as you may be disappointed. It is important not to consciously become dependent on anyone – that could result in unhappiness. You may need the help of others from time to time to tide you through difficult times, and that is acceptable – you need to ask for advice when you need it.

Job security, or inheritances are no longer certain. It is up to each one of you to determine how best to plan for and create your own financial freedom. Even if you are fortunate to have a job that you enjoy now, your salary stops when your job stops. It is unlikely that your job will enable you to create enough income, and build enough capital including superannuation, in the long term, to enable you to survive, and live well, after you stop working.

There is no such thing as a "get rich quick" solution. Be sure that whatever vehicle you choose, as the tool to create your financial freedom, it will not be too stressful for you to cope with. This means knowing your risk profile. It is never too soon, or too late to start to create and implement your plan, but the sooner you start the process the easier it will be to achieve your goal. Plant good seeds and watch them grow – with patience – and make changes along the way, as necessary. Live within your means. You can have both money and whatever else you need to make you happy. However, financial freedom at the expense of happiness can result in illness and unhappiness.

Example:

Alan was born into a family without much financial wealth and was given an opportunity to pursue an education that resulted in him becoming an engineer. He wanted to provide a larger home for his parents, as well as succeeding in his career. He decided to save 10% of his income to donate to a charity of his choice, and a further 10% for the family home. By making this decision early in life, over a period his savings — that were wisely invested — grew and enabled Alan to place a deposit on a larger home. This was an easy decision for Alan to make at that early stage in his career and provided a sound financial foundation for his future — no matter what circumstances he encountered later in life.

Abundance of wealth is not an issue; the lack of it can be an issue. Abundant wealth can provide you with freedom to enjoy your time and with choices for how to spend your time. It is empowering. It can enable you to share your success with disadvantaged people.

Amassing wealth, can become an issue if it is not used wisely for the benefit of those who are disadvantaged and need help, or for community causes. In giving you receive the satisfaction of knowing that your success has changed someone else's life for the better. Whatever you share with love, benevolence, and goodwill, will surely be returned in abundance.

Examples:

- *Jane who recovered from cancer and now works full-time contributes at least 10% of her income to cancer research thus enabling others to benefit from her unfortunate experience.*
- *Peter, a successful IT guru and business entrepreneur established a charitable foundation, with the object of enhancing some of the building structures in his home town, to be used for medical research. He has become a well-respected contributor to his local community.*

Several tools are available to help you navigate the process of attaining financial freedom.

A *budget* is a tool that can help you to understand how much income you can expect to receive for a period, say twelve months, and the expenses you will need to pay during that period. Creating an Excel spreadsheet can enable you to create this tool that can help you to become aware of your current financial reality, and adjust it, as necessary, to be able to achieve your ideal goal. *Refer to the Example below.* You can see the big picture, and know whether you can pay all your expenses as they become due. If not, you may be need to supplement your income in some way and, or, reduce certain expenses.

You can also prepare longer-term budgets, say for five years, and ten years. Once you have listed the budgeted income and expenses, this tool will ensure that you can provide for daily needs, set aside funds for a rainy day, replace assets that wear out, and for other irregular expenses – example: annual vacations. It can also make you more aware of how you are currently earning income and spending it, and consider whether there are ways in which the income can be increased, and, or, the expenses reduced.

You need to keep a record, on a separate Excel spreadsheet, of all *actual* income received and expenses paid – your personal income and expense account – to monitor the income you receive and expenses you pay. At regular intervals – for example: monthly, quarterly, half-yearly, and annually – you can compare the actual figures with those listed in the budget spreadsheet.

You need to separately write down what the *variances* were – the differences between the budgeted income and expense, and the actual income and expense. This process will enable you to adjust and make changes in your future budgets, to make them more meaningful and realistic – refer to the Variance template – Exercise Eight (at the end of this chapter).

Example:

James' short-term personal budget, for the first six months, looks like this -

	Jan	Feb	Mar	Apr	May	Jun
	$	$	$	$	$	$
Projected / Budgeted Income:						
Salary (A)	5,000	6,000	6,000	6,000	7,000	7,000
Projected / Budgeted Expenses:						
Insurance	−200	−200	−200	−200	−200	−200
Car and travel	−500	−500	−500	−500	−600	−500
Food	−300	−300	−300	−300	−300	−500
Entertainment	−600	−600	−600	−600	−600	−700
Mortgage	−800	−800	−800	−800	−800	−800
Medical	0	0	0	−100	−100	−100
Totals (B)	−2,400	−2,400	−2,400	−2,500	−2,600	−2800

Excess Budgeted Income:

(A)−(B)	2,600	3,600	3,600	3,500	4,400	4,200

Total Excess Budgeted Income $21,900

James owns his own home and plans to start his own business within the next six months. He will need a lump-sum of $10,000 to start the business. Although the above budget indicates that James will have an excess of income over expense of $21,900 at the end of the six-month period, which is more than the initial start-up cost of his business — he will need to factor into the second six month budget the fact that his new business may expect to make a loss for the first ten-month period.

By becoming aware of the total projected income and expense — both personal and business — James will know whether it is the best time for him to start a new business now or whether to wait until he has accumulated additional income from his current employment.

You need to prepare separate budgets for your business activities. Your accountant can help provide you with the details. It is important to keep your personal budget records and business budget records separate. Always keep two separate bank accounts – one for personal income and expenses, and another for business income and expenses. Never mix personal with business funds. Your business records need to accurately detail business income and expenses, together with proof to back up each item of income and expense – to validate the figures reported on your annual income tax returns.

Example:

Wayne chose to rebuild a boat with the aim of starting a business of tuna fishing. He did not prepare a budget and frequently ran out of funds to finish the project. He mixed personal income and expense with business income and expense. He became depressed and was unable to cope with life for some time. It was a huge disappointment for him and he abandoned the project. It took him a long time to rebuild his confidence and financial credibility.

Without this tool – this forecast and tracking device – James and Wayne may have no way of knowing their financial capacity and current financial status, and – worst case scenario – could later become bankrupt and suffer needless stress.

Example:

Don was a science graduate and wanted to specialize in animal feedstuffs so he set up his own business. Outside of his business he enjoyed playing golf. Although he had a brilliant scientific brain he had no business training. He relied on his accountant for advice. The accountant understood that his role was to prepare the books for Don's business and the year-end accounts. The missing link was the budgeting process. There was no financial control and, sadly, Don went bankrupt and soon after that event he died from a massive heart attack. That was a tragic event I mentioned above that could have been prevented.

You need to plan to pay off bad debt (that which does not generate income), as soon as possible. That usually includes the mortgage on the house where you live, unless you are renting. Bad debt, in the following example, includes: the home mortgage and car loan, both of which are incurring ongoing interest expense, without earning any income against which it can be offset for tax purposes.

The following sample profit and loss account and balance sheet illustrate what a household financial position might look like.

Jones Family – Profit & Loss Account for the year ended 30 June 20.

	$	$
Income:		
Salaries	30000	
Bank interest	100	
Dividends	1000	
Rental income	12000	
Total income (A)		43100
Expense:		
Mortgage interest	−12000	
Rental expenses	−11000	
Living expenses	−12000	
Insurance	−500	
Car	−3200	
Total expense (B)		−38700
Income less expense (A) − (B)		4400

Jones Family – Balance Sheet at 30 June 20...

	$	$
Liabilities:		
Home mortgage	−295000	
Rental property loan	−200000	
Car loan	−12600	
Bank overdraft brought forward	−35000	
Total liabilities		−542600
Assets:		
Profit & loss account surplus	4400	
Shares	8000	
Family home	300000	
Rental property	230200	
Total Assets		542600

(Note: All above figures are fictitious for illustration purposes only.)

Refer to the financial templates – Exercises Nine and Ten (at the end of this chapter) – that you can replicate on Excel spreadsheets, to complete, review and update every three months or more often as required.

You have considered daily financial needs, and the need to plan for daily survival when you no longer wish to work. Another important exercise is to determine how much capital and income you will need to create, before you can stop working.

Your ultimate aim is to generate an abundant cash flow that you can live off, so that one day you will not *have* to work – although you may *choose* to do so. You will need to build capital in the form of assets – example rental real estate, shares, or managed funds – that can generate that income, and provide funding for specific projects that you may like to include in your free-time, such as travel, and provide for your loved ones when you are no longer here.

Firstly, write down how much income you will need to receive each month once you are no longer working. Bear in mind, we are now generally expected to have an increased life expectancy. How many years do you want to work? Write down how much income you will need to enable you to retire, the date you plan to retire, and your estimated life-span. This exercise can provide you with an indication of the gap that exists between what you can generate now and what your needs will be once you stop working, at a specific time in the future. Then you can decide how you can best bridge that gap. Without doing this exercise you will never know whether, and when, you may be able to retire. It is wise to consult with your financial advisors to discuss what you have in place now, then review what you may need to change, or adjust, to ensure your retirement needs can be achieved within the chosen time-frame.

The younger you are when you start this process the sooner you could stop working, if you desire to do so, and the longer you will have to enjoy more precious time with your family and friends. Do not quit your day job until you have created other means to replace that regular income. Although you may have superannuation, it may not be adequate to provide for you throughout your retirement years, but it does need to be included in your planning.

You need to gain knowledge of how investments made by your superannuation fund can best be accessed, and when – this is a complex area. Be aware of the conditions of the global financial markets and how they impact on your investments.

You can benefit from a template to help you through this process. In Australia, the Property Club can provide such a template, and introduce you to the system devised by its founder, Kevin Young, that can enable people to generate wealth for their retirement, using rental property as the vehicle. It would be well-worth your time invested to attend one of the educational information sessions where you can connect with people who have successfully created financial wealth in this way, even if eventually you choose a different vehicle than rental property, as your preferred method of generating wealth to create your financial freedom (www.propertyclub. com.au).

Should you prefer to invest in shares or managed funds, you need to determine how best to gain maximum return on your investment. It is prudent to spread the risk and not invest all your funds into one basket.

Those of you who own your own home need to be aware that it is a liability and not an asset – refer to the above balance sheet – as it does not generate income, and the mortgage requires regular monthly repayments. Hence, by itself, it is unable to provide retirement funding. However, depending on when the property was bought, or inherited, its current market value could be worth more today than it was when it was acquired by you. This appreciation in its market value could perhaps be put to better use by "reinvesting" that value as a deposit into another property – to be rented out – to generate additional income.

In this way, you could create a rental property investment, to form part of the foundation of your wealth creation. You need to be certain how this potential opportunity might work for you. Such transaction needs to be carefully planned to ensure the outcome best meets your needs and circumstances. The way in which the increase in value is channelled into a deposit for a rental property is complex. You need to fully understand how this concept works and not rely on advice given by those who may not be qualified to provide such advice.

Expenses incurred in directly earning rental income, including mortgage interest and real estate taxes, plus tax depreciation, may be deductible from the rental income reported on your income tax return. The cost of the building may also be deductible over the number of years prescribed by tax law. You need to stay updated on the current tax law, as it changes from time to time, to learn how changes may affect your investments. The excess of income over tax-related deductions is taxable, or deductible in the case of a loss. In that way, your home can be converted from a liability to an asset and over time, through repeating the process of reinvesting appreciation in the market value of additional properties to be acquired in the future, an investment vehicle can be created to provide for your retirement. This is a complex area. You will need to consider how best to own the property – this is a legal issue and can differ depending on personal circumstances.

Residual, or passive income – income that you will continue to receive when you are no longer working – can enable you to maintain your existing lifestyle during your retirement years, and enable you to travel whenever you wish. Residual income begins to flow once you have created its source – such as, rental property, shares, and managed funds, and it continues to grow by compounding. Compounding means that what is earned is re-invested and continues to generate additional income, which can be converted into capital assets. That means you allow the residual income to continue to earn additional income, and do not spend it now. This passive income needs to be reinvested to generate more assets and income, rather than remaining idle.

It is not necessary to own assets to generate income – you may wish to research and consider other types of opportunities that are available, example: hiring assets, and adding a unique service before making them available to be sub-leased.

Example:

Certain of Richard Branson's entities hire aircraft and generate income from adding value, providing a service, and lease them out to other entities for use by travellers and for shipment of cargo.

You can create wealth through real estate development provided you understand the various types of opportunities, risks involved, structuring, time factors involved, and financing issues. This vehicle is not suitable for everyone but may work well for those who have the passion, knowledge, and resources to make it work.

Never compare yourself, or your situation, with others as you may become confused and demotivated. You need to build your own retirement investment vehicle portfolio, and legal structures, taking into account your risk profile and unique personal needs.

Second: the next step is to decide what type of vehicle could best provide the passive, or residual, income you need to generate. This will depend on your level of adversity to risk, and your preference.

Before you choose your preferred vehicle to create your retirement funding you need to conduct due diligence – become certain what each type of investment can offer, and consider the risk profile to ensure you are comfortable with the level of risk involved. You need to become knowledgeable about the various products that are available. You can consult with a financial advisor to gain a general knowledge of what assets are available that may best provide you with your required outcome; and you need to do your own research and ensure that you fully understand all the implications of each method before making an informed decision. A business needs a strong foundation to function optimally and provide a sound investment choice – by reviewing its balance sheets and annual reports you can determine whether its financial foundation is strong. You also need to check the credibility of its operators, their core values and the mission statement of the business before you consider whether the organisation meets your investment criteria.

When you have chosen your preferred investment vehicle, you need to determine which type of legal structure will work best to own and manage the investments in your personal circumstances.

In addition to the traditional assets, such as shares, managed funds, and rental property, several other types of opportunities are offered by network marketing companies. Do your own research – visit websites and organisations, and meet with the founders and their officers, to gain more information and consider whether such an investment could meet your needs. Be sure the services that the company provides are compatible with your ideals and vision. Example: everyone in the world needs a telephone service so there is likely to be no conflict of interest with your ideals. Whereas, if the company markets health foods, you cannot be sure that the components would be suitable for everyone, hence you may find it difficult to market them.

Understand what support services, and ongoing training, are provided by the organisation. There will likely be testimonials on the corporate website that will enable you to connect with and learn from those people who are successful and willing to share their experiences with you. If the company is endorsed by a successful business person that can be advantage. Attend a few of the overview meetings to learn more about how the organisation operates, meet the leaders, and listen to testimonials before making a decision. Does the company support a charity, as part of its vision? Find out how much time you will need to devote to managing this venture to make it successful – generating the income, and managing the income.

Sometimes, due to circumstances beyond your control – such as a global financial or family crisis, floods, bush fires, or illness – you may find yourself with no financial wealth. Hopefully, your assets will be fully insured. This unfortunate and traumatic outcome can become an opportunity to rebuild your financial foundation. You may need to take a break, live within your means, and appreciate your other aspects of wealth – wellness, a good education, close family and friends – whilst considering what to do next. When rebuilding your financial foundation, you can make it stronger by considering what you need, rather than what you want, which could be the same, or different. Accept the adversity as a blessing in disguise, even if it may not appear to be such at the time. You are wiser for the experience, so can plan to do things differently the next time.

~ ~ ~

Remember that, although financial wealth is important, it does not necessarily create happiness. You need to take time to appreciate the beauty of nature, enjoy the present moment, simplify your lifestyle, focus on mindful eating and ensure you have optimum health. You need to take time to recognize and accept what has happened, understand the consequences, realise that it is not the end of the world, start to consider how best you can turn the seeming disaster into an opportunity, and look beyond this situation knowing that it is only temporary. You need to stay positive, meditate, visualise a successful outcome, with hope in your heart, and use this time wisely. Make sure you can survive financially during this time of transition. Do not blame yourself for the adversity. Accept it as part of your life. Learn from the experience. Maintain hope for the future and persevere to rebuild a strong financial foundation.

Change is always inevitable, the will to succeed needs to be harnessed to a greater connection with the Divine self to enable transformation to take place within, and stabilize a harmonic synthesis between the inner and outer worlds – again allowing the world to become your oyster.

Timing

The timing of each action is one of the most important criteria that determines whether the venture will have the most effective outcome. When you are planning the right moment when an outcome is expected to happen, you need to consider:

+ The gestation time it will take, between planting the seed, and harvesting the fruit
+ Whether the economic climate is favourable, or whether you need to wait to buy or sell
+ Regularly review and monitor progress made, so that changes can be introduced to keep the venture on track
+ Put an effective exit strategy in place so, that if circumstances change, the project will be protected against loss

The general rule is never to sell assets when their values decrease, and to purchase when the assets are undervalued. Of course, there may be exceptions to this rule.

Build time into your goal planning to allow for underperformance of assets as, like everything else, seasonal and other fluctuations can impact on expected outcomes.

Abundance

With a mind-set of abundance, appreciation for all that you currently have, and a strong focus on what you need in your life, you can become a money magnet. You need to focus on positive actions, rather than allowing negative thoughts to affect your ideals. Aim to conserve your energy rather than allowing it to be depleted on issues that may be of no benefit.

Example:

Andy's job was made redundant during one of the economic financial crises hence he had trouble meeting his monthly payments. Instead of worrying about this unfortunate outcome he consulted his financial planner and together they devised a new plan that helped see him through this crisis. Andy was also fortunate to find another suitable employment option with a higher salary than the one he lost.

If Andy had allowed himself to worry about his loss rather than taking positive action to enable him to ride the wave and expect something better to materialize, his health and well-being could have suffered.

Persistence

Only you know what will make you happy, and the role financial freedom can play in providing a balanced lifestyle. Regularly review your financial plan, and the performance of your assets, to ensure they are in line with your current needs. Be prepared to make changes, as appropriate.

Financial freedom and responsibility:

As a child, I was influenced by my family's vision relating to finance – the necessity to find a job that would provide adequate income for everyday living expenses, whilst enabling me to progress my career, and an annual holiday. Dad passed away the year before he was due to retire, and Mum managed to get by with the age pension. There was no evidence of any planning in place to enable them to attain their financial freedom. Although I experienced no real hardship when growing up.

The schools I attended provided no education on managing finances and planning for financial freedom.

Having determined that my career would be as a chartered accountant, my main thought at that time was to become qualified and all would be well. During the initial training, the pay was minimal, I made my own clothes, went to the movies, and managed to do everything I had time to fit in. I was happy.

After the initial training was completed, my pay increased significantly and I bought a car, with the aid of a bank loan, and the banks also provided credit card facilities. Hence, I did not establish full control of my finances at that time. Although I had plans to earn as much as I could throughout my working career and to make investments, I had no financial mentor. I did not save a percentage of my salary each month. I lived at home, contributed to the weekly budget, and travelled in my free-time.

Once I had established myself in my career, I decided to focus on that – just like Dad had done. I enjoyed my job, and it was not until much later in my life that I questioned the wisdom of focusing all my time working as an employee, rather than also focusing on other ways to provide financial freedom.

When I lived in Singapore I decided to use investment property as the vehicle to build a retirement asset. I observed that most people there owned their own properties and, with the aid of the Central Provident Fund, which enabled me to use the balance to invest in residential property, I successfully invested in a rental property in Singapore. Prior to my relocation to Melbourne, Australia, I chose to sell the property, making a substantial profit.

Mistake, number one — never sell, unless you need to. In fact, due to my relocation to Australia I required funds to relocate and fund my Master's degree studies.

My most successful property investment in Australia, whilst working in Queensland, was an investment property in Sunnybank Hills. This investment was made through the Property Club (at that time known as The Investors Club). Mistake number two — I sold this property when it made a profit, due to the need to relocate and provide funds for living expenses, whilst searching for a new job role and establishing myself in continuing job moves.

After my job in Queensland was completed, I returned to live and work in Melbourne and finish my Master of International Tax degree with The University of Melbourne.

During this time, I found a job in Adelaide, relocated there, and stayed for five years, until the job was made redundant. I made a few property investments on my own that, in hindsight, one of them ought never to have been made. I was in a new environment, and needed to spend much more time than I did on establishing a reliable team of advisors, and considering the current conditions of the global financial stability, prior to committing to any investments. I trusted the advisors for the projects, who turned out to be inexperienced and unreliable — I did not carry out adequate due diligence, and made decisions that should never have been made, taking into account the global economic climate at that time. After the job in Adelaide was made redundant, I returned to Melbourne to pursue a job there. That job was later made redundant due to a downturn in the global economy. My major investments were traumatically affected by circumstances beyond my control — the banks had been eager to lend money in the past but were unwilling to continue to extend financial assistance during this devastating time. Hence I, like many other people, am experiencing the need to review and refocus my life plan, and rebuild a strong financial foundation.

Timing:

As demonstrated above, the timing of all events is of the utmost importance. For ten years, I successfully invested in rental properties, starting when I lived and worked in Singapore. Due mainly to the relocation to Australia, and the various career moves within Australia, I was unable to keep the properties.

In future I will be mindful – to the extent possible – of potential life changes before entering into or selling investments. Sometimes, it is advisable to refrain from entering into a transaction if there is any doubt about the overall implication, and heed my intuition.

Abundance:

Although there are many different groups that claim to have a similar philosophy, the Property Club ("PC") is the only one I am sure of their integrity. Its founders are caring, committed and willingly share their time and knowledge. Its property developments are built to the highest standard, using only reliable builders. PC also has a team of dedicated researchers that can procure developments suitable for its members. The Club provides tools for members to use to track property investment performance, and educate existing and potential new members. Educational events are held regularly, and run at a modest cost, unlike some of those provided by certain other property groups. New members are mentored by more experienced investors.

This organization was founded by Kevin Young whose vision is that every Australian can benefit from owning their own home and creating a portfolio of property investments as a retirement vehicle, and thereby not have to rely on the age pension to fund their retirement. Kevin is also a philanthropist and, together with his wife Kathy, established PC Club Cares, a not-for-profit organization that supports families in need. I was introduced to this organisation whilst working in Queensland.

Kevin's vision of integrity resonates with mine. In the long-term, my vision includes establishing a charitable foundation – when the timing is right – to enable disadvantaged people to benefit from my experiences in life.

I plan to rely on my existing network when planning future investments. There is an abundance of knowledge available from which I can benefit.

My most valuable assets are my health, a few very good friends, and a BIG dream for the future. Whilst rebuilding my financial foundation I am enjoying a simplified lifestyle in country Victoria, continually upgrading my skills, as well as focusing on and enjoying all the other areas of life.

Persistence:

My overall vision remains the same — to build financial freedom using rental property as the main vehicle, with carefully chosen additional types of investment to diversify the risk.

I am gaining additional knowledge of the current financial market, and planning a strategy that will work best for me. I recently made contact with a financial adviser, with proven integrity, who provided me with renewed confidence to pursue my dream and stay focused.

~ ~ ~

Financial harmony provides a foundation from which I can live my life according to my needs and aspirations, with intuition. Finance is a means of exchanging energies, values, and time, whilst fulfilling my needs, and enabling a flow of abundance to prevail in my life. The more I give, the more I receive. Instead of having limited expectations, I need to allow synchronicity to play its part, and keep an open heart and mind to welcome an abundance of unlimited opportunities to emanate in my life.

Space for you to write in:

Give thanks for what you have now, keep your vision in mind at all times, and you will attract abundance. Choose your advisors wisely.

Financial Harmony

Exercise Eight – Budget Variance Template

Use this tool to track the variances of budgeted income and expense, say, every three months (suggest you create the template on an Excel spreadsheet and modify to suit your needs):

Budget Variances – Income – Year ending 30 June 20..:

Months:	*Jan*		*Feb*		*Mar*	
	Budget	*Actual*	*Budget*	*Actual*	*Budget*	*Actual*
	$	$	$	$	$	$
Salary						
Other income						
(List separately)						
Totals						

Note: Analyse the reason(s) for the variances

Budget Variances – Expense – Year ending 30 June 20..:

Months:	*Jan*		*Feb*		*Mar*	
	Budget	*Actual*	*Budget*	*Actual*	*Budget*	*Actual*
	$	$	$	$	$	$
Insurance						
Car and travel						
Food						
Entertainment						
Mortgage						
Medical						
Other expense						
(List separately)						
Totals						

Notes:
+ *Analyse the reason(s) for the variances*
+ *Determine whether you need to revise the budgeted figures going forward*

Exercise Nine – Profit and Loss Template

Use this tool to track your income and expenses at regular intervals, say, every three months (suggest you create the template on an Excel spreadsheet and modify to suit your needs):

Profit and Loss Account for the Year Ending 30 June 20.., as at (*enter date*)

Income: $

Salary, wages

Business income

Bank interest

Investment income (other than rental)

Rental income

Other income (explain)

Total income   (A)

Expenses:

Deductions against salary, wages

Business expenses

Investment expenses

Rental expenses

Mortgage interest

Living expenses

Insurance

Motor vehicle expenses

Other expenses (explain)

Total expense   (B)

Total Income less Total Expense (A) – (B) = (C)   _____

Exercise Ten – Balance Sheet Template

Use this tool to track your assets and liabilities at regular intervals, say, every three months (suggest you create the template on an Excel spreadsheet and modify to suit your needs):

Balance Sheet for the Year Ended 30 June 20.., as at (*enter date*)

Liabilities: $
Home mortgage
Rental property loan
Car loan
Profit and loss account – (C)
Bank overdraft brought forward
Other liabilities (*list separately*)

Total Liabilities   _____

Assets: $
Bank balance brought forward
Profit and loss account – (C)
Investments (*list separately*)
Family home
Rental property

Total Assets   _____

Note:
Total assets should be equal to total liabilities.

A final comment on the above exercises. Above, I wrote that energy follows thought: that what you think about manifests. So, if you spend time every few weeks working on your exercises, with confidence, mindfully monitoring the performance of your investments, with belief that your assets are growing, then I can assure you that they will grow as energy does follow thought. By completing the exercises you are putting the focus on growth, and that is what will happen.

Chapter Nine
Spiritual Harmony

Take the first step in faith. You don't have to see the whole staircase.
Just the first step. — Martin Luther King Jr.

What lies behind us and what lies before us are tiny matters, compared to
what lies within us. — Ralph Waldo Emerson

Man is asked to make of himself what he is supposed to become to fulfil
his destiny. — Paul Tillich

Through our eyes, the universe is perceiving itself. Through our ears,
the universe is listening to its harmonies. We are the witnesses, through
which the universe becomes conscious of its glory, its magnificence
— Alan Wilson Watts

I have a room all to myself; it is nature. It is a place beyond the
jurisdiction of human governments. — Henry David Thoreau

Happiness depends more on the inward disposition of mind than on
outward circumstances. — Benjamin Franklin

I shut my eyes in order to see. — Paul Gauguin

Man, know thyself. — Socrates

The good of people is the chief law. — Cicero

The words that enlighten the soul are more precious than jewels.
— Hazrat Inayat Khan

As we grow as unique persons, we learn to respect
the uniqueness of others. — Robert Harold Schuller

Meditation is painful in the beginning but it bestows
immortal bliss and supreme joy in the end.
— Swami Sivananda Saraswati

If you want to make beautiful music, you must play the black and the
white notes together.
— Richard Milhous Nixon

Never compete, create. — Earl Nightingale

Let there be peace and love among all beings in the Universe.
— Sri Ramana Maharshi

What we play is life. — Louis Armstrong

Love is the recognition of Oneness, of knowing yourself as other.
The Oneness is love. — Eckhart Tolle

- Connection – inner and outer worlds
- Inner self
- Conscious mind; Subconscious mind
- Balance
- Joy

Connection – inner and outer worlds

The spiritual connection needs to be the main foundation in life. It can be experienced by living consciously, practising regular meditation, correct breath awareness and control, specific body postures, and mindfulness in action. Without a strong spiritual connection, your life will be no more than a roller-coaster ride, based on uncontrollable ups-and-downs, and like a boat with no rudder drifting aimlessly in the sea – with no destination, or stability.

The world is the home of the Divine Self, your home, the home of every person, and living being – all are connected and all contain the same five elements – earth, water, fire, air, and ether. The spiritual being lives in the heart of the physical body. The human mosaic contains the frequency of abundance that is available to all through daily devotional meditation. There needs to be a harmony between the inner and outer worlds for you to experience happiness – one without the other results in inner chaos, and a feeling of despair, unfulfilled and unhappiness. Passion and joy comes from connection with the Divine self. The two states need to be balanced. It is never too late to rebuild the foundation, and start anew to discover or rediscover the real purpose for your life.

The soul, spirit, and heart are the stronghold – your connection between the inner and outer worlds. Like a house, the body, mind, and Soul need a strong foundation – a spiritual temple. This foundation may need to be rebuilt if the connection to the Divine self has been neglected in the past. This can often happen when you are working in the outside material world with a routine that leaves little time for maintaining the spiritual connection.

Example:

Steve grew up in a small community in North America and during his international business career he became successful and made a lot of money. He spent much of his time travelling and staying in hotels away from his family and friends, maintaining an unhealthy diet, and without a regular exercise regime. He neglected to maintain a Spiritual and Social harmony – spending all his money on new "toys"; a large car, a yacht, and worshipping greed, without sharing any of his wealth with less fortunate people. In due course Steve eventually lost his job and was forced to reconsider his real purpose in life and rebuild foundations in his spiritual and social areas of life to allow harmony to return.

Materialism – seeking contentment in earthly enjoyments and pleasures and resulting in temporary oblivion of difficulties, and focusing on greed – can lead to boredom and loss of inner happiness.

The mind is attached to outcomes and expectations, whereas, the heart is free from those conditions. The heart can be expanded to enable you to feel deeply, and act for the benefit of others. You are spiritual beings within an earthly experience. The elements of your body, mind, and Soul are interconnected and interdependent.

Spiritual harmony enables you to feel connected to the universe, and nature, as well as in your relationships with others. Spirituality is a connection with the Divine Self – the heart is the home of the spirit. Spirituality does not mean religion. One of the differences between spirituality and religion is that spirituality can be experienced every moment of each day and is not merely a ritual that is performed once or twice a week. It can be beneficial to study comparative religions to become more aware that each religion has a similar focus based on truth, and good living. Many people are initiated into a religion at an early age, and some people choose to change their alliance to a different religion later in life. However, spirituality is much more than religion as it synchronises the whole of life experience. It integrates the inner and outer worlds, light and darkness, male and female. When you have spiritual harmony, harmony within the other areas of life can follow. You each need a Guru – teacher / adviser / inspirer – to learn from, to show you the way. The Guru can be the inner Guru.

The inner and outer worlds can be likened to a tree – the roots provide its foundation, the source of its being; and the branches and leaves are its outer world that are fed by the source. The tree trunk connects the roots with the branches. You need to create a bridge between the two worlds. With a unity of body, mind, and Soul all things become harmonious and possible. The inner – spiritual world is everlasting, whereas the outer – material world has a limited lifespan. By living with an awareness of the universal divine nature of the soul, and manifesting divinity in your daily actions – through your words and deeds – you can see the Divine everywhere, in everything and everybody. It is possible to remain dutifully employed in the world, and at the same time maintain a mental detachment by acting as a willing instrument of the Divine, rather than as a servant of your ego. Thus, you can experience life from a higher state of consciousness that encompasses harmony of inner and outer worlds.

You can have it all – happiness, prosperity, and well-being – provided there is a balance between the inner and outer worlds – sharing time with family and friends, and sharing wealth (including time) with less fortunate people. That is the ultimate blessing. And, if you happen to lose everything in the outer world it is never too late to start all over again to rebuild the appropriate foundation. The whole of life is a vibrating energy that needs to be kept in motion to prevent stagnation.

Example:

Jim is a director of an international company and is required to travel, during his work. He regularly attends a social organization and contributes a portion of his salary to its charitable fund. Jim attends a local gym wherever he is based. He stays physically, mentally, and spiritually connected and experiences a strong feeling of well-being and peace throughout each day, whether he is at home or away from home. He has built a spiritual home within that always goes everywhere with him.

Not everyone can relate to the concept of life before physical birth, or life after death. Surely, there must be something more than just the physical being in this awesome world. Physical life is merely a transition – the present. The soul in eternal. There has to be a link between the two.

You need to create a temple within your heart – that will enable you to experience, receive, and transmit each of the internal states:

- divinity
- beauty
- sound
- love
- energy
- feeling
- form

and build a foundation to reclaim the life-force from the ground up. You need to nourish your self – physically, emotionally, and spiritually – to be able to maintain the energy channels free of blockages and experience abundance rather than lethargy in life each day. You can connect with the young child you once were that is protected within the heart, by taking time to mentally focus on that vision and embrace it. The question, "Who am I?" is a spiritual enquiry not an intellectual enquiry. There is an equilibrium within each of you that needs to be unveiled and appreciated – it is natural and it is your right.

You were born with a doorway to the Divine self – the Soul. In between the body, mind, and soul is a bridge – a vibrating field, a linking process – a power. The soul connects with the mind.

The principal seven energy centres – chakras – located within the spinal region, integrate body, mind, and spirit. Each chakra energy corresponds to glands in the endocrine system. The main seven chakras correspond to the twelve astral signs of the zodiac, and are interrelated with the Sun. Hence, all beings are affected by an inner and outer universe.

Chakras can best be described as vibrational energy wheels that monitor the cosmic force fields within the body. There are many chakras but seven main ones, and all have a dual purpose that needs to be kept in balance. The higher chakras control the lower ones. The physical, mental, and spiritual health of an individual depends on harmonious energy balance between the chakras and the endocrine glands to which they are each related.

The energy from Chakra Seven controls thoughts and connects the head with the heart – to the divine intelligence or Source within, thereby unifying the eight elemental qualities of reality – earth, water, fire, air, ether, motion, mind, and individuality, that are manifested as consciousness and enlightenment. This is the gateway that allows liberation through universal consciousness. Attachment to limited forms provides obstacles on the path to attaining spiritual growth. Movement of energy freely and harmoniously, up and down the chakra energy passageways in the spinal cord region, enables this harmony – when all the energy blockages have been removed.

Regular Yoga practices can balance the swirling wheels of energy – the seven major chakras that align the spine – to eliminate energy blockages in the related nerve centres, and major organs of the body, thereby preventing stagnation. Each chakra needs to be kept in balance to allow harmony to flow throughout the body. These centres impact psychological, emotional, and spiritual states of being. If unsuitable asanas (yoga exercises) are performed the body's energy balance can be adversely affected. Specific asanas that focus on individual glandular constitutions need to be prescribed by a qualified yoga instructor.

~ ~ ~

How do you treat the universe? It also has a soul that needs to be respected. The environment needs to be kept clean and pure. When its equilibrium is challenged, its physical balance is also challenged.

Each day, you need to connect in some way with nature, for example: appreciate the beauty in flowers, the sky, the stars and their formations. This can help you to recognise there are seasons in all of life, and realise that these natural events are perpetual and cannot be changed by humans. You can begin to comprehend the miracle that you are only a small part of the whole universe, and your physical body is here for a limited time only. The physical body is a vehicle that enables its user to experience life for a definite time after which what is left? The Soul is eternal and needs to be purified during each lifetime to enhance the process of evolvement, thereby making the world a better place for future generations to experience. How to make the world a better place? Start with yourself. Each of you is unique – born with inherent talents – and has a special contribution to make.

You need to develop compassion for others – all have the Divine within – even though there may not always be harmony within, due to some disconnection. You are each part of the brotherhood of man. All beings are interconnected. You are each in the game of life together. You each need to recognise the dark side that is within you that is also inherent within all beings.

Fear nobody. Do not allow anyone to interfere with your evolution process, fulfilment of your duty, and rendering service to fellow men. The further you evolve, the greater the blessing you can become to those around you and to future generations.

Inner self

Tools are available to help you to connect with the inner self, one of which is the Science of Yoga, which encompasses the whole of life experience.

By reconnecting to your Source, your True Self – your inner centre of harmony – you can create wellness and attract abundance. If you have those two blessings, all else, including creativity and intuitiveness, can follow. You can discover your ideal path in life that may have been hidden up until now. This ideal can change over the years as you evolve. Unlimited success can always be yours.

Yoga is a tool that can be used to purify the body, and mind, and unify them with the spirit. Yoga can be practised every day, anywhere, by everybody. It is a discipline, without which life is unbalanced.

Yoga is a science, an art and a philosophy that encompasses the whole of life. It is not a religion. It originates from the Vedic tradition of ancient India that recognized the multi-dimensional aspects of the human being. Yoga encompasses a system in which the body, breath, and mind are integrated and synchronized. When these systems are in harmony within themselves and with each other, calmness of mind is experienced, together with inner peace, a greater depth of self-awareness, and a higher level of consciousness.

Yoga is a process of mastering the self and attaining harmony within. It contains a step-by-step procedure by which the body and mind are disciplined, and the soul is liberated. As it is experiential, it enables you to discover and explore a new expression of movement and energy when practised regularly. It joins, with integrity, that has been separated, and expands your awareness to explore further dimensions of life, and connection with others and the universe. Your body and mind act as your personal laboratory.

The yoga system – Eightfold Path – as outlined by Rishi Patanjali, contains the following eight steps, which form a vital part of Raja Yoga:

1. Yamas: five self-regulating restraints – moral principles involving interactions with people and the world at large:

   + *Ahimsa, or non-violence* – being tolerant of people's differences – having a complete absence of violence, inducing harmony in your-self and others
   + *Satya, or truthfulness* – in communication with others – discriminating between real and unreal, resulting in realistic perception
   + *Asteya, or non-stealing* – not taking what is not given – being honest with your-self and others
   + *Brahmacharya, or preserving vital energy* – not wasting energy – development of emotional security
   + *Aparigraha, or non-grasping* – having an absence of greed – letting go of envy and jealousy, and acquiring only basic needs, resulting in inner peace

2. Niyamas: five personal practices that relate to the inner world, which contain negative and positive moralities – personal discipline both physical body and mental aspects:

   + *Shauca, or cleanliness* – in the body, environment, home and mind, promoting mental and emotional purity
   + *Santosha, or contentment* – accepting your situation in life with grace – resulting in a state of peace, happiness, and joy
   + *Tapas, or austerity* – commitment to transform yourself and improve your life, to be able to experience the true essence, reduce anxiety, and tackle difficulties with confidence
   + *Swadhyaya, or self-study* – spiritual education and learning-witnessing thoughts and emotions, to discover the true self
   + *Ishwara prandidhana, or surrendering yourself to a higher essence* – whatever you believe in and love, to manage the ego and develop potential for love

3. Asanas: right postures to promote well-being and prepare the body and mind for meditation.
4. Pranayama: control of the breath and subtle life currents, to promote concentration and mental balance.
5. Pratyahara: withdrawal of the senses from external objects, opening the potential and possibility of enlightenment and internal peace that can promote happiness and well-being.
6. Dharana: one-pointed focus that eliminates actual awareness of meditation.
7. Dhyana: meditation, which can lead to ultimate self-knowledge – a deeper state of Dharana.
8. Samadhi: super conscious perception, by total absorption and one-pointedness of mind, resulting in bliss.

The final goal is Kaivalya – realization of the Truth, which is beyond intellectual knowledge and transcends consciousness.

Styles of Yoga:

There are more than eight hundred styles of yoga, so everyone can benefit from the ancient teachings – based on their personal temperament and goals. These types of yoga include:

Hatha Yoga – the yoga of physical discipline that embraces asana practice (physical postures), and encompasses various breathing techniques that cleanse and strengthen the body and purify the nerves, to preserve youth and prolong life, in preparation for the practice of meditation;

Meditation – to prepare the body and mind for higher states of meditation, and fine-tune and harmonise the internal organs of the body. Regular practice results in better health, more energy, better sleep, improved circulation, and a more positive outlook on life.

Once mastery of purification of the body has been attained by the regular practice of Hatha Yoga, spiritual wisdom and insight can be developed.

Bhakti Yoga – the yoga of devotion, the path of the heart – enables the student to conquer and master the emotions of desire, passion, love, hatred, pride and anger through chanting and singing – and experience a deeper feeling of connection with the Divine self.

Karma Yoga – the yoga of action in work through a discipline that is mastered by purification of the mind, to achieve one-pointed focus, and efficient completion of the task with perfection and consciousness of a higher level. The aim is to complete the task at hand, for the sake of serving humanity selflessly – without selfish expectation.

The whole of life can thus become a meditation and Divine connection and, thereby, more interesting and insightful – each moment being experienced fully, with awareness and mindfulness, and without expectation or boredom.

Jnana Yoga – the yoga of pure wisdom, and intellect, that manifests in attainment of liberation through gaining knowledge of the absolute, and realizing oneness with the Divine. It is practised in three stages, and considered to be the most difficult path of yoga.

Raja Yoga – the royal path of yoga, a discipline that focuses on attaining a direct connection with the Divine by the study, integration, and systematic mastery of the eight steps contained in Rishi Patanjali's Yoga Sutras. Mudras and Bandhas are used to gain control over the physical body.

It provides a link from the inner world – the inner nature of everyone – to the outer or external world, which is merely a reflection of the inner nature; and, through a release of intuition, in which inherent talents can be activated, allows a state of bliss, calmness, serenity and peace to be experienced.

Kriya Yoga – includes the practice of breathing exercises, Mantra chanting, mudras, and advanced meditation techniques to rejuvenate the brain and spinal centres by recharging and decarbonizing the human blood with oxygen. It clears the mind of sensory obstacles, by preventing accumulation of venous blood, and lessening or preventing tissue decay. This process can be a powerful release, thus the practice needs to be conducted by an experienced qualified yoga teacher to ensure a natural and safe outcome.

Tantra Yoga – involves the study of the universe – macrocosm – through the study of the self – the microcosm, with the aim to expand awareness in all states of consciousness.

Regular practice of any type of yoga can help you to improve your physical, mental, and spiritual well-being.

Yoga provides a middle path of activity and spirituality. The synthesis of head, heart, and hands is simultaneously combined. By allowing the higher intelligence to intervene in your life you may experience a freedom, attained by your mind becoming detached from everyday ups and downs. This state of equilibrium enables you to calmly accept where you are at now and deal with issues rationally, rather than feeling that you are on a roller-coaster ride over which you have no control.

By encompassing an integrated practice of yoga, on a regular basis, with awareness and mindfulness, the whole of your personality can be positively transformed, over a period of time. Your life experiences may become subtler, and less gross – enabling you to feel a greater depth of awareness and connectedness. With this integrated practice your physical and mental health can benefit, and you can gain peace of mind and realise a vision for your ideal life direction. A yoga practitioner tends to be more self-aware and interacts harmoniously with others.

Asanas affect both the body and mind. When practised with a qualified teacher you can gain a greater understanding on how each pose can benefit the body and mind, and ensure that postures your body can best benefit from are included in your regular practice.

You need to be aware of potential injuries that can be caused by incorrect practice of certain asanas – hence it is advisable that initially you find a qualified yoga teacher, who can advise which asanas are most suitable for you, based on your current medical condition, flexibility and overall body fitness. Injuries to the joints, especially the knees, need to be prevented. You need to be aware that each day your body can have differing capacities – what it is capable of at any particular time – due to varying weather conditions and other factors, and never try to achieve anything that puts too much strain or stress on any part of your body. If you are attending a general yoga class, it is best you advise the instructor of any of your concerns before the class starts – so that they can advise specific contra-indications.

Meditation allows the mind to become quietened through discipline and devotion, which enables you to disconnect from a state of restlessness in your life – and helps you to connect with the peaceful state of the reality that is within you. The creative part of your mind will then be free to focus on visualising your real needs in life based on your inherent talents.

The mind holds an ignorance about reality, identifies with the ego, attracts and repulses objects of desire, and the fear of death. By mastering the mind the body's vitality and energy can be conserved, resulting in a healthy body. You need to eliminate the emotions of fear, guilt, shame, grief, lies, illusions, and attachment through the practice of meditation – to experience self-esteem and joy. In this state of calmness, you can become distanced from material forms and the senses can be re-aligned with your divine nature. Thus, although you may have to deal with difficult life experiences they need not destroy your equilibrium. Ordinarily, the individual acts as a puppet of past actions and environment.

Being detached from issues and objects does not mean you renounce them from your life – it means that you renounce your attachment to them, and thereby do not allow them to rule your reason for being, and do not focus on them unduly. By achieving this state of equilibrium and non-attachment – providing a distance – the mind can become disciplined and remains calm throughout both pleasant and unpleasant experiences, thereby enabling you to feel calm and at peace. You can choose to keep all your possessions and appreciate them without worshipping them, bearing in mind the ongoing need to diminish any clutter that exists in your life.

Example:

Keith owns several properties as part of his retirement planning strategy, and supports a charity. He does not worship these assets. Keith appreciates what he has but is not affected by the objects, and does not feel attached to them. He regards them as a vehicle that provides for the welfare and benefit of himself and others. In fact, he will not have to rely on the age pension or anyone else for financial assistance when he retires.

Meditation is a technique for energising, calming, and clarifying the mind – to allow it to enter higher states of consciousness, transcend petty concerns that otherwise occupy the mind, and allow it to accept and experience a greater, deeper state of hope and awareness. Regular practice of meditation enables the mind to sort through stored data and discard outmoded belief systems and unnecessary information, and reset the personal matrix to leave more space to allow new and relevant information to be stored.

Imagine your future new life story, and how it feels to be living it now. The gap that currently exists between where you are now and where you want to be can be bridged – by a journey that is yours to begin. How can this process start to happen?

Meditation can help you to:

+ still your mind, enable you to access your creativity, and oneness with the Divine self within
+ develop your concentration and focus, providing clarity and insight and, when practised daily, enable you to reap these benefits

Whilst your mind is in this quiet state, ask "What is it I need to understand? What is my path?"

The more deeply you meditate, over a period of regular practice, you may:

+ gain a closer connection with the Divine Self within, and your intuitive powers; feel a deeper state of peace within
+ feel an ecstatic surge of love that can bring tears of joy
+ perhaps you will see vivid colours, and / or other visions; and
+ feel an overall sense of calmness and clarity

Remember – you need to use your intuitive powers for the benefit of society, and not misuse them against society.

Intuitive awareness, and not intellectual awareness, is based on pure knowledge. This knowledge and awareness provides a spiritual awakening of humanity, which is the only real purpose of the human birth. The process of meditation eradicates influences by the lower qualities, that include attachment to worldly objects and issues, and unfolds the higher state of divine qualities that include peace and joy.

The practice of *Mouna* – noble silence – where you choose not to speak for a designated period can conserve your energy and help you maintain your connection with the inner world, enabling you to witness your thought patterns and impulses. It nourishes the mind and body.

Mantra chanting is effective in altering the state of the body and mind. Om – Aum – is the primal sound and, when chanted, can align and invigorate the whole of the body's energy systems, calm the nerves, and energise the mind. It can lift negativity and depression. Silent chanting is the most powerful, and can be practised daily with deep abdominal breathing (explained in more detail in Chapter One) – while sitting at your desk or wherever you spend most of your time. It vibrates into the Sri Yantra – the blueprint of all life.

The practice of yoga enables the devotee to unite the mind at will with the divine realm, thus switching on and off the life current to the five senses: sight, sound, smell, taste, and touch: the world of matter – as and when required and appropriate.

Other tools are available that can provide a link between the Self and the Divine but Yoga is one that integrates the whole of life.

Conscious mind; Subconscious mind

There are several levels of consciousness. For the purpose of this discussion the states of the conscious and the sub-conscious are analysed.

The five patterns of consciousness are:

+ Right knowledge: that which you know is true
+ Wrong knowledge: that which you think you know but is not true
+ Fancy: fantasies that cause worry about things that do not exist, and will not happen; or dwelling on the past and feeling guilty
+ Sleep: disturbances that generally occur when you are asleep
+ Memory: stored in the subconscious mind that causes physical, mental, and emotional disturbances

The first three patterns are generally experienced at the level of the conscious mind, and are controlled by logic.

The *conscious*, objective, thinking mind can hold only one thought at a time, and has no memory. It has four functions, to:

+ identify information
+ compare the information with what is stored in the sub-conscious mind
+ analyse the data available; and
+ make a decision

The last two states are generally contained within the subconscious mind.

The *subconscious* part, stores:

+ negative habits
+ bad experiences; and
+ conditioning from the past

It can be likened to the hard drive of a computer that needs to be cleaned and reprogrammed.

How can you achieve spiritual harmony? By recognising what it is that is stored in your subconscious mind and reprogramming your mind by eliminating the harmful and useless contents, and filling the empty space with positive expectations. Then your energy can vibrate on a higher frequency.

Suppression of harmful thoughts and experiences become submerged in the subconscious mind and they need to be "weeded" out by the roots to alleviate the unhappiness and pain. Like weeds in a garden, if the unwanted weeds are not entirely removed, they will remain and multiply.

Unless these obstructions are removed from the subconscious mind – together with the pressures created by daily living in a stressful society – you remain full of mental tensions that manifest, as:

+ anxiety
+ nervousness
+ guilt
+ lack of self-confidence
+ loneliness
+ fear; and
+ obsessions

Some people choose to temporarily escape from these tensions by using harmful substances, such as alcohol and drugs, or else opt for costly psychiatric help. You are all looking for some form of change, relief from inner conflicts and turmoil, and need to feel at ease with yourself, to experience contentment, peace, and bliss.

Antar Mouna is a powerful tool that you can use to understand, tame, and befriend the mind, enabling you to train it, and eradicate deep-rooted tensions, harmful thoughts, and experiences. Thus, the mind can be purged, and peace and calmness induced. This practice needs to be facilitated by a qualified yoga instructor.

Antar Mouna consists of six stages – it forms a fundamental part of the Buddhist practice of Vipassana, used in a modified way. The first three of the six stages of Pratyahara, are the most important:

+ In the *first stage* the mind is focused on external awareness, enabling it to detach from bodily sensations and perceptions, and become undisturbed

+ The *second stage* focuses on internal thought processes to distract the mind. This stage consists of three steps, whereby the mind is initially encouraged to think what it wants; then becomes bored and subsequently quietens; and finally, the "journey" continues along an empty road, allowing the process to continue – at this point the mind has gained the courage, openness, and honesty to accept the hidden and suppressed parts of the personality that will be revealed – we become friends with the mind and accept our self as we really are.

- In *stage three*, the mind is guided to consciously create and dispose of thoughts at will, and by focusing on confronting negative and difficult issues, the mental knots can be slowly released.

This process may need to be repeated several times so that the mind can be purged of past negative habits, bad experiences, and conditioning. As each barrier or blockage is removed, the mind is purified and the truth becomes clearer; and experience of unconditional love becomes natural – enabling you to live a richer and fuller life – deepening the texture of life's experience.

Quietening the analytical mind and awakening the heart, allows unconditional surrender of the ego and intellect – a humbling and fearless process.

Balance

Spiritual harmony – the balance between your conscious and subconscious mind is the key to attracting harmony in all other areas of your life. It comes from within – you do not have to look to external factors to experience it.

An understanding, and mastery of one's Self is the key to spiritual harmony. You each contain the same blueprint. The physical body is affected by the mind and its thoughts, bad habits that cause physical and psychic disharmony, the experiences you encountered in the past, and the food you eat. The way you breathe affects the efficiency of the working of your internal organs and their overall harmony within the body's framework. Your thoughts affect your whole outlook on life – whether you are positive or negative – and impact on the state of your body. The purer your body becomes, the healthier it becomes, and it can vibrate at a higher energetic frequency.

Spiritual and mental healing, resulting in harmony of the mind and Soul, can eradicate disease from the body for example, by eating holistic food at regular meal times, in a quiet environment.

There are several different levels of awareness, ranging from gross to subtle. These states include:

- Being awake
- Being asleep
- Dream state
- Experiencing psychic awareness through the chakras
- Connection with the Divine Self

Invisible veils created by the mind need to be removed so you can fully experience the state of being awake in its full capacity.

Spiritual awakening allows you to experience things with a deeper vision, and this state is often preceded by darkness. You need to reach into the depths of your soul – beyond where you have been before – to create a new reality. Darkness always precedes the dawn / light.

Light and darkness are inherent in everyone and everything, and the key to understanding the way forward is to accept that both attributes are present in every situation and person. Neither is right nor wrong. There needs to be a balance between the two states.

With a deeper state of awareness, you can:

* realise your true nature and potential, the final stage of your journey to freedom, and the means to get there
* witness miracles, via a state of meditation
* become one with the Divine Self within, via observation, going with the flow and letting go
* witness from a state of detachment rather than from a state of attachment. Attachment forms the basis of suffering or addiction as it fixates on energy outside of the self, which needs to be released; and
* have an ability to allow abundance to manifest in each area of your life, learn to master your relationships, and adjust your knowledge through wisdom

You need to:

* visualise success, enable your expanded awareness to manifest, plan for it to happen, believe it will happen, and allow it to manifest
* believe in miracles, have faith, and remain positive; and be patient, knowing that the good seeds you have planted will take some time to germinate
* examine your belief systems – the belief created by your experience; and
* look into spaces, rather than at solid shapes, and discover that anything is possible

Each day, you need to take time out to appreciate natural miracles – the trees, flowers, colours of the sky, the stars. You are one of those miracles. Take time out to relax into a quiet state and take a few deep breaths to connect with this Divine miracle. Learn to appreciate the sound of silence. Develop an attitude of gratitude and give thanks – recognise that you form a very small part of the whole world, and count your many blessings. As you change yourself, you change the world.

You need to recharge your battery from time to time, to be able to transcend present limitations.

By accepting the capitalist ways of the West, and integrating the spiritual ideals of the East you can experience an integrated and balanced lifestyle, by allowing faith and hope to outweigh fear.

Joy

The gold within is your unique inherent talents. What may have been latent until now can be discovered to allow a transformation to take place. Your new vision needs to be awakened, so you can live life fully. Only then can you use those talents fully for the benefit of mankind. You need to approach the future with hope, trust yourself, and leave behind regret and fears. With ongoing effort, a disciplined lifestyle becomes an integral part of the personality. Everything in the future can improve if you make a spiritual effort now. The journey of discovery awaits.

Life is like a tapestry, or painting, that can have many colours, and depth, depending on your level of connection with the Divine self. Never compare yourself with others – you are unique. Never compete with the main intent of winning, where someone else stands to lose or fail, which will stifle your creativity. Maintain a state of humility – go all out to play the game fairly – there is enough of everything in the world for everyone to benefit from and enjoy. Love your neighbour – and develop compassion for others.

When you surrender to a higher power, going beyond self-centred ideas, fears, and insecurities – by living in the present and expressing yourself in an integrated way – life can become more pleasurable and enjoyable for others. At that level, the aspect of giving joy and happiness is not limited only to one person – as in a normal relationship – but can penetrate the entire world. This state of being is the greatest living truth that can be experienced. You can become like a lotus flower – in the world but not part of it – that opens anew each day.

Connection – inner / outer worlds:

When I was young I recall experiencing a vision of three sages' heads sculpted into the Himalayas – akin to the US Presidential heads that are sculpted into Mount Rushmore – I just knew they were there. Whereas the presidential sculptures symbolize freedom and hope for America, despite them desecrating the natural landscape – per Native American environmentalists, the Himalayan vision and peaks are sacred. It was not until later in my life that I gained a deeper awareness of the reality of the ancient teachings embodied in my vision. Unbeknown to me at that time I had been experiencing a state of meditation – connection to spiritual harmony – freedom and hope. The vision was so profound that I never mentioned it to anyone – I doubt they would have understood the true significance, which I revered for later awakening. In that state, I experienced a feeling of peace within that I shall never forget.

On another occasion, on a skiing trip in the Pyrenees in Northern Spain, I recall witnessing the pristine snow glistening in the sun – that was real beauty – a sight I will never forget – pure and awesome.

During my teens, I attended a spiritual retreat in the Lake District in England, organised by the Salvation Army. Youths from all over the world attended and the fellowship was an uplifting experience, amid the beauty of nature and the songs of praise. We sang and we danced to the tune – Lord of the Dance. I will always remember the peace and special friendships formed during that time.

Whilst visiting Hong Kong on a business trip, I flew to Guilin in southern China, a picturesque region of limestone karst hills – dramatic landscape – that can best be viewed from taking a boat trip along one of the meandering rivers. The scenery is breathtakingly beautiful and needs to be seen to be believed – some of the scenic paintings depict the scenery of the region during different seasons of the year. Meandering along the River Li by boat felt like being part of a far distant world remote from any commercialism, except for a few market stalls half-way through the journey.

After that, I was fortunate to meet a master painter who had studied art in Japan, and I bought one of his paintings, which is hung on my wall at home, that portrays that area during Spring-time. The painting radiates light, peace, hope, and a harmony of nature.

More recently I felt harmony when floating above the vineyards, North of Melbourne, in a hot-air balloon. That was on the second attempt – after the first hot-air balloon became caught up on, and ripped by, a eucalyptus tree branch. The local Boy Scout troupe had never witnessed such a spectacular occurrence before, and hopefully never again. Can you imagine the feelings of the pilot? He had never experienced this situation before, as it is usual for eucalyptus branches to bend upwards – he must have been devastated but did not show it.

I noticed the faces of the other balloonists turned white, but I had faith that the pilot could handle the situation without too much trouble – he was forced to land amid a field of startled cows running anti-clockwise around the field that was surrounded by an electric fence – no harmony there! It took a lot of care and patience to get out of the field – not sure whether everyone in the group stayed for the second successful attempt to fly. It was well worth persevering to experience the peace, and a feeling of divinity, floating above the vineyards away from the madding crowds and traffic below. I would do that again.

During a drive to the Yarra Valley, following the fires that devastated Marysville and many trees in the region, I felt the solitary quietness and stillness in the environment – as though the eucalyptus trees had taken refuge to rejuvenate internally and recover from the experience. Fire is a normal process for the eucalypts. We can learn from the trees – how to survive the storms of life.

Inner self:

When I first arrived at the ashram in April 2011, after my job in Queensland had been made redundant, I was exhausted from the drive from Queensland, and totally shattered. I felt demoralised – loss of job, loss of regular income, and, eventually, loss of all material possessions. It was high time for a lifestyle change. I had no idea how long my stay at the ashram would be, but it lasted for almost five years. During that time, I renounced most of my connection to the outside world, to immerse myself into a different lifestyle and focus on reconnecting with the inner world, away from distractions.

The ashram is located in a State forest and, as well as the other human visitors, my neighbours included kangaroos, and various native birds. It has a wonderful library facility and I read many of the books in my free time. The days there were long, filled with Yoga practices and spiritual studies. At the same time as working six days a week in the ashram, I chose to pursue a two-year full-time course in yogic studies, and fitting that into the daily ashram schedules required a huge amount of discipline and perseverance. In addition to the yogic studies program, I attended several programs, conducted by outside presenters, within the ashram environment, including mindfulness, effective communication skills, and Hindu cultural festival activities.

My initial studies incorporated a four-week program – Living Consciously – that consisted of weekly teachings and discussion sessions with a Yoga instructor, and a review of observations made during Karma Yoga, whilst living in the ashram.

Having spent most of my professional life working as an accountant and tax adviser I felt a strong connection with Karma Yoga – serving others selflessly in performing my duties mindfully, with awareness. It became possible for me to stay focused on each task at hand without being attached to the outcome in a way that resulted in the best outcome with minimum stress and within the allotted time frame. Each moment is a meditation. In that state, I can create a positive environment and empower others to achieve the same outcome for themselves, without experiencing stress. During my role managing the kitchen I learnt a lot about which herbs can be used to flavour different food types, and witnessed the organic food cycle – from seeds planted in the ashram garden, to food on the table at meal times, and back to the garden, via the composting process.

I also feel strong connection with Bhakti yoga – aiming to experience a direct connection with the Divine in all activities in life. Soon after I commenced my studies and regular yoga practice and experience, I felt a real connection and synchronicity between the head, heart, and hands – whereas previously I had connected mainly from the head (intellectual) and hand awareness, focusing on intellect and actions, without synchronising inclusion of the heart. Other branches of yoga I resonate well with are Jnana yoga, Raja yoga, and Kriya yoga.

My mind now is calmer – much less stressed, my body is more flexible, and I am continuing to evolve with the help of spiritual teachers and like-minded friends, some of whom have much more knowledge and depth of awareness than me. Yoga provides me with a strong foundation and tool with which to strengthen the bridge between the inner and outer worlds. Whilst living in the ashram I gained more confidence and strength in the face of extreme situations, enabling my intuition to deal calmly to resolve whatever actions needed to be taken. There is now a harmony between the mind and the heart. My mind became detached from the issues that needed to be resolved in a logical manner without experiencing undue stress, and I proceeded to take the most appropriate actions. It was the start of a new phase in life and a more balanced lifestyle. Generally, I lived most daily experiences in a mindful and meditative state.

I also studied the basics of other related practices, including Ayurveda, which is ongoing. An appreciation of how the body, mind and soul work together deepens my understanding of any internal disharmonies, and provides a means to regularise any imbalances of energy.

My first real experience of meditation in the ashram, within a class conducted by a qualified yoga teacher, gave me a feeling of total inner peace and timelessness. I sat cross-legged on the floor with my hands in my lap and focused on natural breathing, witnessing the cold air flowing into my nostrils on inhalation and the warmer air flowing out of my nostrils on exhalation. Once the body was settled, focusing the mind at the point between the eyebrows, and the imagination on the blank space above the eyebrows, we were guided through a journey. My journey took me to a waterfall at the top of a hill. I was sitting on top of the hill near the source of the waterfall, and slowly walked down the hillside to a rocky ledge behind the waterfall where I rested for a while, before walking down to the bottom of the hill and sitting at the foot of the waterfall, near a green meadow. I will always vividly remember the sight of the waterfall and hear the powerful gushing sound of the water cascading down the hillside. I experienced a feeling of bliss and universal love, during which time stood still. The teacher then slowly guided us from the state of meditation back into reality. That was an example of being in the NOW.

After another of my meditation sessions, I witnessed several white lights moving around in my darkened room. This phenomenon lasted for about fifteen minutes – it was enlightening, and peaceful.

Prior to these experiences in the ashram, during the process of surgery in Singapore to remove bunion joints, I had witnessed an out-of-body experience. From a position above my body, I witnessed my body below bathed in white light, and recall being told "it was not my time yet" after which I returned to my sleep state and awoke. Following that experience I have never been afraid of dying.

Conscious mind; Subconscious mind:

My ability to review, analyse, and see the big picture is an inherent talent that has been invaluable when practising my profession. I had to be certain that facts were correct, based on logic, and without fantasising.

The practice of, and experiencing, the science of yoga has enabled me to free the mind from memories that disturbed my mind, and include: asanas, breath control, meditation, withdrawal from the outside world, and concentrated focus. This enabled me to experience each task as a meditation and live life mindfully.

I had plenty of time to reflect on and practice what I had learnt by completing the two-year intensive yoga training program, which changed my life.

Balance:

Ashram life enabled me to re-connect with and strengthen my spiritual foundation — distinguishing between intuition and impulse: expressing and not suppressing emotions, and distinguishing between adequacy, addiction, lack, and oversupply, and their effects, especially as they affect the intake of food, sufficiency of sleep, and a healthy acceptance of financial needs.

One of the experiences I particularly enjoyed, was observing the different species of birds in the forest — nothing changes their life patterns. The fairy wrens are joyful; the sulphur-crested cockatoos are boisterous and destructive; the kookaburras laugh, rule, and let live — all have differing personalities.

The friendships I established are lifelong — there is a common denominator and bond in each friendship, a higher dimension — a mutual trust and respect among people, who are like family. Time out to observe my reactions to situations encountered has made me a stronger person with more confidence, self-esteem, and peace of mind to face the future.

I miss the ashram lifestyle. Although it was not easy, it had its own rewards. Especially, I miss meeting and working with people from different cultures, and backgrounds in life — each have their unique purpose for visiting the ashram. I learnt a lot living in that community. I remain in contact with several friends I met there. However, the time came for me to integrate into the outside world, with a different mind-set, and I realise that this process can take some time.

I chose Yoga as a tool and a step to reaching a closer connection with the Divine. There are other tools but I found yoga to be all-encompassing, integrating the body, mind, and soul — synchronising head, heart and hands — it provides an insight into the true nature of all beings, and throughout my lifetime the experiences will deepen with continued practice, and deepening awareness. Although I had that profound vision early in life, and studied comparative religions during my working life, I had never been fully exposed to the ancient spiritual teachings of the East and the all-encompassing experiential science of Yoga.

I chose to study and teach Yoga, so I can celebrate life's goodness, and help other people to gain from the benefits the practices can provide. I feel privileged to act as a facilitator to share some of the ancient teachings and wisdom with you so, hopefully, you can gain some benefit from them.

The two-year Diploma of Satyananda Yoga Training (Bihar School of Yoga, India) tradition, consisted of 1440 hours, conducted over four semesters – each with residential teaching sessions conducted in the ashram, followed by individual practices with on-line submissions. The overall syllabus, as outlined in the Student Handbook, included:

- Anatomy and Physiology – promoting coordinated movement patterns to ensure safe performance of yoga postures
- Yogic Physiology – subtle dimensions and energy systems of the human organism, including nadis, prana, and chakras; gestures and techniques for harnessing and redirecting energy and awareness
- Philosophy, Ethics, and Lifestyle – cultural origins and underpinning philosophies; theory and practice synthesized into life skills through living and working in the ashram environment
- Yogic Psychology – analysis of major structures and systems of the human body, and the effect of yoga practices on them
- Techniques
- Teaching Methodology; and
- Integrative Practice and Teaching

The first semester included:

- an overview of the multiple branches of yoga
- basic yoga practice and lifestyle; analysing strengths and weaknesses from a physical, emotional, and mental perspective.

The second semester included:

- exploring dimensions of human experience, energy flow, workings of the mind, and the nature of subtler spiritual experiences
- progressive development and investigation of asana – postures including the Pawanmuktasana series, pranayama – balancing, tranquillising and vitalizing practices, and meditation – recognizing that different personality types have affinity with different meditation practices
- practical application of skills, and yogic awareness relating to the functioning of a yoga centre; and
- nutrition, the cardiovascular, respiratory, digestive, and nervous systems

The third semester included:

- a deeper understanding of the theory and practice of yoga
- an in-depth study of the Yoga Sutras of Patanjali, Kundalini Tantra, and the Bhagavad Gita
- planning and progressing my own yoga practices
- the nervous and endocrine systems; and
- I elected to research the effects of stress on the brain, an area that has always impacted my thinking, and has opened up a wish to learn more about how the brain can change

The fourth semester focused on teaching practices, developing yoga programs, and sharing experiences with other student teachers and trainers, as well as teaching classes outside the ashram.

I am required to keep my First Aid Certificate current, and complete regular ongoing education updates.

Whilst living at the ashram, I was initiated into the Saraswati (which means "knowledge and the arts") tradition of the monastic order by my Guru. There are ten subdivisions, each of which traces their spiritual lineage to Lord Shankara. I was given a spiritual name – Kripadhara – a Sanskrit name which, translated, means "flow of grace". The purpose of the spiritual name is to provide a spiritual goal to aspire to throughout life.

The yogic journey is for life, I am an eternal student, and whatever direction my path may take in the future – the tapestry of life will become even more vivid, and the journey more enriched and exciting. I hope I can prepare tailored yoga programs to include specific needs of students, as well as conducting general yoga classes in the community.

Joy:

One of my favourite poems is "Samadhi" by Paramahamsa Yogananda, which is reproduced below:

"Vanished the veils of light and shade,
Lifted every vapour of sorrow,
Sailed away all dawns of fleeting joy,
Gone the deep sensory mirage.
Love, hate, health, disease, life, death,
Perished these false shadows on the screen of duality.
Waves of laughter, scyllas of sarcasm, melancholic whirlpools,
Melting in the vast sea of bliss.
The storm of maya stilled
By magic wand of intuition deep.
The universe, forgotten dream, subconsciously lurks,
Ready to invade my newly-awakened memory divine.
I live without the cosmic shadow,
But it is not, bereft of me;
As the sea exists without the waves,
But they breathe not without the sea.
Dreams, waking states of deep turia sleep,
Present, past, future, no more for me,
But ever-present, all-flowing I, I, everywhere.
Planets, stars, stardust, earth,
Volcanic bursts of doomsday cataclysms,
Creation's moulding furnace,
Glaciers of silent x-rays, burning electron floods,
Thoughts of all men, past, present, to come,
Every blade of grass, myself, mankind,
Each particle of universal dust,
Anger, greed, good, bad, salvation, lust,
I swallowed, transmuted all
Into a vast ocean of blood of my own one Being!
Smouldering joy, oft puffed by meditation
Blinding my tearful eyes,
Burst into immortal flames of bliss,

Consumed my tears, my frame, my all.
Thou art, I am Thou,
Knowing, Knower, Known, as One!
Tranquil, unbroken thrill, eternally living, ever-new peace!
Enjoyable beyond imagination of expectancy, Samadhi bliss!
Not an unconscious state
Or mental chloroform without wilful return,
Samadhi but extends my conscious realm
Beyond limits of the mortal frame
To farthest boundary of eternity
Where I, the Cosmic Sea,
Watch the little ego floating in Me.
The sparrow, each grain of sand, fall not without My sight.
All space floats like an iceberg in My mental sea.
Colossal Container, I, of all things made.
By deeper, longer, thirsty, guru-given meditation
Comes this celestial Samadhi.
Mobile murmurs of atoms are heard,
The dark earth, mountains, vales, lo! molten liquid!
Flowing seas change into vapours of nebulae!
Aum blows upon vapours, opening wondrously their veils,
Oceans stand revealed, shining electrons,
Till, at last sound of the cosmic drum,
Vanish the grosser lights into eternal rays
Of all-pervading bliss.
From joy I came, for joy I live, in sacred joy I melt.
Ocean of mind, I drink all creation's waves.
Four veils of solid, liquid, vapour, light,
Lift aright.
Myself, in everything, enters the Great Myself.
Gone forever, fitful, flickering shadows of mortal memory.
Spotless is my mental sky, below, ahead, and high above.
Eternity and I, one united ray.
A tiny bubble of laughter, I
Am become the Sea of Mirth Itself."

Note: Samadhi means "Bliss" in Sanskrit.

The tapestry of life is vast. My adventure in life has just begun, and I am here to share it with those I love, being guided by the Divine self within. The transformation continues.

Since my reconnection to the outside world, I have learnt to trust myself, communicate and connect more deeply with others, celebrate the beauty deep within, and love myself unconditionally. I have hope in my heart for peace, and harmony in the world. The river of joy runs deep. My life is more balanced now. I am happy. I need to be mindful how the universe can be protected – it is the body and soul – the temple of mankind. It needs to be understood and respected.

Space for you to write in:

Rediscovering your true self brings peace of mind, and harmony within both the inner and outer worlds.

Spiritual Harmony

Chapter Ten
Goals and Taking Action

Go slowly in the direction of your dreams! Live the life you've imagined.
As you simplify your life, the laws of the universe will be simpler.
– Henry David Thoreau

I have never hit a shot, not even in practice, without having a very sharp,
in focus picture of it in my head.
– Jack William Nicklaus

Nothing can stop the man with the right mental attitude from achieving
his goal; nothing can help the man with the wrong mental attitude.
– Thomas Jefferson

If one does not know to which port one is sailing, no wind is favourable.
– Seneca

If you do not know where you are going, every road will lead to nowhere.
– Henry Alfred Kissinger

If you fail to plan, you are planning to fail.
– Benjamin Franklin

A journey of a thousand miles begins and ends with one step.
– Lao Tzu

The secret of success in life is for a man to be ready for his opportunity
when it comes.
– Benjamin Disraeli

Continuous effort – not strength or intelligence – is the key to unlocking
our potential.
– Sir Winston Leonard Spencer Churchill

Life is like riding a bicycle. To keep your balance you must keep moving.
– Albert Einstein

It does not matter how slowly you go so long as you do not stop.
– Confucius

The time is always right to do what is right.
– Martin Luther King Jr.

Today is the first day of the rest of your life.
– Charles ("Chuck") E Dederich Sr.

- How does it feel to be a winner?
- What goals will help you bridge the gap to living your ideal goal?
- What actions will you take?

How does it feel to be a winner?

You have a dream that can become reality. Whatever you believe in passionately can be achieved. Assume your passion is so strong that your dream is now reality – you are living the future in the present – you can witness this reality by focusing your mind on the imaginary screen above your eyebrows and watching it on the "screen". Being able to visualize the dream on the screen is the secret to enabling it to become reality. Enjoy the future in the present. Believe you have already achieved it. Feel it, taste it, smell it, see it, and enjoy it. Treasure it. Keep this experience in your mind until it becomes reality. Allow your intuition to help you. Do not impose any limitations.

Example:

Visualise yourself winning the Gold Medal at an Olympic event, or some other event that you may relate with more closely. How do you feel now? Celebrate that feeling now. Smile! Breathe deeply and allow the feeling to permeate your whole body and mind. Accept success.

You need to build a life from the circumstances in which you find yourself now: steadily persevere, plod on, do not look back, and bravely march forward. By not allowing obstacles to discourage or disappoint you, you can always remain passionate and enthusiastic. Character is built by your thoughts.

When you develop humility and courage, all the other virtues can follow. Passion can enable you to succeed at whatever you want to achieve. But, you need patience. You need to serve, love, and give – unconditionally, with all your heart.

Example:

Pearl is a business person who has worked hard to be successful in her executive role. Her dream is that one day she can empower disadvantaged women, with a family, to support, to gain confidence and self-esteem that will enable them to work and provide for themselves and their families.

Pearl is passionate about her dream becoming a reality and can feel how the reality will work. This vision leads her to connect with like-minded people who agree to provide a venue where the young families can live, and where programs can be conducted to provide them with the training they need to establish their road to financial independence. Pearl opened her heart to seeking a team, without which the venture could not have succeeded.

Pearl's reward for this successful venture is the smile on the faces of the young families who feel safe and cared for whilst they build a life for themselves and become contributing members of the community in which they live.

You will have determined with passion your true potential in life, based on your latent inherent talents, and what your reason for living means to you. Now, you need to set some meaningful goals to channel your passion into reality.

What goals will help you bridge the gap to living your ideal goal?

You need to stay focused on the big picture and use your goals as tools to help you attain your dream – rather than pre-setting goals that impose limitations on reaching your desired destination. Anyone can set goals and achieve them – but be certain your goals will help you achieve what you really need in your life. Will they help you to attain freedom, happiness, and peace of mind, in all areas of life?

Write down your goals in Exercise Eleven (at the end of this chapter). List all the main goals that will help you get from where you are now to where you want to be. Take time to complete this exercise. At this point in time some of the goals may appear to be unattainable. Your goals may be anything that will challenge you to live your life fully, based on the current stage of your journey.

Examples, to:

- *become well – what steps do you need to take?*
- *find a more challenging and fulfilling job – list your needs, update your CV / resume. How do you plan to find a new role?*
- *take the family on a long vacation – discuss where you would like to visit / plan the timing of this holiday / determine the cost and how you can meet that*
- *start a new family – make sure each party is ready for this commitment, and make your plans together. Be sure you each share the same needs and aspirations. Make no assumptions.*
- *build a relationship with a new partner*
- *rebuild financial freedom – revisit the steps outlined in Chapter Eight*
- *travel around the world – where do you want to stay / what type of accommodation do you need? How long do you want the journey to last? Determine the cost / prepare a budget. Plan to get inoculations from the doctor. Plan your wardrobe / weight of your luggage. Include enough time for research so you can make the most of your time away.*

Do your goals connect with the power of your body and spirit? Do they truly reflect your vision? Take some time to ponder these issues.

When you have listed each goal, give each one a priority. Which one do you want to achieve first, second, third, etc.? Give each one of them a number from one – twelve (assuming you have twelve main goals).

Examples:

- *Mike wants to compete in a marathon in two years' time. Currently he walks each day but has not yet started training for the marathon. He finds out when the marathon will take place and where. He decides to start practising running each morning at 5.00am for one hour before he eats breakfast and goes to work. He knows that with regular practice he can build the strength and fitness needed to perform well and enjoy running in the marathon, without stress.*
- *Sally has never travelled overseas and wants to visit a pen friend who lives in New York. She needs to save enough money for the trip and plan the places she would like to visit as well as visiting her friend. She starts to save each month for the trip and has budgeted that it will take her eighteen months to save enough to fund her trip. During that time, she spends much of her spare time in on the Internet researching places she would like to visit.*

Go back to Exercise Eleven, and set realistic time frames in which to achieve each goal so you can monitor your progress, and enter the dates by which you plan to achieve your twelve main goals.

You now have some meaningful goals, and potential time frames. These will help you stay focused, to keep the big picture in mind. Without this plan, you will be like a rudderless boat adrift at sea, and get nowhere.

Monitor your progress on a regular basis to enable you to make changes / modifications, as necessary.

Expect to encounter obstacles and challenges along the way – that will inevitably happen. In Exercise Eleven, make a list of potential or imaginary obstacles that may challenge you along the way to achieving your goals. Your resolve to manifest successful outcomes in your life will enable you to stay focused on your goals, and overcome those obstacles and challenges. Allow time in your schedule to enable you to cope, deal with, and overcome those potential obstacles.

Examples of potential obstacles:

- *Lack of experience of certain team members – you may need to recruit additional team members*
- *Feeling physically unfit – you may need to take time to focus on your health, to prevent stress and enable your body to heal*
- *Fear of success – take time each day to meditate and stay focused on your goals becoming reality. Spend your time and conserve your energy wisely – take time to recharge your batteries*

While you are focusing on your goals you need also to continue doing whatever you currently do to earn a living, support yourself and family.

What actions will you take?

Your first goal needs to be a "stretch" goal that may appear not yet achievable. You need to set mini-goals to act as stepping stones to help you to systematically achieve the main goal – in Exercise Twelve (at the end of this chapter). Carefully think through the practical steps needed to get you from where you are now to reaching your main goal, to bridge that gap. Be specific and include all the details. Highlight the potential obstacles. This will make the process attainable, easier and more fun, keep you committed, and guide you along the way.

You need to spend 80% mind time – visualizing and setting goals – and 20% action time. Always expect the best, but be prepared for the worst to happen. That way you will be ready to deal with obstacles when they crop up, and not be disappointed, whatever happens.

Be sure you remain physically fit, by including a fitness program in your daily routine schedule. Communicate additional activities in your lifestyle to your family members and close friends, so they are aware why you may be unable to spend as much time with them as in the past. Get them on board before you make any changes, so they feel included and not neglected.

Once you have made the decision and the effort to make that first step your new journey can begin.

Then *you* need to take action – do it now. The first step is the most important one, so make it a small one, so you will not get discouraged. That is all it will take to get the ball rolling, and once the process has started you can gradually gain momentum and the passion to continue. Changing the status quo can, at first seem daunting – do not allow procrastination to take over – you will become more excited and committed as the process gains its own speed. It is like the ripple effect in a pool, when a stone is dropped into the pool the effects can be seen far wider than at the spot where the stone was dropped, and nothing can stop that ripple.

Example:

John is eager to start the project that will provide him with financial freedom before his retirement. He has chosen to focus on rental property investment. He currently has a mortgage on his family home. The first step is for John to contact as many property groups as he can, to research the services they provide, the training they offer, and the cost of their services. Then John needs to contact the appropriate person in each group to ascertain whether they have the same integrity as he has. Once he has gathered all the information he needs, he can determine which group can provide him with the support he needs to build his property portfolio. The group he chooses should be able to provide tools that can help John plan the timing of each property acquisition, financing, cash flow, and capital appreciation, and a link to back-up professional services he needs.

Be realistic at all times. If at first you fail, keep trying. Persevere – you may be closer than you think to reaching your goal. You deserve to reach your goal – all you need to do is to be persistent, and never give up. Be patient. Sometimes you need to go with the flow and have faith in Divine timing. Allow things to happen. Sometimes certain other things must fall into place before you get the results you want. Sometimes the seeds you sow may take time to germinate and ripen, and you may need to do some weeding. Be thankful for all you have now. Keep the big picture in mind. Hold on and hang in there. Enjoy the journey of each day.

Treat each day as the first day of the rest of your life. If things did not go as planned yesterday – they rarely do, due to unforeseen circumstances – refocus on your goals, be determined, and persevere. Go the extra mile to succeed – go all out. Visualise having achieved each step along the way, having successfully achieved your goal – experience the feeling now. Celebrate as you go so that you enjoy some down-time in your new schedule. That process can be very powerful. Small adjustments that could help, may come to mind during this time.

Your friends may tempt you to take time out to join them in pursuits they will still be doing in many years' time. Remember, you need to stay focused on your goals now, knowing that your lifestyle will be different than theirs in the future, due to the extra effort you are putting in now. Stay on track and settle for nothing less. You will reap the benefit in the long term. Then your friends may say that you were lucky – whereas you will know it was due to your regular effort and perseverance to change your life for the better. You will not be disappointed. You can then empower your friends to change their lifestyle, if they so wish.

Example:

John followed his dream and after ten years he owned a total of seven properties that in time will provide him with financial freedom and enable him to retire within the next ten years. He stayed focused on his dream, spent time educating himself, and spent his vacation time with his family at local events to conserve his cash reserves. His friends spent their vacation time with their families at overseas locations.

John knows that once he has achieved his goal, he will have financial freedom and can spend his time with whom he wants, when he wants, and where he wants. On the other hand, John's friends, will have barely enough superannuation on which to retire and be forced to rely on the age pension. John and his family are happy with their decision, and they feel closer as a family as they have enjoyed their time together along their journey. They have achieved success as a team.

It may take more than one attempt to gain the results you need. Overcome any discouragement. Take the necessary actions. Be calm and stay focused on the required result. Trust that you can do it. You are not alone – you are supported by your inner light. Relax, have hope, and gratitude for all your blessings. Remember to breathe, and smell the roses along the journey.

Go with the flow – feel the unseen Divine hand guiding you.

Celebrate your health; your wealth; each day. You were each born with joy and the basic needs of peace and happiness.

Now you have prioritised your goals, proceed to Chapter Eleven to consider who you need in your team, and the resources you need.

How does it feel to be a winner?

It took a while for me to overcome certain disappointments experienced in the recent past. I needed to overcome this feeling, accept the disappointments as part of my growth and education, and start to refocus on rebuilding certain foundations in my life. Prior to that, I had achieved successes with my investments, and weight management so am confident that success in those areas can be achieved. It feels good to experience harmony in each area of life.

I have no regrets that things did not turn out as I had hoped – maybe my expectations had been unrealistic, or the timing unsuitable. Having accepted that, I updated my goals and action plan – allowing time for my body to heal from the toxins of disappointment. Also, I needed to establish boundaries on my time and energy, to avoid stress.

I feel fulfilled, being able to make a difference in the lives of others. I feel happy to have worked my way through accepting the setbacks from the past as reality, and am ready to face the future with an open heart and mind.

With a quiet mind I was able to visualise what it feels like to be a winner, and celebrate my inherent talents, experiences to date, values, family and friends. I feel refreshed and ready to tackle the challenges of each day.

What goals will help me bridge the gap to living my ideal goal?

My most recent main goal was to settle into my new homeland of Australia. On my magnetic board, I attached pictures of houses, cars, and motivational sayings, and visualized an abundant lifestyle every day. The initial focus was to pursue my career, and become an Australian citizen. I overcame settling-in difficulties encountered along the way, keeping my mind focused on this successful outcome. I never doubted that I would succeed. Once I started on this journey, supportive people miraculously appeared in my life. I was not concerned how long the settling in process might take – it was the journey that counted, knowing that everything would turn out for the best in the long run.

I have hope and know that as I continue to consider potential ways to use my time and energy most efficiently, my intuition will guide me to make the most appropriate decisions. In addition I prepare a daily To Do list that ensures I achieve the essential operating tasks.

I need to refocus my mind on the goals to create financial freedom and optimum health and consider what additional training is required to rebuild and strengthen these foundations.

What actions did I take?

I am working with a food diary to ensure I stay on track with attaining my ideal weight; and have tailored a yoga program to help my body achieve more strength and flexibility, as well as practising daily meditation.

I am grateful for where I am today, and am systematically considering potential ways I can achieve my goals to making the world a better place, regularly monitor the progress.

Each day, I review what has been achieved and go to bed with a quiet mind.

Space for you to write in:

**Believe in yourself. Stay focused on the positive.
Take action. Celebrate each day.**

Exercise Eleven – Goals

Date:

	Main Goals:	Priority:	Estimated Achievement	Potential Obstacles
1.				
2.				
3.				
4..				
6.				
7.				
8				
9.				
10.				
11.				
12				

Signature................................

Name: ....

Date: ....

Exercise Twelve – Action Steps

Prioritised Goal – Goal One (repeat process for each goal):

Potential Obstacles:

_____

_____

_____

_____

_____

_____

Mini-goals – Action Steps:

Estimated Achievement Date

1.				
2.				
3.				
4.				
6.				
7.				
8				
9.				
10.				
11.				
12.				

Signature...............................

Name: ....

Date: ....

Spiritual Harmony

Chapter Eleven
Your Team / Resources

No man is an Island, entire of itself.

– John Donne

Alone we can do so little; together we can do so much.

– Helen Adams Keller

I not only use the brains I have, but all I can borrow.

– Thomas Woodrow Wilson

The whole is greater than the sum of the parts.

– Aristotle

Our faith must be alive, always growing like a tree.

– Thich Nhat Hanh

- Who can help you to achieve your goals?
- Networking
- Be accountable
- Learn new skills

Who can help you to achieve your goals?

Detail the project you have chosen as your first goal, including the steps that need to be taken for the project to become reality in Exercise Thirteen (at the end of this chapter). Depending on the size of the project, you may need to draft a Business Plan to include your mission, vision, and a financial budget of income and expenses to show to your team so they are aware of what exactly you plan to achieve.

You need to build a world class team. Prepare a profile of the desired backgrounds, vision, achievements, talents and integrity you require from potential team members.

Make a list of people who may be suitable to provide those services, and meet your team requirements, in Exercise Thirteen. Research their profiles. Find out what they are currently doing. Do you need them to act as directors, team leaders, or production people?

Always be open to learn from others who are qualified and able to help. Learn to accept all the help you need, and ask for support from the most reliable sources available. You need to take time to ensure your targeted team members share the same life values and integrity that you have, and have the required experience, before selecting them to help you. You may also need a mentor to help you to stay on track.

In addition to the operating team, you will also need a lawyer, accountant, banker, and other professional service providers.

In addition to your business team members, take the opportunity to review your other team members, including – medical, dental, fitness, finance, and family. Make sure they are kept informed of your venture and you meet with them as often as necessary to stay fit and maintain harmony in your life. You are the master of your life – plan time for your R & R.

Example:

Richard's initial goal is to become fit and lose twenty kilograms so he can feel healthier before commencing his second goal of running a marathon in two years' time. After informing his family of his intention, Richard considers who else he needs to include on his team.

The first step is for Richard to inform the doctor of his plan, to find out whether any health issues need to be addressed. Then, Richard needs to meet with one of the gym instructors to record his weight, height, and fitness now, and make a plan to ensure his fitness can meet the needs of the marathon within the two-year period. What it needs to be going forward. Richard's progress needs to be monitored by the gym instructor on a regular basis.

Richard intends to enrol on a course on mindful eating to learn more about his body type and the food it needs. He also needs to complete a daily food diary to monitor his progress.

Ask how you can achieve what you want, and the Law of Attraction will bring to you those people who can help. This may sound spooky – I can tell you it can happen if you believe it can. Whatever you think, with passion in your mind, will provide a magnetic attraction via the universal vibratory energy field, and enable this to become reality. You need to make known what you plan to do, by informing people you can trust. It has happened to me. Successful people are always willing to share their knowledge with you – if only you will ask. Have faith in yourself.

Example:

Julie needs to choose a team of directors for the organisation she intends to set up to manufacture educational toys for children, to enhance the more traditional teaching methods available. She also intends to provide a safe and supportive environment where children can spend time learning from working with other children and building their life skills at an early age.

There are two stages to Julie's plan, to:

- *Obtain funding for manufacturing / obtaining the toys; and*
- *Obtain the space required for teaching / supervising the children; teaching staff.*

Stage One includes creating a business plan and feasibility study, obtaining financial backing, marketing the product, and providing the product.

Stage Two includes finding the facility, and staff required, the budgeted cost of which needs to be included in Stage One.

Networking

When you have designed your ideal team, make a list of contact details and make contact with them to introduce your venture and determine whether they are interested and willing to discuss it in further detail at a meeting. Arrange a meeting with each one of those who is interested. When you meet with them consider their personalities and whether they could work well together as a team. Could you work with them? List the qualities you need for your team to work well. Once you have a picture of the team in your mind, make a list of people you think could fulfil the roles you have in mind, and your criteria. Make a list of areas in which your ideal team is deficient.

At your discussion meetings, ask your potential team members if they are aware of other people who could fit the profiles for the other vacant roles. Otherwise, you may need to advertise for people to fill the vacant roles. You may need to enlist the services of a recruiter or executive search firm to help you conduct this process.

Target functions where you can meet potential team members or people who may know of such people. Networking time can be time well spent.

Be accountable

As part of the process when selecting your team members, carefully consider whether each of them could effectively communicate with both you and each other. Do they each possess effective interpersonal communication skills, as well as the other professional skills required? Do you trust their judgement, as advisors? Are they leaders or followers? Do they have the relevant experience?

The final choice of team members must be made by you. They will each require a job description.

Your choice of team members can make the difference between enabling your goal to become a reality, rather than merely a learning experience. Choose wisely and never accept anyone at face value. You need to do your own research, and make your own decisions before making the final selection. Your team members are there to act as consultants – you need to make the final decisions.

Take time out each day to visualise the success of your new venture, how it can make a difference to your life, and that of your family, and your employees. What plans can you introduce to benefit the members of staff, to make sure they feel committed and will remain loyal? What difference could it make to the community?

When you delegate tasks to team members, first make sure they can perform them, as expected, within the required time-frame. You need to monitor the progress on a regular basis to ensure the goals can be met within the indicated time frames. You always need to fully understand what transactions are in process, and the overall effect of the outcomes. You also need to be kept aware of issues that arise throughout the organisation so you can take appropriate action.

Learn new skills

You may need to acquire new skills related to your new venture, and update your existing knowledge, or acquire new knowledge. List these in Exercise Fourteen (at the end of this chapter).

Check available courses that can benefit you. Attend courses, acquire new skills, and read books that can help bridge your knowledge gaps. Be sure these resources are the best available – either within the local community or on-line.

Consider whether attending a course on team building could benefit you. Do you need to acquire additional business skills? Do you need to gain experience in conducting team meetings, or in presentation skills?

Read books that can enhance your knowledge.

Who can help me achieve my goals?

Building the best team, and fully understanding their competencies, took me longer than I expected at my first attempt. Gaining credibility in a new country and updating the foundations for my dreams was often disheartening. It took courage, patience and perseverance. The will to succeed carried me along, and I took regular breaks for rest and recreation. My close friends provided invaluable support throughout the whole process.

I decided I need a mentor to help me stay on track to rebuild the foundations in the areas of physical harmony and financial harmony.

Networking:

I have experienced my fair share of setbacks, and now need to rebuild my team, in light of my current goals. To some extent, I realise I may have had some unrealistic expectations, and perhaps been somewhat impatient. With that in mind, I determined that first of all I may need a mentor.

Once I had decided that I need a mentor, the opportunity arose and I registered my interest. The organiser contacted me and advised that they had received more applications of interest from potential mentees than mentors, and asked whether I would be willing to participate as a mentor in view of my life experience and learning. On the basis that you need to become a friend to make a friend – this time I felt the need to become a mentor to later become a mentee. I feel this could be a life changing and enriching experience.

It meets the criteria of my goal – operating as a mentor and providing a service that can empower others to reach their goals in life. I can gain experience in a new role and learn new skills, whilst growing my network.

Choose my team wisely:

I am in the process of considering whether any members of my previous team can meet my current requirements and, if so, ascertain whether they are still available and able to help.

Be accountable:

I need to monitor the performance and relevance of my team members, on an ongoing basis, and be open to expanding my team as I go. This process will take time to research and document.

Learn new skills:

Whatever I do I will always need to update my current skills and be ready to learn new skills to keep up to date with current requirements and ongoing technological changes in the world. I need to choose the most relevant courses to attend, groups to join, and books to read.

Space for you to write in:

Now you are fully prepared for success. You need to accept your team's capabilities, stay on track, and persevere.

Celebrate Your Gold Within

Exercise Thirteen – Team / Resources

Details of project:

....

....

....

....

....

....

Potential team members:

Date of contact:

....

....

....

....

....

....

Signature............................

Name: ....

Date: ....

Spiritual Harmony

Exercise Fourteen – Team / Resources

New skills to be acquired:

....

....

....

....

Courses to attend:

....

....

....

....

Books to read:

....

....

....

....

Signature…………………………..

Name: ………………………………….

Date: ………………………………….

Chapter Twelve
Celebrating Your Progress / Success / Gold

We must cultivate our garden.

— Voltaire

To me, every hour of the light and dark is a miracle. Every cubic inch of space is a miracle.

— Walt Whitman

How poor are they who have no patience.

— William S.5hakespeare

Have no friends not equal to yourself.

— Confucius

If anything can go wrong it will.

— Murphy's Law

You may have to fight a battle more than once to win it.

— Margaret Hilda Thatcher

Only those who dare to fail greatly can ever achieve greatly.

— Robert Francis Kennedy

Anyone who has never made a mistake has never tried anything new.

— Albert Einstein

Effort only releases its reward after a person refuses to quit.

— Napoleon Hill

Never to suffer would have been never to have been blessed.

— Edgar Allan Poe

Keep your eye on the sunshine, and you will not see the shadows.

— Helen Keller

I have a list of things to prove myself. One is that I can live my life fearlessly.

— Oprah Gail Winfrey

The Journey, not the arrival, matters; the voyage, not the landing.

— Paul Theroux

Enjoy all you have while pursuing all you want.

— Emmanuel James ("Jim") Rohn

- Analyse your progress each day
- Have patience
- Celebrate your Progress / Success / Gold
- Who is important in your life?
- Sharing your success

Analyse your progress each day

Each day when you return home, or at the end of the day, sit down and analyse your progress – your successes and failures. Did you achieve what you set out to do? Did you encounter any obstacles? Could you have done anything differently that would have provided a more favourable outcome? Do you need to modify any of the results in any way, going forward? Do you need to take a break if you are sick or feeling stressed?

Write down your achievements, no matter how small or insignificant they may seem. Also, write down your lessons learned, and disappointments – treat these experiences as opportunities to adjust your planning – analyse what you can learn from them and how you could have done things differently. Never be disheartened, and never give up. Write down your thoughts. Do your homework, and prepare for tomorrow. If necessary, adjust your Plan to take into account experiences encountered and lessons learnt. Celebrate today – you have created it. Celebration is important. It helps you to stay present, to create space between the past and the future – sacred time. There is a difference between celebrating on your own and celebrating with others.

Make sure you enjoy the food you plan for dinner. Relax after dinner to allow the food to properly digest. Include a meditation session that will quieten your body and mind to enable you to sleep well. Avoid loud noises and TV programs that may provide stress. Make sure you feel calm before you go to bed. Sleep well.

It is important to find a few people with whom you can share and discuss your life experiences, and with whom you can share successes as well as setbacks, without fear of judgement; with whom you can express your gratitude and feelings, knowing that others will not question your intent, and accept you as you are.

This needs to be your process / your system – to be followed each day – after completing your other daily routines. You need quiet time to enable you to prepare for tomorrow, recharge your mind and rest your body.

As you achieve each goal tick it off in Exercises Eleven and Twelve (at the end of Chapter Ten). Celebrate each success, no matter how small it may seem in the overall scheme of things. Each step is important. Enjoy the journey – savour each moment, each day. Meditate, give thanks.

Have patience

As long as you have the right mind-set, a good reason for bridging the gap from where you are now to where you want to be, and have faith in yourself, you will reach your goal. You will need patience throughout the journey. Do not expect instant results. Allow time for other events to take place before your goal can be achieved. If you have unrealistic expectations you may be disappointed.

Example:

Jean has completed all the planning she can put into place for now to achieve her goal to change her lifestyle by changing her career path. Her new job will start in November, which means she has two months of free-time before starting that job.

She decides to conduct a major clutter-clearing project at home that will take two weeks; spend time with friends for two weeks; and enrols for a meditation program for the remaining month.

Enjoy each day. Life is not meant to be difficult – lighten up. Laugh, have fun. Smile.

Winners are ordinary people with extraordinary determination.

Celebrate your Progress / Success / Gold

Amid all the tragedy and unhappiness in the world today, you can rejoice as good things are also happening out there and it is on the good things you need to focus – on abundance, and on your ability to mindfully live each day, and make a positive contribution in your universal home. Should you currently be embroiled in tragedy of any kind, know that it will not last forever, try to envisage what your ideal life looks like going forward, and have hope in your heart. There is always darkness before light, and neither are inseparable. There needs to be a cleansing, a breakthrough, a balance re-established.

Congratulations on discovering your Gold within. Be grateful for all you have in your life. Enjoy the benefits available to you. Sit back and review how much you have transformed, from your new perspective, since your journey began. What do you treasure most? How do you feel? Be proud of the new you. You deserve to have abundance in each area of your life. Discover the simple pleasures in life. What have you learnt?

When you have achieved success in your life, it is likely you will want to share it with those who are less fortunate than you. With humility, you can share how you feel now with the way you used to feel before you discovered your gold – your freedom in each area of life – thereby encouraging others to seek their gold and giving them confidence to fully use their inherent talents, live life with passion, and make a positive difference in their own lives and in the lives of others.

Be aware, now you have succeeded, and come so far on your journey, you may find that other less motivated people may consider that you are "lucky". Be compassionate and try to motivate them to gain confidence to become successful by sharing with them your formula for success. Have empathy with them. Let them know that you were prepared to accept failure along the way but expected the best to happen and you always focused on that. Let them believe that they also can feel successful and empower others who are less fortunate to feel successful and achieve their life goals. They need your encouragement now, when they may be feeling disheartened. Humbly empower them to start their journey of self-discovery, like you did, by questioning what will make them truly happy. Listen, in silence, to their real needs. Show them you care. Inspire them. Include them in your celebration.

How do you plan to share your success with others, some of whom may appear to be less fortunate than you? Listen, and discover their needs. Have compassion and aim to bridge the gap that may exist between you and them. Consider how you can make a positive difference in the universe. Maybe you can become their mentor.

Example:

Imagine you have taken time to write a book – fact or fiction – you may want to share the story with the world so that whoever reads it can benefit in some way. You need to consider the best options for having the book edited and published.

Be grateful for this opportunity to share your experiences, lessons learnt, caring, and self-confidence.

Who is important in your life?

List those people with whom you want to share your success in Exercise Fifteen (at the end of this chapter).

Example:

- *Your children — how can you show your appreciation for them?*
- *Your spouse / partner — how can you thank them for being there for you?*
- *Your parents / grandparents / brothers / sisters — how can you communicate your appreciation for them?*
- *Like-minded friends — let them know they have played an important part in your success*
- *Disadvantaged people — how can you share your success with them?*
- *The whole world, or targeted projects — maybe there is a group of people who you would like to share your success with — with whom you closely feel connected?*

When an opportunity arises for you to spend some time:

- in a yoga centre, either for a short or extended period
- working in another country
- sponsoring someone, for example a foreign student or family; or
- volunteering to participate in well-chosen projects in a lesser-developed country

Seriously consider accepting that opportunity, as it could dramatically enrich your life experience, and the lives of others. The sharing can be a privilege. There are no boundaries — the world is your oyster.

You need to remember that you are inter-connected with all other beings in the world. Accept them for whoever they are, where they are at, and without judgement. How can you communicate your harmony and bridge seeming gaps? Take time to listen to your inner guide, and your intuition. Honour your place in the world. Be open to new possibilities with an open mind and heart. Visualise the reality, and allow it to manifest. Take action.

The tapestry of life is vast. Every little helps to enhance the depth in your reality of life. It is up to you to decide how best to proceed — accept the inner guidance, and trust in life. You are never alone. Remember, charity begins at home.

Take time to stop, be still, and breathe deeply. Dream, live well, and love much. Live with passion, act now, enjoy. Question what you have learnt so far, give thanks for all your blessings and support in the miracle of life.

Review your energy levels. Empower others who are not as fortunate as you to experience harmony in their lives. Be their friend and mentor. Have compassion.

If it is meant to be – it is up to you and me. What we sow we will reap – and we need to be sure the soil is fertile. There is no point in having unreasonable expectations of those who do not share our vision. The world is hurting, and it needs us to manifest the positive change that can be achieved by each of us acting as a responsible global citizen, and by reaching out to others. We are all in this game together.

None of us, by ourselves, can change the world. We are each a small part of the global family, and together we can change our environment, our world. We need to take this responsibility seriously. We can each make a difference in whichever way we choose, and are able. The change needs to start within each of us.

Have you noticed how – since the World Trade Center disaster in New York, the bush fire and flood disasters in Australia, floods in the UK, earthquakes in New Zealand and Japan, and other major traumatic global events, the citizens of the world have become closer? They have bonded. Everyone who is able, wants to help those who are less fortunate to survive, and live well.

It is not only about taking – it is also about giving. What can you give? What are your real needs? Let the boundaries disappear – whatever they may be. You need to learn to give and receive with an open mind and heart, trusting in your vision.

You may need to revisit the foundations you have built in each area of your life and strengthen them, making necessary adjustments. Also, consider taking a well-deserved break, before starting the process of choosing another goal and starting the process all over again. Allow time for rejuvenation, assimilation, and enjoyment.

Analyse my progress each day:

When I relocated from Singapore to Australia I had collected a container-full of Asian artefacts, technical books, and paperwork. Imagine – during the settling-in process – it took me several years to decide what I really needed to keep and to sell, donate, or throw away the unwanted items. Only then could I truly start to master / manage my life process in my new country with the passion it deserves.

Without that physical and mental clutter, I feel much lighter. But there is always more to clear! So, I will keep at it to allow space for more change and growth. This is an important stage of transitioning from the past to the future.

It is a roller-coaster of a different kind! Time to celebrate a life of abundance and beauty, a simplicity, an indescribable joy, of happiness and peace within. There is an incomparable richness and no need to rush into anything new.
I am grateful for each day. Life continues to get better. I am excited.

Have patience:

Patience is a virtue – I think I was on the back row of the class at school when it was being taught.

Exercising patience pays off. I love my new homeland and am grateful for the opportunity to live and work here, despite the various challenges I have encountered. I knew very few people when I arrived here and it took some time to become familiar with different ways of doing things.

I need to take one day at a time, open my heart and mind to allow change to take place, have trust and allow people to help me. Each day is an exciting and new learning experience. It is fun, yet challenging. I sometimes feel like Alice in Wonderland.

Celebrate my Progress / Success / Gold:

I always maintain a vision in my mind of what I want to achieve and what that means to me. When I sit still and ask for guidance someone magically always appears to help.

It is impossible to go backwards – the only way to go is forwards, being wiser for past experiences.

Who is important in my life?

My family, friends – including you – my new friends, are important in my life. Also, those people who are less fortunate than I and those who may be able to benefit from ongoing medical research are important.

It never ceases to amaze me how small the world is becoming – people are all basically the same at heart and in needs, with only a different set of circumstances to work within. We are like a global family. There are abundant riches everywhere – life is a miracle.

Space for you to write in:

Have fun each day, along the journey. Expect the best, review the reality, adjust your expectations, and enjoy life's harmony; Remember to share your success with people who are less fortunate than you.

Celebrate Your Gold Within

Exercise Fifteen – With Whom Do You Want to Share Your Success?

List down all those people / organisations / projects, with whom you want to share your success:

....

....

....

....

....

....

....

....

....

....

....

....

Signature...

Name: ....

Date: ....

Chapter Thirteen
What Next?

Life's most persistent and urgent question: What are you doing for others?
— Martin Luther King Jr.

The life which is not examined is not worth living. — Plato

Live each day as if your life had just begun. — Johann Wolfgang von Goethe

Tough times never last, but tough people do. — Robert Harold Schuller

The golden rule is that there are no golden rules. — George Bernard Shaw

As human beings, our greatness lies not so much in being able to remake the world …. as on being able to rework ourselves. — Mahatma Gandhi

You give but little when you give your possessions. It is when you give of yourself that you truly give. — Kahlil Gibran

We are one, after all, you and I. Together we suffer, together exist, and forever will recreate each other. — Pierre Teilhard de Chardin

We must be aware of the real problems of the world. Then, with mindfulness, we will know what to do and what not to do to be of help. — Thich Nhat Hanh

One does not discover new lands without consenting to lose sight of the shore for a very long time. — Andre Gide

Wherever you go, go with all your heart. — Confucius

The universe will reward you for taking risks on its behalf. — Shakti Gawain

There is nothing like returning to a place that remains unchanged to find the ways in which you yourself have changed. — Nelson Mandela

Your work is to discover your world and then with all your heart give yourself to it. — Buddha

Learn to be silent. Let your quiet mind listen and absorb. — Pythagoras

From the standpoint of daily life, however, there is one thing we do know: that man is here for the sake of other men. — Albert Einstein

Luck is a matter of preparation meeting opportunity. — Oprah Winfrey

Many persons have a wrong idea of what constitutes true happiness. It is not attained through self-gratification but through fidelity to a worthy purpose. — Helen Adams Keller

There were two classes of charitable people: one, the people who did a little and made a great deal of noise; the other, the people who did a great deal and made no noise at all. — Charles John Huffam Dickens

"What moves men of genius, or rather what inspires their work, is not new ideas, but their obsession with the idea that what has already been said is still not enough. — Eugene Delacroix

- Your legacy
- Your message to the world
- You can make a difference

Your legacy

Congratulations on staying the course – it is a huge achievement. I hope you are feeling excited. When you have discovered harmony in each area of your life, and overall, and feel at peace with yourself, it is likely time to consider sharing your experience with others. How best can you do this?

Thank you for allowing me into your life. Whatever you choose – there are no rules – may you have harmony, joy, abundance, fun, and happiness each day of your journey.

Your message to the world

Communicate your message to the world – your Eulogy. Turn to Exercise Sixteen (at the end of this chapter), consider how to showcase your life, and be remembered, when your body fails. What message do you want to leave on your tombstone? What is your message for your family, friends, and neighbours when they gather together to celebrate your life?

You can make a difference

Now is the time to fine tune your Blue Print for success. What changes do you need to make before embarking on the next stage of your journey in life? The past is not the future. Now is the time for action – the present. Go for it, with all your heart. There is only one of you – you are unique. Celebrate your success, your Gold.

Together, we can make a difference. Love is the greatest gift.

I hope you have enjoyed reading the book.

My legacy:

Part of my legacy is the difference this book can make in each reader's life.

With this mind-set, I recently received an expanded vision of how I could make the world a better place – by establishing a wellness centre where people can gain healing and mentoring to strengthen their hope and confidence to live life fully, amid whatever misfortune they may currently be experiencing. I continue to seek further intuition to allow this focus to become reality. This centre can be mobile and exist in many different places – waiting to be discovered.

My message to the world:

I am happy for my eulogy to contain the following:

"Kathy, dreamed big, lived with passion, travelled the world in her pursuit of happiness, and abundance, and empowered others to connect with their Gold within and manifest their ideal dreams.

She encountered many obstacles, which became learning experiences and opportunities for growth, never gave up, nor lost her sense of humour. Kathy mindfully challenged seeming traditions, and beliefs, to uncover the truth.

Kathy treasured her family, and friends and the opportunity to make the world a better place. She opened her heart and mind to the world, both in the West and the East, and her life became enriched in the process.

Join with me in the celebration of life. All my love."

I can make a difference:

In the meantime, I intend to live each day with passion, and joy, and question how I can continue to make a positive difference, with joy, have fun, and communicate my wealth of understanding to others to empower them to experience life with a greater depth of awareness and joy. Life is a blessing – a miracle – it is awesome, and humbling. It is a gift, to be shared.

I am open to a world of new opportunities, new perspectives, new knowledge, and experiences. The adventure continues.

Space for you to write in:

This is your life. Live it with Passion, Harmony, and Joy. Happiness and Health is the greatest wealth of all. Celebrate your Gold within.

What Next?

Exercise Sixteen – Your Message to the World

Write your Eulogy here: How do you want to be remembered?

....

....

....

....

....

....

....

....

....

THIS IS YOUR LIFE PLAN
LIVE YOUR LIFE WITH *PASSION*, WITHOUT REGRET

GO FOR IT!

Signature.......................................

Name: ....

Date: ....

Epilogue
The Light Within

Can you hear?
Silence and love
Miracles both
Listen, dear.
Gold within
Gold without
Limitless,
Knows no bounds.
Your heart is precious
Keep it pure
Let it be open
To receive divine love.
Breathe deeply,
Smile much more
Spend your time

Wisely now.
Be grateful,
Kind and true
Quietly
In your space.
You are home
Deep within;
Hope and Joy
All you need.
Share your love.
Forever free
Riches abound
For you and me
Outside now

At the top;
Help those below
Find their heart.
You have done it,
So can they.
We can do it,
Together always.
No beginning
No end;
Always there
Shine and glow,
Can you see
The light within?
Always there
To show the way.

Inspirational Reading – Resources

A Brief History of Time – *Stephen Hawking*

Ageless Body, Timeless Mind – *Deepak Chopra (and other books)*

An Open Heart – *The Dalai Lama*

A Spiritual Renegade's Journey to the Good Life – *Lama Marut (and other books)*

A Systematic Course in the Ancient Tantric Techniques of Yoga & Kriya – *Paramahamsa Satyananda Saraswati (and other books)*

Autobiography of a Yogi – *Paramahamsa Yogananda*

Awaken the Giant Within – *Anthony Robbins (and other books)*

Ayurveda – *Gopi Warrier*

Ayurveda and Acupuncture – *Dr Frank Ros*

Back to the Truth – *Dennis Waite*

Beyond Words – *Swami Satchidananda (and other books)*

Bill Gates: Entrepreneur and Philanthropist – *Jeanne M Lesinski*

Buddha's Brain – *Rick Hansen, PhD with Richard Mendius, MD*

Chinese Medicine – *Ted J Kaptchuk*

Clear Your Clutter with Feng Shui – *Karen Kingston*

Crystal Ascension – *Catherine Bowman*

Dare to Fail – *Billi P S Lim*

Divine Soul Songs – *Dr. Zhi Gang Sha (and other books)*

Eastern Body Western Mind – *Anodea Judith (and other books)*

Eating for You – *Sallyanne Pisk*

Essays on The Gita – *Sri Aurobindo*

Feng Shui for the Soul – *Denise Linn*

Getting Past the Pain between Us – *Marshall B Rosenberg PhD*

Getting That Job – *Geoff Morgan & Andrew Banks*

Harmony: Radical Taoism Gently Applied – *Eulalio Paul Cane*

Hatha Yoga The Hidden Language – *Swami Sivananda Radha (and other books)*

Heal Thyself – *Edward Bach MB, BS, MRCS, LRCP, DPH*

Hope – How Yoga Heals the Scars of Trauma – *Helen Cushing / Swami Ahimsadhara Saraswati (and other books)*

Horizon Beyond – *Julius Tahija*

How To Get What You Want – *Wallace D Wattles (and other books)*

How to Make Friends and Influence People – *Dale Carnegie (and other books)*

How To Write Your Block-Buster – *Fiona McIntosh*

Into the Heart of the Himalayas – *Jono Lineen*

Journeys East – *Dr Harry Oldmeadow*

Journey of the Mind – *Paramahamsa Pragyananda (and other books)*

Leadability – *Rowdy McLean*

Live Right for Your Type – *Dr Peter J. D'Adamo with Catherine Whitney*

Living for Health – *Dr Gillian McKeith*

Living with the Himalayan Masters – *Swami Rama (and other books)*

Living Your Dreams – *Jack Canfield and Mark Victor Hansen (and other books)*

Longevity The Tao of Eating and Healing – *Aileen Yeo*

Losing My Virginity – *Sir Richard Branson (and other books)*

Maximum Achievement – *Brian Tracy (and other books)*

Mindfulness – *Craig Hassed, MD (and other books)*

Moksha Gita – *Swami Sivananda (and other Books)*

Money And The Law Of Attraction – *Esther and Jerry Hicks (and other books)*

Networking Magic – *Robyn Henderson*

No Future without Forgiveness – *Desmond Tutu*

Peaceful Living – *Mary MacKenzie*

Pole to Pole – *Pat Farmer*

Professional Women in City Life – *London Junior Chamber of Commerce*

Program for Reversing Heart Disease – *Dr Dean Ornish*

Property, Prosper, Retire – *Kevin Young (and other books)*

Raw Juices Can Save Your Life – *Dr Sandra Cabot (and other books)*

Rich Dad Poor Dad – *Robert T Kiyosaki (and other books)*

Rich Woman – *Kim Kiyosaki*

River of Compassion – *Paramahamsa Prajnanananda*

Robinson Crusoe – *Daniel Defoe*

Sacred Sounds – *Alanna Kaivalya*

Sage of Arunchal – *Sri Ramana Maharshi*

Schweitzer – A Biography – *George Marshall & David Poling*

Shakti Manifest – *Barbara Pidgeon*

Storyshowing – *Sam Cawthorn*

Swiss Family Robinson – *Johann D Wyss*

The Abundance Book – *John Randolph Price (and other books)*

The Alchemist – *Paul Coelho*

The Angel Bible – *Hazel Raven*

The Artist's Way – *Julia Cameron*

The Barefoot Investor – *Scott Pape*

The Body is the Shadow of the Soul – *Marcilio Facino*

The Brain that Changes Itself – *Norman Doidge MD*

The Buddha in Me, the Buddha in You – A Handbook for Happiness – *David Hare*

The Chakra Handbook – *Shalila Sharamon & Bodo J Baginski*

The Complete Book of Herbs & Spices – *C. Loewenfeld & P. Black*

The Dragon's Blessing – *Ian Gawler (and other books)*

The Great Australian Diet – *Dr John Tickell (and other books)*

The Heart of Love – *Dr John F Demartini (and other books)*

The Herbal Drugstore – *Linda B. White and Steven Foster*

The Hidden Messages in Water – *Masaru Emoto (and other books)*

The Invisible Branson – *Louise Woodbury & William de Ora*

The Key – *Joe Vitale (and other books)*

The Life of Mahatma Gandhi – *Louis Fischer*

The Love You Deserve – *Dr Scott & Shannon Peck*

The Nature Doctor – *Dr. H C A Vogel*

The Power is Within You – *Louise L Hay (and other books)*

The Power of Chi – *Geoff Pike*

The Power of Now – *Eckhart Tolle (and other books)*

The Power of One – *Bryce Courtenay (and other books)*

The Power of Positive Thinking – *Norman Vincent Peale*

The Prophet – *Khalil Gibran*

The Richest Man in Babylon – *George S. Clason*

The Secret of Getting a Job – *Philip Garside*

The 7 Habits of Highly Successful People – *Stephen R Covey (and other books)*

The Snow Leopard – *Peter Matthiessen*

The Spontaneous Healing of Belief – *Gregg Braden (and other books)*

The Untethered Soul: The Journey Beyond Yourself – *Michael A Singer*

The Yoga Tradition: Its History, Literature, Philosophy and Practice – *George Feuerstein, PhD*

Think and Grow Rich – *Napoleon Hill (and other books)*

Think Like a Tycoon – *W G Hill*

Three Cups of Tea – *Greg Mortenson & David Oliver Relin*

Tools for Tantra – *Hamish Johari*

Treasure Island – *Robert Louis Stevenson*

25 Years of Whitt & Wisdom – *Noel Whittaker*

Upanishads – *Juan Mascaro*

Wheels of Life – *Anodea Judith, PhD*

Where Have All The Leaders Gone? – *Lee Iacocca (and other books)*

Why People Don't Heal and How They Can – *Carolyn Myss, PhD*

Wisdom of the Heart – *Alan Cohen*

Yoga Darshan – *Swami Niranjananda Saraswati (and other books)*

Yoga for Dementia – Tania Plahay

Yoga for Health – *AA Acarya*

Yoga for Healthy Living – *Baxter Bell, MD & Nina Zolotow*

Yoga of Sound – *Paul Russill*

Yoga Psychology – *Dr Rishi Vivekananda*

Yoga the Essence of Life – *Alix Johnson*

Yogini – The Power of Women in Yoga – *Janice Gates*

You'll See It When You Believe It – *Dr Wayne Dyer (and other books)*

www.ingramcontent.com/pod-product-compliance
Lightning Source LLC
Chambersburg PA
CBHW072010110726
47910CB00005B/1709